R Riddell

**A Manual of Gardening for Western and Southern India**

R Riddell
**A Manual of Gardening for Western and Southern India**
ISBN/EAN: 9783744661775

Printed in Europe, USA, Canada, Australia, Japan

Cover: Foto ©Andreas Hilbeck / pixelio.de

More available books at **www.hansebooks.com**

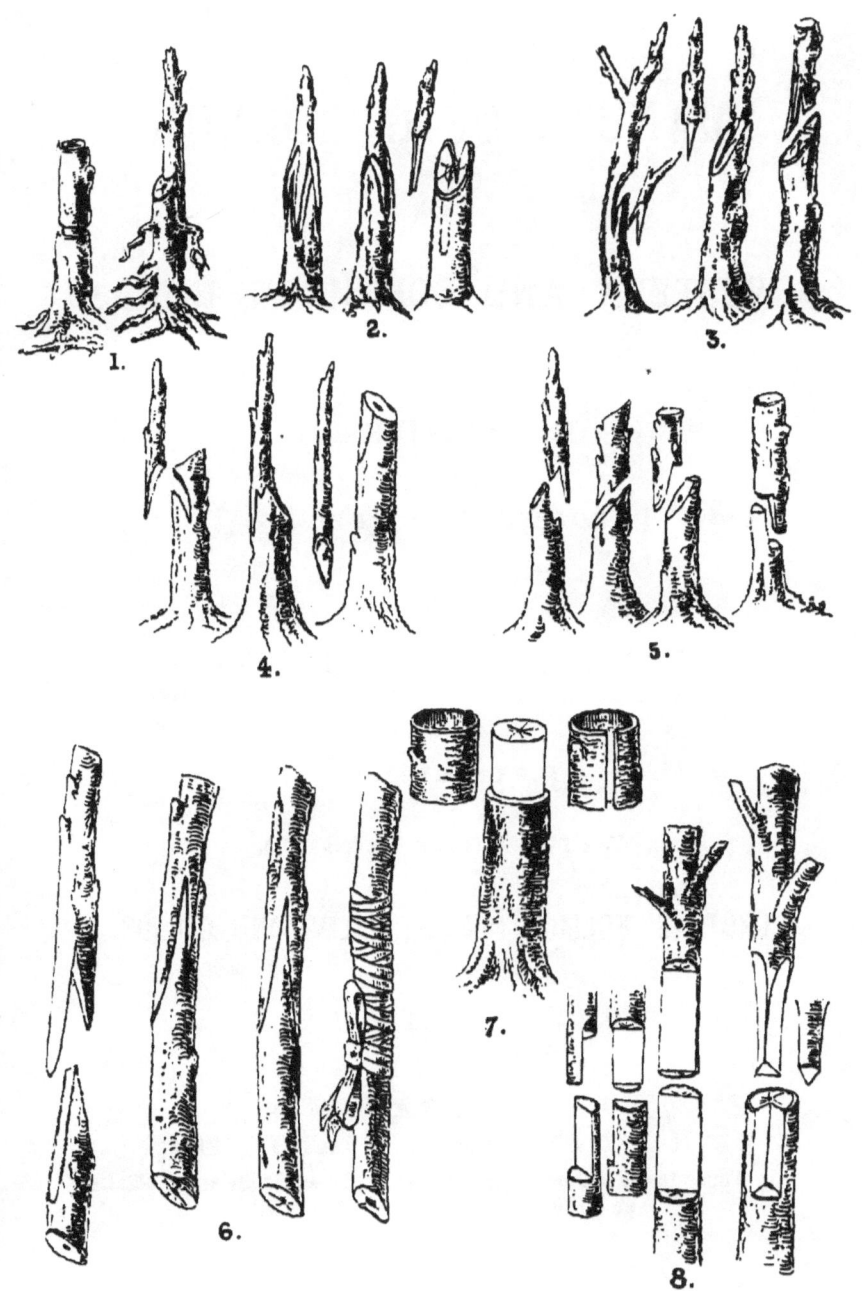

DIFFERENT MODES OF GRAFTING.

A

# MANUAL OF GARDENING

FOR

## WESTERN AND SOUTHERN INDIA,

BY

### R. RIDDELL.

*EDITED AND REVISED*

BY

#### LIEUTENANT-COLONEL BODDAM,
HONORARY SECRETARY, MYSORE AGRI-HORTICULTURAL SOCIETY.

FIFTH EDITION,

WITH CHAPTERS ON

CROTONS, FOLIAGE PLANTS, PALMS AND CYCADS.

MADRAS:
HIGGINBOTHAM AND CO.
By Appointment in India to His Royal Highness the Prince of Wales,
and Publishers to the Madras University.
1884.

MADRAS:
PRINTED BY HIGGINBOTHAM & CO.,
164 & 165, MOUNT ROAD.

# PUBLISHERS' PREFACE.

The Fourth Edition of RIDDELL's Manual of Gardening was revised by Lieutenant-Colonel BODDAM, Honorary Secretary, Mysore Agri-Horticultural Society, who brought the work up to date as regards many newly introduced Plants and Flowers, and their treatment.

To the present edition, the Fifth, chapters on Crotons, Foliage Plants, Palms and Cycads, are added.

# TOOLS
## DESIRABLE FOR GARDENING.

Axe or Pick.
Bill Hook or Pruning Bill.
Bleaching Pots..
Beetle or Rammer.
Broom.
Budding Knife.
Digging Hoe.
Dibble.
Flower Pots.
French Flower Pots.
Fruit Preservers.
Fumigating Bellows.
Garden Trowel.
Garden Water Engine.
Grafting Knife.
Gathering Scissors.
Hoes.
Hedge Shears.
Ladders.
Long Pruning Shears.

Mallet.
Mattock or Kodallee, Hoe Axe.
Native Hoes, Nurance and Koorpah.
Pins and Line.
Plough.
Powrah.
Propagation Pots.
Pronged Hoe.
Pruning Hook.
Rake.
Ringing Knife.
Shade Baskets or Pots.
Saws.
Spade.
Spud.
Transplanter.
Wheel Barrow.
Watering Pots.
Three Pronged Hand Grubber.

The trowel is a most useful instrument for lifting young plants with a ball of earth round their roots, so as to avoid their receiving any check, several young seedlings require a move, should be lifted with the tip of the trowel put into the new place very carefully so as not to disturb the earth immediately round them. The three pronged hand grubber is the best implement for loosening the soil round plants and exactly suited to the Native gardeners' fancy, they do not as a rule take kindly to European implements, the spade they cannot use as they do not wear shoes, and besides it is generally too much for their strength. Watering pots with large moveable necks are very desirable for watering large beds obviating the men trampling over the surface.

## GLOSSARY OF TERMS, ETC.

ALBUMEN—is a thick, glairy, tasteless, fluid, resembling the white of an unboiled egg; and is a substance deposited in the cells of vegetables. It abounds in the papaw (Carica papaya) tree; it also exists in the seeds of many plants, and in the fungi.

BLANCHING OR ETIOLATION.—The process of whitening plants, by which we deprive them of much of their bitter quality. It is performed in several ways—either by earthing them up so as to exclude the light and air, or by covering them over with boards, which is a bad plan in this country; or else by placing over the plant earthenware pots, open above and below, and filling up the space at the bottom with dry sand,—but I by no means recommend doing the latter, as it gets between the leaves, and is sometimes difficult to remove. A couple of half circular tiles, placed round the plant, with the earth brought up around it, is the method I generally pursue. Salad only requires that the leaves should be brought together and tied with plantain leaf or other substance, and if rain falls, the leaves must be occasionally opened and the water shaken out, else they soon decay.

BLIGHT.—A common term for injuries received by the vegetable kingdom when in a state of growth, which cannot always be referred to any obvious or certain cause, and coming suddenly, is said to give them the appearance of being blighted. Attacks of insects, fogs, clammy weather, and frost, are said to be some of the causes.

BUDDING—should be performed in the morning or evening: the natives give the preference to the last and first quarter of the moon for the operation. The cuttings from which buds are taken should be from healthy trees, and such as have borne fruit. The best season for budding is at the commencement of the rains, and during the cold weather, though much will depend upon the state of the tree from which you take your bud, and the forwardness of the stock on which it is to be inoculated,—whether the sap is rising in it, and the bark separates with ease from the wood when opened.

*Process.*—Provide yourself with a good sharp knife, (*vide Fig.* 29.) and shreds of linen tape, or plantain leaf, about one-fourth of an inch in breadth; also have a thin blunt piece of flat ivory or bamboo, cut round or smooth at the end, for introducing between the bark and separating it from the wood. Having your knife, shreds, and cuttings, ready, you are to proceed in the following manner:—

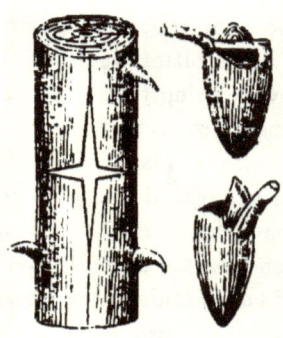

With your knife make a cross cut in the smooth part of the bark, rind off the stalk, and be careful to make it no deeper than the bark; let another be made down the centre about two inches long, so that the two cuts form the figure of the cross, in which the bud is to be inserted. Then from your cuttings or shoots take off the bud in the following manner: begin at the lower end of the shoot, having removed all the leaves, but leaving a small part of the stalk remaining; then about an inch below the lower bud, or eye, make a cross cut in the shoot, half way through, in a slanting direction, carrying the cut upwards in a clean manner to about half an inch below the bud; here separate it from the stalk with a cross cut; then with the point of your knife clear away the wood inside from the rind, very gently, and observe if the inside of the eye of the bud be left; for if there appears a small hole, the eye is gone, and the bud for insertion useless, therefore take another, and when ready, insert it immediately in the stock prepared for its reception. Be careful to place the bud in the centre of the perpendicular slit from the cross above, observing that the bud is in no ways injured or pressed upon by the sides or the bark of the stock; then let that part be immediately bound round with the tape, or shreds, beginning a little below the cut and proceeding upwards, drawing it closely round to the top of the slit, but carefully observing that the eye of the bud is not included or pressed upon. When you have thus surrounded the whole, bring the end through a slide of the fastening and leave it: thus the operation is done. A piece of plantain leaf tied about four inches above the bud, so as to drop over it, will shade it from the sun and promote its growth. In the course of a fortnight, you will be enabled to judge if it has taken, by its full and green appearance: if otherwise, it looks black and shrivelled. When the shoot is six or eight fingers long you may then cut off the heads of the stocks, leaving about two inches above the insertion of the bud.

Shield budding or T budding differs from the preceding merely in the form of the incision.

Observe, as soon as your buds have shot out strong, that you loosen the bandages below, suffering the upper to remain a short time longer; hemp or string should on no account be used, as they cut through the rind and injure the growth of the shoot.

In Niche budding the incision is made in the form of an inverted U, this mode is applicable to rose bushes.

A bud of sweet brier grafted on the stock of a Rose Edwards threw out a shoot full three inches long in the course of twenty days after the bud was first tied on, in the month of February, at Hyderabad, in the Deccan.

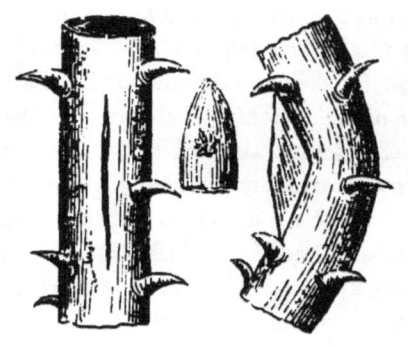

*Native Method of Budding.*—This is very simple, and in general most successful. An incision of the length required is made perpendicularly in the stock; they then take hold of it with their hands, both above and below the cut, and bend the stock forward towards them, the bark is thus separated and forms an opening sufficient to introduce the bud, which is placed in its right position, the stock is then allowed to regain elasticity, and the bark or rind closes tightly round the bud: a ligature of plantain leaf shreds is bound round the perpendicular incision, omitting of course the bud, and allowing it free space to grow, no cross cut being required.

When you remove these plants into the situations in which they are to remain, and they appear to have taken root well, then you may cut off the head of the stock in a slanting direction, near the bud, in a clean and careful manner.

CIRCULATION OF WATER IN SOILS.—It is necessary for the due nourishment of plants, that the water by which soils are moistened have a proper movement or circulation. When the soil is so loose and porous as not to retain moisture, the circulation is too rapid, so that the water is carried off before it can be taken up by the root fibres and conveyed to the plants, on the other hand, when the soil is stiff and compact so as not to allow the water it imbibes to circulate, the mouths of the minute tubes are pressed upon and obstructed, so that no nourishment obtains admission, both conditions are of course detrimental. If a soil is very porous, the water naturally sinks into it and moves towards the bottom, which, if not of a firmer texture, the water will naturally drain away; and as the heat expends the water nearest the surface into vapour, and raises it into the air, as soon as by this means the surface becomes dry, the moisture below will gradually rise in the same way, leaving little or no further nourishment for the plant. But again, if in such a soil there is at a little depth, of two feet or so, a stiff clay or rock, the water then settles, and being out of the reach of the sun's influence to raise it, it becomes necessary to drain it off, otherwise, for want of circulation, it becomes deleterious to the growth of the plant: water should never be allowed to stagnate round plants, but always have a free movement or circulation, otherwise the mouths of the suckers become pressed upon and obstructed, and of course the nourishment is checked in its progress. Water, when stagnated, soon becomes exhausted of the nutritive material with which it may have at first been mixed and it then becomes destructive.

CLEARING OF FRUIT TREES, &c.—This is a very necessary part of the business of a gardener who wishes his trees to look well and produce a good crop of fruit. In the first place, keep all the space round your trees, if possible, clear of weeds, which only can be done by cutting and hoeing them up, and then removing the same—or scatter under your trees a small quantity of hemp stalks; this not only prevents the growth of weeds, but, when it decays, forms a very beneficial manure. All dead branches should be cut away in a smooth manner, either with a saw, or knife, and suckers never allowed to spring up from the roots, unless wanted for stocks. Another important thing to attend to, is, to observe if any insects have bored holes in the woody part of the trees, and which may immediately be known by seeing their holes, or a quantity of dry saw-dust, in appearance, hanging by light filaments of thread from the entrance, in which an insect like a caterpillar has taken up its quarters, and will be found working its way either into the sap of the tree or along the bark, both of which are equally injurious; it is necessary to remove them as soon as possible. The method to effect this is very simple. Provide yourself with a strong infusion of assafœtida, and some dough made with common flour and water: pour a small quantity of the infusion into the hole, enough to fill it up; then after having removed all the dirt round it, stick a small piece of the dough, about the size of a pigeon's egg, over the hole, and let it remain. In the course of an hour or two, if you take off the dough, you will find the insect to have embedded itself in it. This plan answers when you have other work in hand cannot wait the result of the infusion which has been put into the hole: if you can, generally in a few minutes, if the insect is there, you will observe a bubble in the mixture; this is occasioned by the insect moving, and shortly after it will be seen crawling up to the top, presenting a thick horny head: then, with a long pin, or thorn, gently run it slanting through the neck and give the insect a sharp twist out. They are sometimes two or three inches long, and very destructive, as they attack every fruit-bearing tree, as well as others. When insects infest the leaves of trees, they must either be picked off, or destroyed by smoking the tree. Sulphur thrown on burning charcoal is very effective method of destroying insects; the fumes must be allowed to pass over the branches. A pound of sulphur will suffice for very many trees.

COLOUR OF FLOWERS.—The colour, smell, and nutritive qualities of plants, depend for their production chiefly on the action of light. The propensity of plants to turn to the light depends solely on the hardening and stiffening of one side, whilst the other remains soft and pliable; the side exposed to the light has its moisture carried off by evaporation, and is rendered more firm, contracted, and shorter, than the one less exposed.

COMPOSTS—Are mixtures of several earths, or dungs, for the improvement of the general soil under culture, or for the culture of particular plants. In respect of composts for the amendment of the general soil of the garden, the quality must depend upon the natural soil; if this be light, loose, or sandy, it may be assisted by the addition of heavy loam, clays, &c., from ponds, tanks, and ditches. On the other hand, heavy clays and stubborn soils may be assisted by light composts of sandy earth, all kinds of ashes, rotten bark, saw-dust, and other similar opening materials that can be procured.

COMPOSITION FOR WOUNDS IN TREES.—The following composition, prepared after the recipé of Mr. Forsyth, has been found to answer extremely well: old fruit trees, such as the mango, frequently derive benefit by having the composition applied, after removing the cankered and decayed parts. It may also be applied to the end of cut branches when pruning trees:—"Take a large basket of fresh cowdung, half a basket of fine lime rubbish from old buildings, half a basket of woodashes from the kitchen, and about four double handsful of the finest sand procurable: the last three articles must be well sifted and mixed together, working the whole up with a powrah or beater until it is quite smooth; then lay on the plaster about one-eighth of an inch thick, all over the part where the wood or bark has been cut away, finishing off the edges to a thin surface." "Then take a quantity of dry powder of woodashes, mixed with a sixth part of the same quantity of burnt bones. Sprinkle this powder over the surface of the plaster till the whole is covered over with it: let it remain to absorb the moisture, then apply more powder, gently rubbing it with the hand till the whole plaster becomes a dry surface."

CUTTINGS.—Propagation by cuttings is simple, and generally successful with fast growing hardy shrubs, such as the Laurel, Grape, Fig, &c., but with many others, such as the Myrtle, Cypress, &c., it is one of the most delicate and difficult modes of continuing the species. The subject must be considered as to the choice of cuttings, their preparation, insertion in the soil, and future management.

CUTTINGS, CHOICE OF.—Those branches of trees or shrubs thrown out nearest the ground, and especially such as recline, or nearly so, on the earth's surface, have always the most tendency to produce roots: even the branches of resinous trees, which are extremely difficult to propagate by cuttings, when reclining on the ground, if accidentally covered with earth in any part, will often throw out roots, as in the Fir, Cypress, &c.: cuttings should therefore be preferred from those shoots nearest the stem and ground. The proper time for taking cuttings, is when the sap is in full motion, in order that, returning by the bark, it may form a callus or protruding ring of granular substance between the bark and wood, whence the roots proceed. As this ring is generally best formed in ripened wood, the cutting, when taken from the mother plant, should contain a part of the former year; or in plants which grow twice a year, of the wood of the former growth; or in evergreens, such wood as has begun to ripen or assume a brownish colour. This is the true principle as to the choice of cuttings as to time, but there are many sorts of trees the cuttings of which will grow at any season in India, if protected from the hot land winds. In some plants, where the sap is comparatively at rest, the principle of life is so strong, and so diffused over the vegetable, that very little care is requisite for their propagation. Cuttings from herbaceous plants should be chosen from the low growths which do not indicate a tendency to blossom, but they will succeed in many cases from the flower stems, and border flowers, as the Dahlia, Rocket, Wall-flower, Nasturtium, &c.

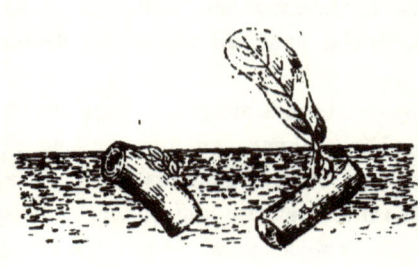

*The preparation of Cuttings* is guided by this principle, viz., that the power of protruding buds or roots resides chiefly, and in most cases entirely, in what are called the axillæ or joints, where leaves or buds already exist: hence all cuttings should be evenly cut across with the smoothest and soundest section possible at an eye or joint; and the choice of a bud should be in wood somewhat ripened or fully formed, and the section should be made in the wood of the growth of the preceding season, or as it were in the point between the two growths. It is true that the cuttings of some plants, such as the Grape, Mulberry, &c., not only throw out roots from the ring of granulated matter, but also from the sides of every part of the stem inserted in the soil; but all plants which are difficult to root, such as Heaths, Camellias, Oranges, &c., will be found in the first instance to throw out roots only from the ring of herbaceous matter above-mentioned: and hence the necessity of properly preparing the cuttings. It is not a good practice to take off the whole of the leaves of cuttings, as the leaves in many instances supply nourishment to the cutting until it can sustain itself. Leaves alone in some instances, will strike root, and form plants.

*Cuttings* which are difficult to strike may be rendered more tractable by previous ringing. If a ring be made on the shoot which is to furnish the cutting, a callus will be created, which, if inserted in the ground after the cutting is taken off, will freely emit roots. A ligature would perhaps answer the same purpose. The amputation, in case of the ring or ligature, must be made below the circles, and the cutting must be so planted as to have the callus covered with earth.

[*Collodion useful for striking Cuttings.*—Many cuttings fail from damping off at the base, using collodion is said to save them. Major Trevor Clarke, a great authority, on the Committee of the Royal Horticultural Society, London, gives the following recipe. Allow the cuttings time to dry off visible moisture from the cut, then dip the ends, in a minute or so dip again, and in five minutes plant them.

Procure the collodion from a good Photographic Chemist and state in your order that it must be capable of giving a strong horny film, with only sufficient Alcohol to ensure solution, and to be twice as strong in cotton as that used for photographic purposes.

*Striking Cuttings.*—All soft wooded and delicate plant cuttings should be struck in sand under a hand glass, not overwatered, the soil kept just moist, if the cuttings are kept in the open, the glass should be covered in the day with matting during bright sunshine, generally a place under a big tree is selected for striking cuttings. It should be well raised so that no over-wet state of the soil is created, from too much moisture cuttings are liable to damp off when they have rooted the hand glass is removed except in heavy rain.—ED.]

*The insertion of Cuttings*—may seem an easy matter, and none but a practical cultivator would imagine that there could be any difference in the growth between cuttings inserted in the middle of a pot and those inserted at its sides. Yet such is actually the case, and some sorts of trees if inserted in a mere mass of earth, will hardly, if at all, throw out roots, while if they are inserted in sand or in earth at the side of the pots, so as to touch the pot in their whole length, they seldom fail of becoming rooted plants. Some cuttings will be found to strike more easily if their lower ends are placed on a piece of broken pot or tile, or when touching a stratum of gravel; therefore with cuttings which are found difficult to strike root, it is advisable they should be so laid in pots as to be made to touch the bottom. A large tumbler or glass bell jar placed over a cutting, if small, will often facilitate its growth.

*The management of Cuttings.*—No cutting requires to be planted deep, though such as are large ought to be inserted deeper than such as are small. In the case of evergreens, the leaves should never touch the soil, otherwise they will rot off from damp: a leaf lying with its under part on a wet soil, or on water, will decay and rot as fast as if plucked and exposed to the sun; and the same difficulty occurs in the case of tubular-stalked plants, which are not in general very easily struck, owing to the water lodging in the tube and rotting the cutting. Both ends of a cutting may in some cases be inserted in the soil forming a half circle in this manner, besides, with a

greater certainty of success, two plants will be produced. Too much light, air, water, heat, or cold, are alike injurious, and to guard against these it is useful to enclose an atmosphere over the cuttings of tender plants by the means of a bell or hand glass. This preserves a uniform stillness and moisture of atmosphere. Immersing the pots in earth (if the cuttings are in pots) has a tendency to preserve a moisture to their roots; and shading or planting the cuttings, (if in the open air) in a shady situation, prevents the bad effects of the excess of light.

DESCENT OF THE SAP.—The simple fact with respect to leaf buds and branch buds seems to be that they are expanded in spring by the sap, and when sufficiently so to permit the air and light to convert this into pulp, it descends into the bark at their base, but it is not until the leaf is fully expanded that any new wood is or can be formed; consequently it is the leaf, not the leaf bud, which is the chief agent in this process.

DESTROYING INSECTS ON VEGETABLES, &c.—Sprinkle the leaves over with very fine pounded sulphur tied up in a muslin bag, or with woodashes from the kitchen. Fumigate also trees with tobacco smoke, or sprinkle the leaves with a solution made after the following manner: to three parts of lime add one of sulphur, and boil both together in one hundred parts of water: you may also soak seeds in this to preserve them.

*For destroying White Ants*, take a bundle of the twigs of the Sarcostemma Viminale; put it into the trough of the well by which the bed or field is watered, along with a bag of salt, hard packed, so that it may only dissolve gradually. Water so impregnated destroys the ants without injuring the crop. Dry twigs answer as well as green. This plant abounds in the Deccan, in Gogah and the coast of Kattywar.—*Hind,* name, Soom.

DEW.—Is the moisture insensibly deposited from the atmosphere on the earth. The moisture is precipitated by the cold of the body on which it appears, and will be more or less abundant—not in proportion to the coldness of that body, but—in proportion to the existing state of the air in regard to moisture. It is commonly supposed that the formation of dew produces cold, but, like every other precipitation of water from the atmosphere, it must evidently produce heat.

DIGGING.—This is almost always performed by the pickaxe and kodallee and is the most effectual method (the spade never being used by natives). When the ground will admit, the plough, probably, is a quicker method. The earth thus turned up admits of being easily worked, and the clods knocked to pieces, the plough also turns out the weeds, only that it is apt to disturb the roots of trees in the neighbourhood, and the bullocks, injure the trees themselves.

EARTH AND SOILS.—Earths are the production of the rocks which are exposed on the surface of the globe, and soils are earths mixed with more or less of the decomposed organized matter afforded by dead plants and animals. Earth and soils therefore must be as various as the rocks which produce them. The surface earth, or that which forms the outer coating of the dry parts of the globe, is formed by the detritus of worn off parts of rocks, and rocky substances. Earths are therefore variously composed, according to the rocks or strata which have supplied the particles. Sometimes they are formed from slate rocks, as in blue clays; at other times from sand stone, as in siliceous soils; and mostly of a mixture of clayey, slatey, and limestone rocks, blended in proportions as various as their situations. In process of time the decay of vegetables and animals form additions to the outer surface of the earth, and constitute what are called soils. As soon as the smallest layer of earth is formed on the surface of a rock, the spores of Lichens, Mosses, and other Flowerless plants, which are constantly floating in the atmosphere, and which have found a resting place, begin to vegetate; their death, decomposition, and decay, afford a certain quantity of organizable matter, which mixes with the earthy materials of the rock. In this improved soil more perfect plants are capable of subsisting. These in their turn absorb nourishment from water, and the atmosphere, and after perishing, afford new materials to those already provided. The decomposition of the rock still continues, and at length, by such slow and gradual processes, a soil is formed in which even forest trees can fix their roots, and which is fitted to reward the labors of the cultivator.

*Preparation of Garden Soil at the commencement of the hot season.* —It is stated by Leibig, that the frequent separation and intermixing of the granules of the soil during suitable weather is beneficial to it chemically and physically, the surface soil has the power of arresting and fixing a large quantity of plant food, especially Ammonia, some of which it gets from the atmosphere, phosphate of lime and potash. The first inch of top soil, (which is 100 tons per acre of earth) gets the best chance of appropriation and then come the next and lower ones. As plants multiply their side fibres near the surface we may comprehend why surface manuring is so often found beneficial. The sub-soil is cold, dense, pale and unaltered, altogether different from the friable and manured surface soil. It is therefore necessary to break up the sub-soil and intermix it with the upper soil. This is best done in this country by digging up the garden beds early in the hot season when the ground is lying fallow and letting the sun's rays act fully on the up-turned clods, which, on the first showers of the monsoon will crumble and be easily worked.

EARTHING UP.—This is performed by the hand and a small spade, or with a large sized hoe; it consists in turning up the ground round the stocks of plants, so as to support and nourish them,—a thing very essential to the growth of all kinds of vegetables, potatoes, peas, beans, &c.

ESCULENT ROOTS—delight in a light, rather sandy, deep and well stirred soil. It must be dry at bottom, but a moist atmosphere and moderate temperature are greatly favorable to the growth of them.

ESPALIER TREES.—Such as are suitable for, or are planted against rails or upright trellis-work, which are much more suitable for India than walls.

ETIOLATION.—A disease of plants which destroys their verdure and renders them pale: it arises from the want of the agency of light, and may also arise from the depredation of insects nestling in the radicle, and consuming the food of the plant, and thus debilitating the vessels of the leaf, so as to render them unsusceptible of the action of light, for on examining with a microscope, the leaves of peas and other plants in this state, the meally greyish appearance evidently arose from eggs and excretions deposited upon them by a minute greenish coloured insect which was seen feeding, and moving in every direction upon their surface; this readily accounts for the destruction of the stem and plant. A similar appearance was observed on Mango blossoms and leaves after a succession of cloudy days.

EXPOSURE AND SHELTER.—Solitary trees become greatly larger than those that are crowded, whilst their roots are always proportioned to the branches, the same is true with regard to nearly all garden plants, which extend in proportion to their room; hence the necessity of wide planting when trees or shrubs with spreading heads are set out to grow.

FOOD OF PLANTS.—Vegetables cannot live without a supply of food, and are incapable of moving to look for it. The food of all plants varies but little.

The difference between some garden plants and others is in their greater delicacy; hence the nourishment given to them requires only a little more delicacy in its preparation.

Young plants require on first germinating from seed, a different nourishment than when more advanced,—after they have exhausted the nourishment in the seed lobes and seed leaves. Plants derive their nourishment from two sources, the earth and the atmosphere, but principally from the soil through the roots. It is chiefly in the form of water holding various solid matters, in solution that the nutritive matter of the soil is received by the roots, which are furnished at their extremities with spongioles or sucking mouths possessing an amazing power of absorption.

FIBRINE—is a peculiar substance which chemists extract from the blood and muscles of animals. This substance constitutes the fibrous part of the muscles, and resembles gluten in its appearance and elasticity, and a substance possessing the same properties, has been found by Vanquelin in the juice of the Papaw tree: it is called vegetable fibrine.

GERMINATING OF SEEDS.—Some seeds, such as Coffee, require to be sown immediately on being gathered, otherwise the nutrient matter contained in the shell becomes too hard to be dissolved in water. Seeds gathered before they are quite ripe, germinate sooner than very ripe ones; because the nutrient matter is less hard, and more easily diluted with water. But though seeds when gathered before they are quite ripe, germinate sooner, it does not follow that they will produce the best plants.

GLUTEN—is that part of the paste formed from the flour of wheat that remains unaffected by the water after all the starch contained in it has been washed off. This is a tough and elastic substance, of a dark white colour, without taste, but of a very peculiar smell: it is found in fruits and grain such as Peas, Beans, Barley, Acorns, Chesnuts, Apples, Quinces; also in leaves, such as Cabbage, Cresses, Saffron, &c.; and also in the petals of the Rose; and is the most important of all vegetable substances.

GRAFTING.—The most common method, and in general use in the Deccan, is by approach, although crown and stock-grafting are both practised by the gardeners in Bombay and Salsette: the latter is done by making a hole in the bark of a stock and inserting the scions therein while the tree is growing, but nine out of ten generally fail.

HAUM OR HAULMN.—The lower part of the straw after the ears are cut off; in gardening the term is generally applied to leguminous vegetables after their produce has been gathered.

HEADING.—The growing of the leaves of a plant into a roundish head or loaf.

HEAT—is essentially necessary for the growth of plants, as it is obvious that no plant could take up frozen liquids. The process of fermentation and putrefaction, by which are produced the supply of Carbonic Acid Gas, Humic Acid,* and Azote, is indispensable to vegetation, as it cannot go on without it.

HERBARIUM.—The dried plants for surpass either drawings or descriptions, in giving complete ideas of their appearance. When plants are well dried, the original forms and positions of even their minutest parts (though not their colours) may at any time be restored by immersion in hot water. The mode or state in which the plants are preserved is general desiccation, accompanied by pressing. The greater part of plants dry with facility between the leaves of books or blotting paper, the smoother the better. If there be plenty of paper, they often dry without shifting, but

* Humic acid—the principal ingredient of all manures.

if the specimens are crowded, they must be taken out frequently, and the paper dried before they are replaced. Some vegetables are so tenacious of their vital principle, that they will grow between papers; the consequence is a destruction of their proper habit and colours. It is therefore necessary to destroy the life of such by immersion in boiling water, or by the application of a hot iron such as is used for linen, after which they are easily dried. The herbarium should be kept in as dry a place as possible, and free from insects.

HYBRIDIZATION.—The process though very simple requires much care and attention as well as patience.

In the first instance, it consists merely in applying the pollen of the flowers of one variety to those of another of the same species. The strange pollen grain resting on the stigma of one of the latter flowers, in process of time, puts forth a microscopic tubule, and penetrating the tissue of the stigma it finally reaches the ovule to which it communicates the principle of life. The ovule finally matured is a seed—in this instance a seed borne of one flower and receiving the vital principle of another. Several precautions are necessary to a successful issue. The flower in which the operation is to be performed, must be deprived of its own anthers before the pollen they secrete is matured and fitted for its functions in the vegetable organism. In some flowers, in which the ripening of the pollen takes place before the expansion of the flower, this is almost impossible, as the flower in such case must be torn open while it is yet unexpanded; in others it may be managed by using a very delicate pair of lady's scissors. Selecting a flower of another variety of the species the pollen of which is just ripe or nearly so, it may be removed by a fine camel's hair brush from the anthers and transferred to the stigma of the first flower. It is then customary amongst some cultivators to tie a little bag of fine gauze or muslin over the flower thus treated to prevent the application of any other farina, by the intervention of insects, or the wind which might interfere with the result. Others are again content with the simple ticketing so as to be able at seed time to distinguish the flower. The usual process then goes on, the flower fades, and in time ripens when it must be carefully collected and stored up in a marked box.

HORTUS SICCUS.—After having collected as good a specimen as possible of the plant, lay it flat, disposing of it in the best manner, betwixt sheets of white paper, so that the flowers and leaves do not interfere with each other : put this on a quire of blotting paper, and also a quire over it, and then apply a weight on the top—books answer this purpose very well. The next day put dry blotting paper as before, first opening the sheet of paper, and making any alterations in the disposition of parts. Dried specimens are to be fixed into slips of paper or glued with common glue. These should be kept in shelves or drawers. To prevent the depredation of insects, Dr. Smith recommends a solution of corrosive sublimate (muriate of mercury,) in some spirits of wine, with which the plants are, when dry, to be gently moistened.

IMPERFECT PLANTS.—Apparently defective in one or other of the more conspicuous parts or organs, whether conservative or reproductive, are denominated imperfect, and are called Cryptogamous, because their organs of fructification are not yet detected, or are so minute as to require the aid of a microscope to render them visible, as in the Filices, Musci, Hepaticæ, Algæ, Lichens, and Fungi.

IMPROVEMENT OF SOILS.—Soils may be rendered more fit for answering the purposes of vegetation by pulverization, by consolidation, by exposure to the atmosphere, by an alteration of their constituent parts, by changing their condition with respect to water, by changing their position with respect to atmospherical influence, and by a change of the kind of plants cultivated. All these improvements are independently of the application of manure. The fibres of roots take up the extract of the soil by intro-susception : the quantity taken up therefore will not depend alone on the quantity in the soil, but on the number of the absorbing fibres. The more the soil is pulverized, the more these fibres are increased : and the more extract is absorbed, the more vigorous does the plant become. Pulverization, therefore, is not only advantageous, previous to planting or sowing, but also during the progress of vegetation, when applied in the intervals between the plants. In this last case it operates also in the way of pruning, and by the cutting off the extending fibres, causes them to branch out numerous others, by which the mouths or pores of the plant are greatly increased, and such food as is in the soil has the better chance of being sought after and taken up by them.

Pulverization increases the capillary attraction, or sponge-like property of soils, by which their humidity is rendered more uniform. It is proved that capillary attraction must be greatest when the particles of the earth are finely divided, for gravel and sand hardly retain water at all, while clays not open by pulverization, or other means, either do not absorb water, or when by long action it is absorbed, they retain too much. Water is not only necessary to the growth of plants, as such, but it is essential to the production of extract from the vegetable matters they contain, and unless the soil, by pulverization or otherwise, is so constituted as to retain the quantity of water requisite to produce this extract, the addition of manures will be in vain. Manure is useless to vegetation until it becomes soluble in water, and it would remain useless in a state of solution if it so abounded as wholly to seclude air, for then the fibres or mouths, unable to perform their functions, would soon decay and rot off; as is the case with flowers or shrubs in pots where there is no opening, so that the air cannot circulate round the roots.

Pulverization leads to the increase of vegetable food. Water is known to be a condenser and solvent of carbonic acid gas; which, where the land is open, can be immediately carried to the roots of vegetables, and contributes to their growth; but if the earth be close, and the water lie on or near its surface, then the carbonic gas, which always exists in the atmosphere, and is carried down by rains, will soon be dissipated. An open soil, therefore, is always suitable for effecting those changes in the manure itself which are equally necessary to the preparation of such food. Animal and vegetable substances exposed to the alternate action of heat, moisture, light and air, undergo spontaneous decomposition which would not otherwise take place.—A very good compost for improving stiff soils is made by equal parts of lime and woodashes with two parts of sand.

In soils that are very light, it is advantageous to roll or beat down seeds, as it prevents the light soil from drifting, and also (a very material point) hinders ants from carrying them away.

Stagnant water may be considered as injurious to all the useful classes of plants, by obstructing perspiration and intro-susception —thus diseasing their roots and submerged parts.

INARCHING, OR GRAFTING BY APPROACH.—This is a very common method all over India, and is performed by bringing the stock you would graft upon close to the tree from which you wish to take a branch, and which remains united until the two branches are firmly connected together: the stem is then divided near the stock and removed.

*Process.*—Either having the stocks and trees designed to inarch from growing in the ground near together, or in pots, or that you wish to inarch some branches of trees, and that the said branches are three or more feet from the ground, and suppose the stocks you would graft upon to be in pots or boxes, in that case you must erect a slight stage close to, and as high as, the branches of the tree, for placing the stocks upon. Thus far, then, in either case, you have proceeded. Take one of the branches you desire to inarch, and bring the body of the said branch to touch that of the stock at such a convenient height, where the stock and graft is nearly of the same size, and mark the parts where the stock and graft will most readily unite; then, in that part of the branch, pare away the bark and part of the wood about three inches in length, and in the same manner let the rind and wood be pared off that side of the stock where the branch is to be joined, the same length and breadth, so that both the cut parts may exactly join, rind to rind, and be united in the middle; let them then be immediately tied together with tape, as closely and firmly as possible; then tie round the whole in a smooth manner. A piece of wax cloth, or else a composition of clay and cowdung, must be fastened round the whole; the objection to the latter method is, that it becomes the receptacle for insects, ants in particular, and you are in danger of having your grafts spoiled. After this, to prevent the wind from displacing the grafts, a strong stake should be driven in the ground, close to the stock, to which they should be tied. The stock and graft should remain in this position for at least ten weeks, though sometimes they will be united much sooner. This method of raising trees may be followed at any season, except in the rains.

INSECTS—which infect the plants are almost as numerous as the plants themselves, almost every species having a particular insect which it seems destined by nature to support. The eggs of insects seldom increase in size from the time they have been deposited by the parent until they are hatched. Different species of insects remain enclosed in the egg for different periods: some continue enclosed in the egg for months, others only for a few days. The insect in its second or caterpillar state is usually known by the name of Eruca or Larva. The Larva of insects differ very much from each other, according to the several tribes to which they belong:—those of the Butterfly (Papilio) and Moth (Phalina) are generally known by the name of Caterpillars; those of the Beetle, (Scarabeus) and those that inhabit the water, are called grubs.

LAWN.—In gardening, a surface of turf or grasses, kept short by frequent cutting, and generally situated near the house.

LIME.—If quick lime, either fresh, or burnt, or slaked, be mixed with moist vegetable substances, it soon destroys their texture, and forms a mixture the greater part of which can be dissolved in water, thus rendering what was previously useless fit for the food of plants. It is much more useful in farms than gardens.

LIGHT—is essentially necessary to the growth of plants, as also its exclusion for blanching or etiolation, as no exposure to cold or fresh air would produce toughness and hardiness, if plants were kept in the dark; and no absence of cold or fresh air would produce blanching if light were admitted. A partial exclusion of light causes plants to be pale and sickly, as in the shade of thick woods or under trees, as is the case where plants shoot out long branches in search of air and light: hence the term is said to be drawn.

*Light* appears to be as necessary to the health of plants as air or moisture. A plant may indeed grow without it, but it does not appear a species could be so continued. Under such a privation, the parts which are usually so grown assume a white colour, as is the case with vegetables grown in a cellar, or protected by a covering for the sake of producing this very effect: thus Celery, Endive, &c., is in this manner blanched or etiolated.

" The part of the process of vegetable life for which light is especially essential, appears to be in the functions of the leaves; these are affected by this agent in a remarkable degree. The moisture that plants imbibe is by their vital energies carried to their leaves, and is there brought in contact with the atmosphere, which, besides other ingredients, contains in general a portion of carbonic acid. So long as light is present, the leaf decomposes the carbonic acid, appropriates the carbon to the formation of its own proper juices, and returns the disengaged oxygen into the atmosphere, thus restoring the atmospheric air to a condition in which it is more fitted, than it was before, for the support of animal life."

"The plant thus prepares the support of life for other creatures at the same time that it absorbs its own. The greenness of those members which effect that colour, and the disengagement of oxygen, are the indications that its vital powers are in healthful action. As soon as we remove light from a plant these indications cease: it has no longer power to imbibe carbon, and disengage oxygen, but, on the contrary, it gives back some of the carbon already obtained, and robs the atmosphere of oxygen for the purpose of re-converting this into carbonic acid."—*Whewell.—Bridgewater Treatise.*

[LIQUID MANURE—is very useful used with caution—when applied in too concentrated a form it is pernicious. A small quantity of fresh cowdung, pig dung, poultry dung, guano, &c., mixed with a large body of water, just sufficient to discolor it is what is required, not a thick muddy liquid. This liquid manure may be applied to the roots of Roses, Chrysanthemums and most plants when they are near their season for flowering, and the soil should be hoed and broken up previously to allow the liquid manure to sink in to the roots. Avoid soiling the leaves and flowers.

POUDRETTE is an excellent top-dressing for Arums, Colocasias, Iresine and Canna, but should not be mixed at all with soil in which seeds are to be sown for it will inevitably kill them. Well rotted leaf mould is an excellent fertiliser and should be used for all composts.—ED.]

*Excellent Dressing for Gardens.*—The use of the following manure is described as being so beneficial as to be followed by a four-fold increase of produce, and is well adapted for the flower and kitchen garden. In a pit about twenty feet long, twelve or fourteen wide, and fifteen or eighteen deep, put a layer of dung, and on that a layer of earth, and so alternately till the pile is elevated a foot or two above the level of the ground, watering each layer of earth with a strong solution of saltpetre—this should be left undisturbed for six months. When this compost is moved, it will be found wholly converted into earth, presenting no trace of the dung.

*Guano*, like farm-yard dung, is variable in its composition. It is the dung of birds which feed on fish, and consists principally of salts of ammonia and phosphates, with a little soda and potash. Attempts are being made to produce an artificial guano by a mixture of the mean of the various salts which it contains, which shall be more uniform in character. In using these concentrated saline mixtures, it is hazardous to drill them in with the seed, as there is a danger of their killing it during germination: they should be used as a top-dressing, and sewn by hand with care, so as to distribute it as equally as possible over the plot of ground.

LOAM—is a yellowish or brownish kind of clay, sometimes containing a considerable proportion of sand. It occurs in immense beds, and is found in almost every part of the world.

MANURE.—This term is applied indiscriminately to all substances which are known from experience either to enrich the different soils, or contribute in any other way to render them more favorable to vegetation.

In an agricultural point of view, the subject of manures is of the utmost importance. To correct what is hurtful to vegetation in the different soils, and to restore what is lost by exhausting crops, are operations in agriculture which may be compared to the curing diseases in the animal body, or supplying the waste occasioned by labour.

Rotted dung is very much superior in imbibing and retaining water to that which is fresh, unfermented, or beginning to ferment. The quantity of humic acid is considerably greater in rotted than fresh dung, and it approaches nearer to the best leaf mould or virgin loam.

Lime should never be applied with animal manures unless they are too rich, or for the purpose of preventing noxious effluvia:

it is injurious when mixed with any common drug, and tends to render the extractive matter insoluble. It is beneficial to all new soils, especially where the salts of iron are found.

Animal and vegetable manures are used to renovate worn-out lands by supplying new soluble and gaseous matter for the nourishment of the plant. This is not a permanent good, and requires to be constantly renewed, as it is found by experience that vegetable and animal substances, used as manure, are consumed during the process of vegetation. The Chinese use every animal and vegetable refuse; everything of disgusting appearance and offensive effluvia they collect carefully and use as beneficial agents in vegetation, thus converting the loathsome and revolting into wholesome and inviting. The great object in the application of manure should be to make it afford as much soluble matter as possible to the roots of the plants, and that in a slow and gradual manner, so that it may be entirely consumed in forming its sap and organized parts. Animal and vegetable manures can only nourish the plant by affording solid matter capable of being dissolved by water, or gaseous substances capable of being absorbed by the fluids in the leaves of vegetables.

The following compost has been used in England, and it is said to have doubled the crops of potatoes and cabbages, and to be far superior to stable manure:—

Raise a platform of earth eight feet wide, one foot high, and of any length according to the quantity wanted. On the first stratum of earth lay a thin stratum of lime, fresh from the kiln: dissolve or slake this with salt-brine from the nose of a watering pot; and immediately another layer of earth, then lime and brine as before, carry it to any convenient height. In a week it should be turned over and carefully broken and mixed, so that the mass may be thoroughly incorporated.

MANURES OF VEGETABLE AND ANIMAL ORIGIN.—Experience shows that vegetable and animal substances deposited in the soil are consumed during the progress of vegetation, and they can only nourish the plant by affording solid matters capable of being dissolved by water, or gaseous substances capable of being absorbed by the fluids in the leaves of vegetables; but such parts of them as are rendered gaseous, and that pass into the atmosphere, must produce a comparatively small effect, for gases soon become diffused through the mass of the surrounding air. The great object in the application of manure should be to make it afford as much soluble matter as possible to the roots of the plant; and that in a slow and gradual manner, so that it may be entirely consumed in forming its sap and organized parts. Mucilaginous, gelatinous, saccharine, oily, and extractive fluids, and solution of carbonic acid gas in water, are substances that, in their unchanged state, contain almost all the essentials necessary for the life of plants; but there are few cases in which they can be applied in their pure form: and vegetable manures, in general, contain a great excess of fibrous and insoluble matter, which must undergo chemical changes before they can become the food of plants.

It will be proper to explain the nature of these changes, of the causes which occasion them, and which accelerate or retard them; also of the products they afford.

"If any fresh vegetable matter which contains sugar, mucilage, starch, or other of the vegetable compounds soluble in water, be moistened and exposed to air at a temperature from 55 to 80 degrees, oxygen will soon be absorbed, and carbonic acid formed: heat will be produced, and elastic fluids (principally carbonic acid gas, gaseous oxide of carbon, and hydro-carbonate) will be evolved, and a dark-coloured liquid, of a slightly sour or bitter taste, will likewise be formed; and if the process be suffered to continue sufficiently long, nothing solid will remain except earthy and saline matter, coloured by black charcoal. The dark-coloured fluid formed in the fermentation always contains acetic acid, and when albumen or gluten exists in the vegetable substance it likewise contains volatile alkali. In proportion as there is more gluten, albumen, or matter soluble in water, in the vegetable substances exposed to fermentation, so in proportion, all other circumstances being equal, will the process be more rapid. Pure woody fibre alone undergoes a change very slowly, but its texture is broken down, and it is easily resolved into new elements when mixed with substances more liable to change, containing more oxygen and hydrogen. Volatile and fixed oils, resins, and wax, are more susceptible of change than woody fibre when exposed to air and water, but much less liable than the other vegetable compounds: and even the most inflammable substances, by the absorption of oxygen become gradually soluble in water.

Animal matters, in general, are more liable to decompose than vegetable substances: oxygen is absorbed, and carbonic acid and ammonia formed, in the process of their putrefaction. They produce fœtid compound elastic fluids, and likewise azote; they afford dark-coloured acid, and oily fluids, and have a residuum of salts and earths mixed with carbonaceous matter.

The principal substances which constitute the different parts of animals, or which are found in their blood, their secretions, or their excrements, have been classed and analyzed by Sir Humphrey Davy and others. It is unnecessary to describe these minutely, but merely to state that a difference exists in each, and that the ammonia given off from animal compounds in putrefaction may be conceived to be formed, at the time of their decomposition, by the combination of hydrogen and azote. Except this matter, the other products of putrefaction are analogous to those afforded by the fermentation of vegetable substances; and the soluble substances formed abound in the elements which are the constituent parts of vegetables, in carbon, hydrogen, and oxygen.

Whenever manures consist principally of matter soluble in water, it is evident that their fermentation or putrefaction should be prevented as much as possible; and the only cases in which these processes can be useful are when the manure consists principally of vegetable or animal fibre. The circumstances necessary for the putrefaction of animal substances, and also of vegetables, are, a temperature above the freezing point, and the presence of oxygen at least in the first stage of the process. To prevent manures from decomposing, they should be preserved dry, defended from the contact of air, and kept as cool as possible.

As different manures contain different proportions of the elements necessary to vegetation, so they require a different treatment to enable them to produce their full effects in agriculture.

All green succulent plants contain saccharine or mucilaginous matter, with woody fibre, and readily ferment. They cannot, therefore, when intended for manure, be used too soon after their death. Green crops intended for enriching the soil, should be ploughed in when the flower is beginning to appear, that being the period when they contain the greatest quantity of easily soluble matter, and when their leaves are most active in forming nutritive matter. Green crops, pond weeds, the parings of hedges or ditches, or any kind of fresh vegetable matter, requires no preparation to fit them for manure. The decomposition proceeds slowly beneath the soil; the soluble matters are gradually dissolved, and the slight fermentation that goes on, checked by the want of free communication of air, tends to render the woody fibre soluble, without occasioning the rapid dissipation of elastic matter.

When pastures are broken up and made arable, not only has the soil been enriched by the death and slow decay of the plants which have left soluble matters in the soil, but the leaves and roots of the grasses living at the time, and occupying so large a part of the surface, afford saccharine, mucilaginous, and extractive matters, which become immediately the food of the crop, and the gradual decomposition affords a supply for successive years.

Sir Humphrey Davy instituted a number of experiments in support of the theory he advanced, that straw should be used in an unfermented state; and there can be little doubt but that great loss is sustained by the farmer under the practice that still prevails to a great extent, of fermenting and re-fermenting the dung-heap by frequent turnings, as much of the gaseous matter is dissipated and lost by every operation.

Dry straw of wheat, oats, barley, beans, and peas, and spoiled hay, or any other similar kind of dry vegetable matter, is in all cases useful manure. In general, such substances are made to ferment before they are employed, though it may be doubted whether the practice should be indiscriminately adopted.

There can be no doubt but that the straw of different crops immediately ploughed into the ground, affords nourishment to plants, but there is an objection to this method of using straw, from the difficulty of burying long straw, and from its rendering the husbandry foul.

When straw is made to ferment, it becomes a more manageable manure; but there is likewise, in the whole, a great loss of nutritive matter. More manure is, perhaps, supplied for a single crop, but the land is less improved than it would be supposing the whole vegetable matter were finely divided and mixed with the soil.

The dung of birds that feed on animal food, such as sea-birds, is considered the most powerful amongst the excrementitious solid substances used as manure. The guano, which is used to a great extent in South America, being the manure that fertilizes the sterile plains of Peru, is a production of this kind. It exists abundantly on the small rocky islands on the coasts, whither sea-fowl resort at certain seasons, and being gathered, forms an article of commerce.

Night-soil is a well known and powerful manure, and very liable to decompose. It differs in composition, but always abounds in substances composed of carbon, hydrogen, azote, and oxygen. From the analysis of Berzelius, it appears that a part of it is always soluble in water, and in whatever state it is used, whether recent or fermented, it supplies abundance of food to plants.

The disagreeable smell of night-soil may be destroyed by mixing it with quicklime, and if exposed to the atmosphere in thin layers, strewed over with quicklime in fine weather, it speedily dries, is easily pulverised, and in this state may be used in the same manner as rape cake, and delivered into the furrow of the seed. The Chinese, who greatly esteem this mixture, mix it with one-third of its weight of fat marl, make it into cakes, and dry it in the sun. These cakes have no disagreeable smell, and form a common article of commerce in that populous empire. We shall hereafter describe the manner in which this and other "fertilizers" are prepared for sale in this country.

Pigeons' dung comes next in order as to fertilizing power. By digesting 100 grains in hot water for several hours, it will yield twenty-three grains of soluble matter; and this affords abundance of carbonate of ammonia by distillation, leaving carbonaceous matter, saline matter, and carbonate of lime, as a residuum. Pigeons' dung when moist, readily ferments, but after fermentation contains less soluble matter than before, as when, in that state,

100 parts will yeild only eight of soluble matter, with proportionably less carbonate of ammonia, making it evident that it should be applied as new as possible. The dung of domestic fowls possesses the same properties as that of pigeons, but in an inferior degree. Rabbit's dung has been used with great success, and is best when laid on as fresh as possible.

The dung of cattle, oxen, and cows, contains matter soluble in water, and gives in fermenting nearly the same products as vegetable substances, absorbing oxygen, and producing carbonic acid gas. The recent dung of sheep and goats afford, when long boiled in water, soluble matters, which equal from two to three per cent. of their weight. These contain a small quantity of matter analogous to animal mucus, principally composed of a bitter extract soluble in water and in alcohol. They appear to differ little in composition, both giving ammoniacal fumes by distillation.

The part of the dung of cattle, sheep, and goats, not soluble in water, is the mere woody fibre analogous to the residuum of those vegetables that form their food after they have been deprived of their soluble materials.

The dung of horses gives a brown fluid, which when evaporated yields a bitter extract, which affords ammoniacal fumes more copiously than that from the dung of oxen.

If the pure dung of cattle is used as manure, there seems no reason why it should be made to ferment except in the soil: or if suffered to ferment, it should be only in a very slight degree. The grass in the neighbourhood of recently voided dung is always coarse and dark green, but this must not be attributed to a noxious quality in unfermented dung, but rather the result of excess of food furnished to the plants.

The dung of horses and cattle is however usually mixed up with straw and other matters, and consigned to a general heap called the dunghill, and as this contains a large proportion of fibrous vegetable matter, a slight incipient fermentation, sufficient to induce a disposition to decay and dissolve when brought upon the land and ploughed in, is certainly advantageous; but although this is necessary to the woody fibre, we must bear in mind that too great a fermentation is highly prejudicial to the composite manure in the dunghill, and it is better in fact that there should be no fermentation before the manure is used than that it should be carried too far. This is a very important matter to observe, for excess of fermentation tends to the destruction and dissipation of the most useful part of the manure, and the ultimate results of this process are like those of combustion.

Woodashes not too much reduced have been used with success as manure. A part of their effects may be owing to the slow and gradual consumption of the charcoal, which seems capable, under other circumstances than those of actual combustion, of absorbing oxygen so as to become carbonic acid.

Animal substances, such as putrid meat or carcases of beasts, require no chemical preparation to fit them for the soil. The object of the farmer should be to blend them with earthy constituents in a proper state of division, so as to prevent their too rapid decomposition. After taking the skin off dead animals, they should be covered with six times their bulk of soil mixed with one part lime, and suffered to remain for a few months, mixing a little more quicklime with the mass at the time of its removal, which will destroy the effluvia.

Fish is a powerful manure, and should be ploughed in fresh, but not in too great quantities, or the crop will be rank. In Cornwall, where this manure is very general in the pilchard season, they mix the fish with sand or seaweed. There is a small fish, called the stickleback, also applied as manure in the fens of Linconshire and other counties. The operation of fish as a manure is easily explained. The skin is principally gelatine, which from its slight state of cohesion is readily soluble in water. Fat or oil is always found in fishes; and their fibrous matter contains all the essential elements of vegetable substance. The effects of a manuring of fish are apparent for several years.

Bones have lately come into great use as a manure, and a powerful auxiliary they are to a tenant entering upon a worn-out farm, being cheap, easy of carriage, available in all situations, and insuring a crop. The more divided they are, the more powerful their effect; but when broken instead of ground to dust, they are more lasting.

The basis of bones is constituted by earthy salts, principally phosphate of lime, with some carbonate of lime, and phosphate of magnesia: the easily decomposable substances in bone, are fat, gelatine, and cartilage, which seems of the same nature as coagulated albumen.

[*Superphosphate of lime.*—One ℔ of bone dust mixed with twelve oz. of sulphuric acid (oil of vitriol) and twelve oz. of water if left to act upon each other for a day form superphosphate of lime, a wine-glass of which has been found beneficial to geraniums. There is little doubt that this superphosphate is excellent manure for flowers, and all kitchen garden crops, being more prompt in its effect than simple bone dust, because it is soluble in water and therefore more readily presented to the roots in a state for them to imbibe. Bones broken into small pieces mixed with charcoal are good drainage for geranium and other soft wooded plants.— To prepare superphosphate puddle and plaster a floor of clay; when dry throw down a quantity of bone dust and surround it with an edging of ashes—on this pour the proportion of Sulphuric acid keeping well to windward in so doing, let the mass seethe a day and it will become superphosphate.—Ed.]

Horn is a still more powerful manure than bone, as it contains a larger quantity of decomposable animal matter: 100 grains of ox-horn yield only 1·5 grains of earthy residuum, and not quite half of this is phosphate of lime. The shavings and turnings of horn form an excellent manure, the animal matter in them appearing of the nature of coagulated albumen, which is slowly rendered soluble by the action of water. The earthy matter in horn, and still more in bones, prevents the too rapid decomposition of the animal matter, and renders the effects very durable.

Blood contains certain quantities of all the principles found in other animal substances, and is therefore a very good manure.— *Magazine of Domestic Economy*.

[*Burnt Earth*—Is a very valuable manure, particularly for Roses, for Fuschias and all delicate soft wooded plants. The following is a good method of burning earth in a large quantity. Collect in a heap a number of rough branches and litter from pruning operations, build a wall of turf about three feet high of a semi-circular form around this litter. Set the branches on fire and when half burnt down, add weeds and other rubbish, and gradually cast earth over them to keep down the flames. The flame should not be allowed to break through and expend itself. Constant watching is necessary. As the fire breaks through, the heap should be opened and a layer of branches and weeds added, and on them again a layer of earth. The fire should be spread through the whole heap and a large amount of earth may be burnt by continually adding to those places where it appears the strongest. The earth to be burnt may be of the stiffest nature.

Mr. Cannell, the great Fuschia grower of Woolwich attributes much of his success to using no soil for his Fuschias until it has been burnt. The following is his plan: "I build up with bricks a rough furnace about one foot high, and if I can get some old bars to form a draught so much the better.

The size of the fire is that of the largest old tea tray that can be procured. A good coke fire is made up and the soil being handy it is put on the tray and with a bricklayer's trowel turned over while hot. In this way a considerable quantity can soon be slightly burnt and purified and can then be stowed away in any old boxes to be ready for use as required. I am convinced that no dung ought to be used for pot plants until it has undergone this process."—ED.]

PARASITIC PLANTS.—Such as root into other living plants, and derive their nourishment from thence.—Some root into the stem or branches, as (viscus) the Misletoe; others attach themselves to the root, as Hypocistus.

PEATY SOILS.—The formation of peaty soils is produced from very opposite causes, and it is interesting to contemplate how the same effect may be produced by different means, and the earth, which supplies almost all our wants, may become barren, alike from the excessive application of art or the utter neglect of it.

PERFECT PLANTS—are divided into conservative and reproductive. The conservative organs are such as are absolutely necessary to the growth and preservation of the plant, including the roots, trunk, branch, leaf and fruit.

PREPARING GROUND.—Having selected your spot, which you wish to prepare for either sowing crops or making a plantation, the first thing to be done is to clear it of weeds by drying or ploughing the whole up well, exposing the earth to the action of the sun and air, then breaking up the clods of earth and removing the weeds, which should be burnt on the spot, as the ashes form an excellent manure, and you are certain that the weeds are destroyed. If your ground is of a clayish soil, which is seldom found in the Deccan, the best thing you can add to it is brick dust or ashes; if of a light nature, the common manure, procurable in almost all situations in the neighbourhood of towns and villages, mixed with mud from the dry beds of tanks. If common manure is scarce, see the artificial compost recommended under the head Manure.

PROPAGATING BY CUTTINGS.—The choice of cuttings should be made from the side shoots of plants, rather than from their summits or main stems, as the strength and health of side shoots being equal to those nearest the ground should be preferred. The proper time of taking cuttings from the mother plant is when the sap is in full motion, in order that when returning by the bark it may form a callus, or protruding ring of granular substance, between the bark and wood, whence the roots proceed. As this callus, or ring of spongy matter, is generally best formed in ripened wood, the cuttings, when taken from the mother plants, should contain a part of the former year; or in plants which grow twice a year, of the wood of the former growth; or in the case of plants which are continually growing, such wood as has begun to ripen, or assume a brownish colour. The cuttings will vary in length, according to their strength and manner of growth, from six inches to a foot; they should be planted in a shady situation, or else protected from the sun by mats or otherwise. The distance of each should be from six to twelve inches apart, or even more where they grow quick and are likely to form large plants; great care is also requisite that, in laying down the cuttings, they are put clear into the ground without injury to the bark.

PROPAGATING BY LAYERS.—The work of laying the branches of trees, or shrubs, is easily performed, though it is not every tree that can be propagated in this manner. The first thing necessary to be done, is to clear and dry up the ground round the tree or plant you propose to take layers from; then gently bend down the branch, after having cleared it of all superfluous shoots, and lay it in the ground about six inches deep, leaving the top uncovered—then put a stone on the earth that covers the shoot, sufficiently large to keep it in its place: wooden pegs are not so serviceable, from being apt to get loose from the mode of irrigation pursued in India, the white ants also generally destroy them. Should the branch be so high, or so strong, as not easily to be bent down, it may be necessary to cut a notch in it, in a sloping direction, so as to make it bend more easily; then split the stem with a knife, towards a bud in that part of the branch which is laid in the ground; this promotes its throwing out fibres, and therefore should be attended to. It is advisable not to remove the layer until it has been separated from the parent stock for a fortnight or more.

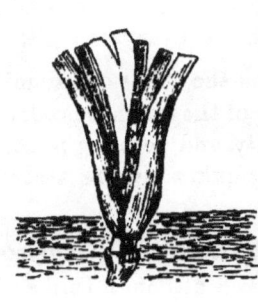

PROPAGATING BY PIPINGS.—This method is mostly adopted for the increase of carnations and pinks, and performed in the following manner: take one of the suckers of either the above flowers and divide the top shoot with a knife, just above the third joint; take the head of the shoot between the finger and thumb of one hand, and with the other hold the lower part of the shoot between a pair of leaves; then pulling the head of the shoot gently it will readily come out of the socket—hence it is called the piping. These pipings are to be inserted in finely prepared earth, to the depth of the first joint or pipe.

PRUNING—consists in removing all superfluous branches either for the purpose of increasing the fruit, enlarging the tree, making it bear better, and more regular in its appearance. Though an operation in general practice, it is nevertheless properly understood by few, and is only to be acquired by practice and observation, bearing in mind the various modes in which each tree is disposed to produce its fruit or flower, and being careful to remove such branches and slips only as may be necessary, without disfiguring or injuring the tree. Be careful in removing decayed branches, that you cut them clean down to the place from which they were produced, otherwise that part of the branch which is left will also decay and prove hurtful to the tree.

RADIATION—is the spreading of heat, which arises from heat passing from a hot body to a cooler one near it. The spreading of heat takes place between the surface of the ground and the air when the air is cold: though the soil be warm it soon loses its heat, and dew or hoar frost is formed on the ground, or grass, by the moisture diffused in the air. But when the sky is covered with clouds, the spreading and loss of heat is in a great measure prevented, and hence there is no dew or hoar frost found on a calm cloudy night. Hence the use of protecting plants by a covering of matting, which stops the heat of the soil from spreading about and being lost in the air.

REPRODUCTIVE ORGANS—are those parts of a plant which are essential to its propagation; they include the flower, with its immediate accompaniments, or peculiarities, the flower, stalk, receptacle, and inflorescence, together with the ovary or fruit.

RUNNERS—are young shoots issuing from the collar or summit of the root, and creeping along the surface of the soil, but producing a new root, and leaves at the extremity, and forming a new individual, by the decay of the connecting link, as in the strawberry.

SAP—is taken up by the tip of the roots, fibres, or spongelets and carried into the interior of the stem, and although thin and clear at first, becomes thicker as it ascends in the plant.

SOWING—is the first operation of rearing; when seeds are deposited singly, in rows or beds, they are said to be planted. When dropped in numbers together, they are said to be sown. The operation of sowing is either performed in drills, patches, or broadcast. In broadcast sowing, the seed is scattered over a breadth of surface previously prepared by digging or otherwise, minutely pulverised. The seed is taken up in the hand and scattered regularly over the surface, so as to fall as equally as possible. A windy day is particularly to be avoided. Dry weather is also essentially necessary for sowing, more especially for covering in the seed.

SPURIOUS PEATY SOILS.—Lakes and pools of water are sometimes filled up by the accumulation of the remains of aquatic plants, and in this case a sort of spurious peat is formed. The fermentation in these cases seems to be of a different kind: much more gaseous matter is evolved, and the neighbourhood of morasses (or tanks) in which aquatic vegetables exist, is usually aguish and unhealthy, whilst that of true peat formed on soils originally dry is always salubrious.

Soils may generally be distinguished from mere masses of earth, by their friable nature, dark colour, and by the presence of some vegetable fibre, or carbonaceous matter. The species of soil is always determined by the mixture of matters, and never by the colour or texture of that mixture, which belongs to the nomenclature of varieties. Thus a clayey soil with sand, is a sandy clay—this is the name of the species: if the mass is yellow or red, it is a yellow or red sandy soil, which expresses at once the genus, species and variety.

The true nourishment of plants is water and organic matter. Both these exist only in soils, and not in pure earth, but the earthy parts of the soil are useful in retaining water, so as to supply it in proper proportions to the roots of vegetables, and they are likewise efficacious in producing the proper distribution of the animal or vegetable matter. When equally mixed with it, they prevent it from decomposing too rapidly, and by these means the soluble parts are supplied in proper proportion.

The power of soils to absorb water from air is much connected with fertility. When this power is great, the plant is supplied with moisture in dry seasons, and the effect of evaporation in the day is counteracted by the absorption of aqueous vapour from the atmosphere by the interior parts of the soil during the day, and by both the exterior and interior during the night.

SUCKERS.—If you desire to get stocks, or plants, by this method, all that is necessary is, that the sucker, or young shoot which springs up from the root of the tree, should be carefully removed with a sufficiency of earth round it, so that the spongioles are in no way injured in the removal to the nursery bed or the spot where they are to remain.

TENDRIL—Is the thread-shaped and generally spiral process issuing from the stem, branch, or petiole, and sometimes from the expansion of the leaf itself, being an organ by which plants of weak and climbing stems attach themselves to other plants or substances for support,—the tendril being much stronger than a branch of the same size.

TEXTURE OF SOILS.—The perpendicular extent of roots are greatly influenced by the looseness or compactness of the soil. As for instance, carrots, beet, &c. All deep penetrating roots, when placed in a hard or stiff soil not easily divisible, are not only dwarfed, but split into branches, or twisted, as it may be. Since, then, the mere texture of the soil, independently of the food of plants which it contains, produces such effects, it must be of the greatest importance to attend to these circumstances.

TICKETING OF FLOWERS.—"When a piece of zinc is rubbed bright with sand or brick dust, and written on with a black lead pencil, the writing in the course of a few hours becomes black and indelible, and will withstand all weathers. Pieces used once may be brightened by rubbing on brick or tile, and employed as often as is desired."—*Bombay Times.*

TRANSPLANTING.— If the object be to remove trees or shrubs, it is essentially necessary that the root fibres should be uninjured, and that a sufficiency of the soil attached to the roots be removed with them. If you are transplanting vegetables, such as beet, carrots, turnips, &c., the best method is to use a straight dibber, place the roots perpendicularly without bending the tap-root, and then gently replace the earth around it. It may perhaps be necessary, should the root fibres be injured, to remove some of the leaves, otherwise the remaining fibres will not be able to nourish the plant.

When it is found impossible to preserve the root fibres from injury, or to replant them exactly in their former position, in order to diminish the loss of sap, the plants ought to be shaded from the light and sun, or a part of their leaves or branches cut off.

The removing of plants or trees depends solely upon circumstances; and the principal facts to be remembered by gardeners are, that all trees and plants derive their nourishment through the tips of the root fibres, and that the sap carried into the leaves passes off by exposure to light and sunshine; therefore the necessity of great care being used to preserve the mouths (or spongioles) entire.

Doctor Oake, M. D., of Southampton, states that it has been discovered that the best method of conveying plants to a distance is, by means of a wide-mouthed bottle, so covered up as to allow only a small aperture for the admission of air.

The exhalation of the plant being condensed beneath the roof or shoulder of the bottle, falls down, or rather distills again upon it, and constantly refreshes it with the results of its own evaporation; while it enjoys the rays of the sun through the transparency of the vessel in which it is confined.

In this way a primrose was conveyed to New Sydney from England.

TRANSPLANTING, OR LAYING DOWN TURF.—Turfing, as the operation is commonly called, consists in laying down turf on surfaces intended for lawns or borders. The turf is cut from a smooth firm part of a bank, or other ground free from coarse grass, in small patches about a foot square, and conveyed to the spot where it is to be used. The surface on which the turfs are to be laid ought previously to be dug or trenched, so as to be brought to one degree of consistency, and then rolled or beaten so that it may not afterwards sink. The turfs being laid so as to fit, are to be first beaten down individually, and then watered and rolled until the whole is smooth; and even then it will require being watered by the hand during the dry season at least once a day.

TRUNK—constitutes the principal bulk of a tree.

WATER.—Water is essentially necessary for the nourishment of plants, and although some will grow and throw out flowers, they never form seed without it.

The material which water holds in solution forms the important part of nourishment, or otherwise causes the decay of plants. All water contains more or less atmospheric air, and water is more or less beneficial in proportion to the quantity mixed with it. Rain water, from its falling, collects a large proportion of air during its descent.

[*Watering.*—Whenever water is necessary it should be given copiously, as slight sprinklings very frequently do more harm, than good. Hoe deeply and frequently leaving the soil light and porous. This is a golden rule. The ground in India has always a tendency to cake from the baking effects of the sun, to keep it open and porous it should always be forked after slight rain, and on the day following a copious watering, nothing could be more apropos than the following extract from Thomson's handy-book of the flower garden on the subject.

"Water being the chief vehicle through which food is conveyed to plants from the soil, and in the atmosphere, the preventive of evaporation from the foliage, in order to be beneficial in these respects must be administered in such quantity as shall penetrate sufficiently deep into the ground to reach the roots in contradistinction to the too common method of merely painting or sprinkling the surface of the soil; and as far as watering can effect the atmosphere, and feed and preserve the strength of plants in that manner during hot weather, its effects must be very limited indeed."

"A mere sprinkling of the surface of the soil is productive of more evil than good. In its necessary rapid evaporation, the soil is robbed of its heat, and on stiff soils particularly, it leaves the surface in a hard and caked condition, rendering it a better heat conductor than when loose and porous; and in proportion as the heat conducting power of the soil is increased, so also is the evaporation of moisture. Therefore not only do surface sprinklings evaporate with the rising of the sun, without ever having reached the roots or materially benefited the plant, but the natural moisture which may rise, by capillary attraction, is also more likely to evaporate by the compact surface produced by daily sprinkling."

One who thoroughly understands what he is about, and waters, when he does water, almost to irrigation, and plies the Dutch hoe among his crops, the next morning, is in a position to assert that his plants do derive unmistakeable benefit from watering, another who rests content with merely sprinkling the surface of the soil frequently, leaving it meanwhile to become a hardened crust, may assert with equal truth, that watering appears to do more harm than good.—ED.]

WINTERING.—Trees are brought into bearing by this process, which consists in carefully removing the earth from the trunk roots and laying them open, and at the same time picking off all the leaves. The tree is left in this way without water for a certain period, and is thus brought into bearing by the nutrient matters and properties of the sap being thickened, and thus stored up and afterwards thrown into the buds, the pulp, wood, root, and crown of the root. The check to the growth of trees by wintering, &c., is thus advantageous—causing the leaf pulp to become thickened by the loss of water and oxygen. When it returns to the stem and crown of the roots, it lays the basis of fresh branches terminating in flower buds. Whereas were a plant to remain unmoved in a rich soil well watered, it would probably send up more sap than the light could readily deprive of its water and oxygen, and thence would push out new leaves to carry off the superabundance; while there would be no pulp formed thick enough and containing enough of carbon to produce flowers.

WORMS—may either be destroyed by picking them up by hand very early in the morning or late in the evening in moist weather, or by watering with lime or salt and water.

WOUNDS IN TREES.—To heal wounds in trees,—make a varnish of common linseed oil rendered very dry, boiling it for the space of an hour with an ounce of litharge\* of each pound of oil, mixed with calcined bones (pulverised and sifted) to the consistence of almost a liquid paste. The wounds are to be covered by means of a brush, after the bark and other substance has been pared off so as to render the whole as smooth and even as possible. The varnish must be applied in dry weather, in order that it may attach itself properly.

---

\* Vitrified Oxide of lead (Moordar Sing.)

# FLORICULTURAL LIST.

*Achimenes, Scrophulariaceæ.*—These are very ornamental species of plants, and of easy culture; the scaly tuberous roots, by which they are propagated must be carefully preserved during the dry weather, by occasionally moistening the earth in which they are kept, and after the commencement of the rains, the imbricated buds which they produce underground, may be divided and planted out.

*Adonis, Ranunculaceæ*—Derives its name from the blood red colour of most of the species, the Autumnalis is more generally called the "Pheasant's eye" and in England much admired, the plants thrive in any good soil, they seldom exceed a foot in height, and being of a bushy nature should not be closer to each other than eighteen inches and planted three or four in a group. They may be raised by seed, or by dividing the root and sown after the monsoon.

*Aerides, Orchidaceæ, A. Odorata.*—These plants possess the power of living almost entirely upon the matter which they absorb from the atmosphere, the flowers are very fragrant and hang in long racemes of a light flesh colour and spotted, from six inches to a foot long, they grow from the axils of the leaves, appearing in April and May, and are found on the Mahableshwar Hills and the Ghauts.

*Agapanthus, Umbellatus.*—This is a beautiful blue Lily brought from the Cape, and requires the same treatment as the other species. Is propagated by dividing the roots. A light peat sandy soil, mixed with old vegetable manure.

*Alternanthera.*—These are very hardy, pretty dwarf foliage plants from Brazil, extremely useful for edging, ribband and carpet gardening, easily propagated from cuttings in sand under glass. At a particular period of their growth, they turn from a dull bronze to a brilliant crimson and pink variegation, as soon as they show symptoms of flowering they should be cut down again and will after a time renew their bright foliage. They stand the heat and drought as well as the wet season.

The varieties are A. Amœna, Sessilis and A. Versicolor or Telianthera.

*Amaranthus.*—A showy class of Annuals with brilliant coloured leaves, natives of India—grow in the rainy season, require rich soil and plenty of moisture. The best kinds are Amaranthus Elegantissimus. A. Tricolor giganteus. A. Melancholeus ruber. Princes' Feather.

*Amaryllis Belladonna, Equestris, Mexican, Cape, American, Asiatica.*—All these blossom during the rainy and cold season, and form a great ornament when judiciously planted amongst other border flowers. The colours are of every variety—red, white, pink, &c. The large flowering sorts are greedily devoured by birds and insects, and require much care to prevent their being destroyed. Is propagated as all other kinds of bulbous roots.

*Amaryllis Frittilaria, or Snake's Head Lily.*—From Amarysso, resplendent. The wild flower hangs pendulous, and is chequered with pale dark purple name from Frittillas, a dice board. Most of the species are natives of China, the Cape of Good Hope, and America; they have become quite acclimated in India, and are found almost in every flower-garden under the names of Mexican Barbadoes, Turk's Cap, Tiger Lily, Parrot, &c. Is propagated by the off-sets of the bulb, which in one year will produce from three to a dozen fresh plants. A good rich, old vegetable soil: if the subsoil is rather porous, the better when grown in pots; be careful that there is a small hole in the bottom, and that the pots are of a sufficient size to admit the expansion freely of the bulbs, which after the decay of the old flowering stalk may be separated and transplanted: if in borders, they will blossom during the rains and cold weather, and many during the hot season.

*Anagallis Indica, Primulaceæ.*—This plant is a native of Nepal colour blue, of easy culture and propagated by cuttings in any common soil.

*Anthemis Purprea Compositæ.*—The "Chamomile" plants flowers yellow, white, and purple, so common in Europe, as to need no further description.

*Aquilegia Alpina, Ranunculaceœ, Columbine.*—The several species are very ornamental, grow in any moderate good soil and increase plentifully by seed.

*Arabis Rosea Cruciferœ.*—These species of plants of which there are seven are chiefly adapted for ornamenting rock work in Europe, being natives of many parts of the world.

*Aralia.*—A class of handsome foliage plants chiefly from Japan, much used in Europe for subtropical or fine leaf gardening, of these the Aralia papyrifera or China rice paper plant, from hot moist parts of China, does well in the Deccan and is reproduced by off-sets, is very hardy only requiring plenty of room, rich soil and abundance of water.

*Ardisia Crenulata, Myrsinaceœ.*—These are handsome species of plants of easy culture in a good soil, and easily increased by cuttings from the root, the A. Elegans, lanceolata, solanacea, are natives of India.

*Argemone, Papaveraceœ.*—Hardy Annuals and perennials growing easily from seed in any common soil. The seeds yield an oil used for common purposes, and the fresh root bruised and applied to the part stung by a scorpion affords relief.

*Aristolochia, Aristolochiaceœ.*—These are mostly climbing plants, some of the species natives of India, growing in any good soil the A. Acuminata bearing large drooping flowers of a dark purple colour, the root is exceedingly bitter, and is said to be an antidote to the bite of poisonous snakes.

*Arums.*—This is a large family comprising Alocasia, Colocasia, Caladium, Calla, Anthurium, Diffenbachia, about which confusion often arises, Colocasia has enormous leaves on tall stems, the type of which we may make Colocasia Esculenta, an Indian plant so much used in Bangalore foliage and called an Arum, there are several kinds, Colocasia, Atroviolacea, C. Alboviolacea and C. Macrorhriza variegata. Following the Alocasia in degree comes the Calla or Richardia, the Nile Lily, with its beautiful large rich green leaves and large pure white spathe so well known here. Alocasia is next in size to Calla and has also a distinct stem from which the leaves proceed, they are large metallic looking leathery leaved plants, Alocasia Metallica, A. Sedeni—A. Veitchi, these do not winter, that is do not lose their leaves, next in order are the Anthuriums—Epiphytes or parasites with beautifully spotted and glabrous leaves. The stem more boldly and distinctly produced, with a palm like habit when full grown—Anthurium Scherzerianum however is a small gem of a plant sending up several vivid scarlet spathes which last for months.

Next the Diffenbachias which are still more palm like in habit and have very beautiful marked variegated leaves and white waxy stalks to their leaves.

Lastly the Caladium which has radical leaves that is, they arise direct from the root, without any main stem, and after six months of growth die down and winter.

Towards the end of the year, when Caladium leaves assume a yellow tint and flag, water should be gradually withheld from the plants, this will greatly hasten the ripening of the roots, when the leaves have perished, the Rhizomes (root stocks) may be taken out of the large pots, repotted in small ones and stored in a godown or shed to winter or rest, receiving a supply of water occasionally to prevent the roots shrivelling. About the middle of April, when the mango showers fall, the plants will awaken from their winter sleep, the Rhizomes plump fresh and beginning to emit roots. When the shoots like spikes appear on the surface, it is time to shift the plants into large pots dividing them into small pieces with 2 or 3 crowns or spikes to each, or retaining the whole according to the requirements of the cultivator. In potting, place the Rhizome low enough to be covered with half an inch soil, press the soil very little over them, good drainage and a rich compost of loam, old manure and sand are indispensable. Few plants delight more in an abundant supply of water at the roots and such should be unsparingly given, when the pots have become filled with roots weak liquid manure may be occasionally applied. Caladiums require shade from bright sun shine. An abundant supply of moisture must also be maintained in the surrounding atmosphere in dry weather, by wetting the stage or floor or by evaporating troughs. If the Caladiums are to preserve their brightness, *the leaves must not be watered overhead*, however careful the selection of water, a sort of incrustation will eventually form over the leaf, if thus watered habitually, of late a great number of Hybrid Caladiums have been introduced, of these some choice ones are described below :

Prince Albert Edward, leaf stems of a rich dark ebony line, streaked and barred with grey white; leaf blades dark emerald green, with a rich crimson mid rib, radiating from the centre towards the margins, the intervening spaces being densely spotted with ivory white.

Madame Houlett, large leaves with clustered blush white blotches on the opposite leaf margins.

Edward Moreaux, mottled green ground with rich lake, red centre.

E. G. Hendeson, rich green leaves, finely marked with transparent rose spots, and brilliantly mottled crimson rays and centre.

President, light crimson centre dark green, margin slightly mottled with grey, fine, very distinct.

Reine Victoria, style of *Belleymei* with elegant green veins and margins, densely spotted or marbled between with white and scattered rich crimson.

Duc de Morny, deep green leaf borders, with large and beautiful crimson rayed centre.

Chelsoni, bright glossy green, suffused with brilliant red and blotched with crimson.

Siebold, rich green, with fiery red crimson rayed centre, green spaces densely spotted with claret red.

Triomphe De L'Exposition, crimson centre with red ribs and green border.

Baron de Rothschild, rich blood red centre and spots on mottled green leaf ground.

Napoleon III, flamed crimson centre with forked rays and carmine red spots on a rich green ground.

Madame Paillet, a beautiful variety, very dark green ground attractively marked with a profusion of large spots, and blotches of pure white.

Auguste Riviere, white centre and rays upon a light green ground interspersed with crimson spots.

Belleymei, pure white with green mid ribs.

Argyrites, beautiful miniature white and green variegated leaves.

Baraquinii, one of the old kind but fine deep green leaves with rich crimson markings.

New Golden leaved Caladiums.

Golden Queen, leaves large, pale green or yellow, uniform in colour; a remarkably chaste appearance.

Princess Royal, leaves large of a pale green or yellow, with crimson centre in the style of C. Brongniartii.

*Asters.*—Among Annuals the Aster is one of the best for pot culture in the rainy season. It is unrivalled for variety, duration of bloom and hardy habit.—The flowers are very beautiful and with care will last nearly a month, while a succession of plants may be kept flowering from the middle of August till March. There are great many varieties of Aster, German and French improvements on the old China Aster. Seedsmen's Catalogues describe them. The best varieties are Victoria, Peony, Perfection Cocardeau, Emperor and Bouquet.

*Asclepias Curassavica, Asclepiadaceæ.*—This genus of tall growing plants thrives well in any good light soil requiring room to spread and show their blossoms, they are readily grown from seed which are produced in abundance. Balm of Gilead,—Vide Dracocephalum.

*Balsams* are very gay but their flowers are short lived and they require a good deal of water. To grow the large double Balsams they should be sown late in May in a spot where they are intended to flower—one seed drop into a richly manured little pit. Watering twice a day is necessary. As the side shoots appear they should be nipped off, and the plant will grow up strong and straight—a mass of flowers up the stem like a giant stock. the best kinds of Balsams are the Camellia flowered of many varieties including the new Solferino Victoria and Caryophilloides.

*Bartonia Aurea, Loasaceæ.*—A beautiful species, flowers of a yellow and white colour, opening at night effusing a sweet odour; they should be planted close together, so that the ground may be covered with its leaves.

*Begonia, Elephant Ears.*—This is a large class ornamental foliage plants for pot culture in partial shade, with ferns and Caladiums, Begonia rex and Begonia dœdala are the two most ornamental foliaged kinds. Begonia fuschioides, B. Almœfolia, B. discolor and many others, have pretty flowers which bloom principally in the cold season easily multiplied by division of the roots and by cuttings of the leaves like Gloxinia under glass.

*Bellis Compositæ, B. Perennis.*—This well known flower is easily cultivated by seed after the rains, it thrives best in a rich loamy soil, and should be grown in pots.

*Bignonia, Bignoniaceæ.*—A class of handsome creepers of which B. Venusta, B. Radicans are propagated by layers.

*Brachycome Compositæ.*—These species of plants can only be cultivated during the cold season, the colours are dark, purple, pink and white, the seed must be sown in a light soil, requiring a moderate quantity of water.

*Briza Graminaceæ.*—Quaking grass, some of the species are interesting and easily grown from seed.

*Brodiæa Liliaceæ.*—These bulbs with lilac blue and white flowers may be grown like other lilies in a rich loam and are increased by off-sets of the roots.

*Browallia Scrophulariaceæ.*—These are handsome plants blue and white flowers, and are easily cultivated from seed in any good soil, both are calculated for borders. The white is an upright, and the blue a spreading plant; both having a pretty and delicate appearance.

*Brugmansia, Solanaceæ, B. Arborea.*—These are ornamental plants of easy culture and propagated by cuttings, they continue to flower several times in succession during the rains and cold season, the number and size of the flowers at one time has a very striking appearance, a large space must be allowed to each plant.

*Bougainvillea.*—A very handsome hardy creeper, the plant flowers in the cold season when its lovely mauve coloured bracts cover the creeper, which assumes a sheet of colour, propagated by layers.

*Cacalia Compositæ, C. Coccinea.*—These plants will grow in any soil and are mostly found in waste places, the species are numerous and found in all parts of the globe.

*Caladium.*—See Arum.

*Calampellis, Bignoniaceæ, C. Scabra.*—This plant is of much beauty, well adapted for training on trellis work, the orange coloured flowers being very showy; any light loamy soil suits it.

*Calandrina Portulacaceæ.*—The species of this genus are very pretty, and only require light rich soil. They are easily cultivated by seed.

*Calathea Zebrina.*—A magnificent maranta with large bright green velvet leaves with dark stripes, likes a moist shady sheltered spot associated with ferns, in the cold weather should be kept in-doors protected from cold cutting wind propagated by off-sets.

*Calceolaria, Scrophulariaceæ.*—These are both shrubby and herbaceous plants, they thrive best in a light rich loamy soil and may be cultivated both by seed and cuttings. The Hybrids raised from this genus are very numerous and showy, the colours are chiefly purple, orange yellow, and spotted.

*Calliopsis.*—There are many kinds of Calliopsis, all very hardy and showy, but as they take a long time growing before they flower it is best to grow them in nursery ground and lift them when nearly full grown with a trowel into the places intended for them in the mixed border. The tall kinds are Calliopsis Tinctoria and Nigra speciosa with their varieties. The dwarf kinds are C. Drummondi and C. Filicifolia also called Cosmidium Burridgi, these two last make very fine masses or clumps. Sow the tall Calliopsis in July to flower in the cold weather, C. Drummondi in October. It is quicker growing and does best in the cold weather having then larger flowers than in the rains.

*Callirhòe, Perennial.*—Two kinds C. Digitata, C. Involucraha trailing, good mixed border plants with crimson cup shape flowers, blooming well in February and March, sown late in the rains, quite hardy.

*Camellia.*—The Camellia has a very annoying tendency to drop its flower buds. This must be attributed to some mismanagement, just as fruit trees lose their fruit and vines their grapes when any thing renders them incapable of perfecting them. Any cause inducing ill-health will produce this effect. Nature is trying to get rid of work the plant is unable to perform. The most common cause, in the case of the Camellia, is bad watering, probably the plant has never been properly watered for months, a little water has been frequently applied which may have reached half way down the pot and even renderd the upper part sour and overmoist, while the lower part of the ball of earth is as dry as dust. Native gardeners rarely observe the simple rule "*never water a plant till it really requires it, and then thoroughly soak it.*"

Camellias will not grow in a strong heavy soil. Leaf-mould and sand should be added to lighten it. Best suited for them are turf sods, cut as if for a grass plot from a sandy loam, chopped up or pulled to pieces; if sand is deficient in the turf it should be added. The buds of Camellia will also drop off when exposed while they are forming to dry hot wind and much sunshine. Naturally it is a plant growing in a cold climate never falling quite to freezing point. In Bangalore it will do best under shade, in hot weather sheltered from dry winds, but getting any amount of moisture from rain in the monsoon, and put out in the open, or a half shady spot in the cold season, attention as before mentioned being paid to the watering.

*Campanula, Campanulaceæ.*—This genus of plants including the Canterbury Bell and Venus' looking glass is well known for its ornamental beauty and profusion of flowers, all the species grow freely in any soil and are propagated by seed and dividing the roots.

*Candy Tuft*, vide *Iberis, Canna Canneæ, C. Indica.*—The Canna or Indian shot was introduced into English parks and gardens some years ago as a bold sub-tropical foliage plant, the flowers bearing but a small proportion to the mass of leaves. Under recent careful cultivation Cannas have made wonderful advances and become really attractive as floral objects, some of the newer varieties have branching flower stems—the flowers themselves broad petalled and bright coloured, twice the ordinary size and habit. The seed to germinate must be sown in great heat with moisture, the plants are easily and quickly multiplied by division of the roots; the finest kinds for size and colour of flowers are Bihorelli, Premice de Nice, Glauca Magnifica, Peruviana; for deep chocolate crimson and striped foliage, Atro Nigricaus, Warcywicksi, Zebrina, Muscœfolio, Sanguinea and tricolor.

*Canterbury Bell*, vide *Campanula Cape Jessamine*, vide *Gardenia, Castilleja, Scrophulariaceœ.*—An ornamental genus of plants growing freely in a good light soil, and may be raised either by seed or by dividing the roots.

*Cantanauche, Compositœ.*—This is a pretty order of small plants, colours yellow, white and blue, succeed well in common soil and may be increased by seed or by dividing the roots.

*Celsia, Scrophulariaceœ.*—This is a genus of ornamental plants growing from two to six feet high, colours yellow and orange, the Coromandeliana a native of India, raised from seed in any garden soil.

*Centaurea Compositœ, C. Atropurpurea.*—The sweet sultan. The various species of this beautiful and elegant genus are easily grown from seed in any light loamy soil, they are of various heights from twelve inches to five feet, the seed may be sown in pots or small beds at the close of the rains, then transplanted and they will blossom during the cold weather. The flowers are fragrant and of different shades of colour, purple, blue, yellow, white, red, brown, &c.

*Centranthus Ruber, Valerianaceœ, Hind, Jallukree.*—This is an ornamental annual, generally grown from European seed, the colours of the different species are red, blue and white, and thrives in any good garden soil.

The valerian grows wild in some of the upper parts of Bengal,

*Cereus, Cactaceæ.*—Night blowing Cereus, Cereus Grandiflorus, white and yellow. From Cereus signifying pliant like wax referring to the shoots of some of the species being pliant. Many of the species produce the most beautiful flowers, the stems are angled and jointed, the blossoms open in the evening or during the night, and die away towards the morning, they are all creepers.

*Cereus Triangularis.*—A creeping plant with triangular stems, sends out roots at the joints which adhere to walls or any support near. The flowers are large of a yellowish white colour with yellow Anthers. It should, if grown in the garden, have a strong trellis work to support it.

*Cereus Truncatus.*—This species produces flowers during the cold season, which are of a rose colour; it is indigenous to the Brazils, the whole of the genus seem to thrive in any tolerable soil, without much watering, young plants may be obtained by separating the branches at the joints, but then they require to be watered daily until the roots have struck.

*Chamomile.*—Vide *Anthemis.*

*Cheiranthus Cheiri, Cruciferæ, Wall Flower, named from Cheir, the hand, Anthos, a flower.*—This flower derives its name from the circumstance of its growing wild on old walls and ruins in England. It is of a light yellow colour, but, when cultivated in gardens, assumes a much richer and darker tint, mixed with brown. The double variety of a yellow colour, and striped with deep orange, is seldom known to blossom here. The name Gitly Flower is given to the stock and a species of pink carnation, these being the only flowers formerly cultivated by dames in their baronial Castles. Is propagated by seed, during and after the rains: space of a foot and a half must be allowed each plant if in beds as it grows nearly two feet high.

*Chelone, Scrophulariaceæ.*—From Chelone a tortoise, to the back of which the helmet of the flowers is fancifully compared, the flowers are scarlet orange, white and purple, the species thrive in any good garden soil and may be increased by dividing the roots.

*Chorozema, Leguminosæ, C. Spectabillis.*—This plant was first found in the west coast of New Holland by Labillardiere, some of the species are scarlet coloured, others yellow and red, they grow best in a rich loamy soil, and may be raised from cuttings as well as seed which they produce in abundance.

*Chironia, Gentianaceæ.*—This genus of plants are all indigenous to the Cape of Good Hope, the flowers are rose coloured, white, yellow and purple, the plant grows to the height of two feet and should be continued by cuttings, they require a light loamy soil.

*Chænostoma, Polyanthum, Scrophulariaceæ.*—These are pretty dwarf plants, of a white and light yellow colour, well adapted for borders, and thrive in any garden soil.

*Christmas flower, Chrysanthemums, Compositæ.*—Have been long well known favourites of the mixed border. But the lately introduced Japanese kinds are particularly desirable, under proper culture they will flower all the year round and are most hardy. The secret in growing the Chrysanthemums is every time to select new shoots, to plant them singly and throw away the old plants, give them rich soil and plenty of water. To grow bushy plants pinch off the head of the main stems as they begin to run up high. They are also easily raised from seed and in four or five months will be in flower. The best kind to sow are the large flowering and Hybrid Japanese kinds—many of which have very curious flowers like tassels and a great variety of colours.

*Cineraria, Compositæ, C. Azurea.*—This genus of plants known by the name of Cape Aster, produce abundance of showy flowers of orange coloured, yellow, purple and red varieties, they grow from two to three feet high, the leaves being covered with a soft white down, grown from seed, and thrive in any good garden soil.

*Cistus, Cistaceæ, Rock-Rose.*—This genus of plants are mostly used for ornamenting rock work, though some grow to the height of four feet, they do well in most garden soils, and may be cultivated either from seed or by cuttings.

*Cladanthus Compositæ, Cladanthus Arabicus.*—These are small dwarf plants, bearing yellow flowers, and grow in any soil.

*Clarkia, Onagraceæ.*—These are handsome annuals which make a showy display in flower borders, their colours are rose, white and purple, they ripen seed in abundance which may be sown in any good soil.

*Clematis.*—Some of the new kinds of Japanese Clematis have been introduced into Bangalore and are doing well, they will be great acquisitions to gardens bearing a profusion of large, single and double purple flowers, which in England present a sheet of bloom.

*Cleome, Capparidaceæ, C. Pentaphylla.*—The species of this genus are very pretty and grow well in a light rich soil, the colours of the flowers are white, red, purple and yellow, cultivated easily from seed.

*Clerodendrum, Thompsoniæ.*—A handsome climbing plant from Central Africa with fine white flowers and bright scarlet coralla, quite hardy.

*Clianthus, Leguminosæ, C. Puniceus.*—From *Kleios* glory, and *Anthos* a flower, an elegant plant, attains the height of 8 or 10 feet, and adapted for a shrubbery, growing well in any moderate rich soil, native of New Zealand.

*Clintonia, Lobeliaceæ, C. Elegans.*—These are pretty border plants, colours white and blue, they flower and give seed abundantly, and thrive in any good soil.

*Clitoria, Ternatea, Leguminosæ.*—There are several varieties. The most common are the blue and white. They blossom all the year round, and being shrubby, twining plants, are well suited for covering trellis work. They are of easy growth, and the blue flowers are used sometimes for colouring boiled rice. Are propagated by seed, and in any soil.

*Clove Pink,* vide *Dianthus Caryophyllus, Cobæ Polemoniaceæ, Cobæ Scandens.*—This is a fast growing creeper, the flowers of which are purple, and the stems attach themselves to any rough surface, like some of the Cereus species, and well adapted for screening walls.

*Cockscombs, Celosia, Cristata.*—Dwarf German Cockscombs have a gay appearance, but are rather stiff and formal as flowers. The seed should be sown in rich soil early in the rains, and the young plants once moved without a check to the place intended for their flowering, require rich soil, and plenty of water, and full exposure to sunshine. The comb forms very early in the plant's growth, plants having more than one such comb when young should be thrown away.

*Coleus, Biennial.*—Popularly called the nettle leaved Geranium, and formerly named Plectranthus fruticosus, has been of late so extensively hybridised and improved, that it became the fashionable foliage novelty of 1868. The leaves are strikingly cut or serrated—presenting a fringed appearance, the colours in different varieties embrace golden yellow, magenta, crimson, purple, claret, black and green, while the leaf markings and blotches are varied almost indefinitely, making them immensely attractive, they are easily raised from seed in the rains or by cuttings in sand under glass.

*Collinsia Scrophulariaceæ, Collinsia Grandiflora.*—These plants are mostly all of a bright colour, and well adapted for borders to a flower garden, the colours are mostly yellow; but the Scabriuscula is red and yellow, these plants require a tolerable good soil with plenty of water.

*Columbine.*—Vide *Aquilegia.*

*Commelyna, Commelynaceæ.*—Some of the plants of these genus are very handsome, the colour of the flowers mostly blue, and propagated by dividing the tubers.

*Convolvulus, Ipomœa.*—Ipomœas are all hardy, and easily raised from seed if annuals, from layers if perennial. Convolvulus Major, of this class Dicksoni, Crimson and Burridgi, deep blue, black and Annei, striped are the best.

Ipomœa Hederacea and Huberi Japanese convolvoli, with white edges to many hued flowers and marbled leaves, are very handsome trailers, do well, sown rather far, apart and pegged down like Verbenas in the rainy season only. They are hardly climbers, flowering near the ground. Ipomœa rubro-cœrulea, the large true blue Mexican convolvolus is a striking object in flower, in September and October. Sown in June and July, it becomes a great creeper; sown in October it is dwarfed to a small trailer, and grows well in a bed, with yellow and orange Nasturtiums.

*Corrœa, Rutaceæ.*—The species of this genus are mostly shrubs, the flowers, white and scarlet, each plant requires a tolerable space to grow in, as it attains the height of six or more feet, and should be placed in a shrubbery where the soil is good.

*Cotula Compositæ, Cotula Aurea.*—This is a common plant with little golden ball like flowers, and is cultivated in any garden soil by seed.

*Crocus Iridaceæ, Crocus Vernus.*—This plant never flowers in the western part of India, the roots when planted, only produce leaves, wither and die.

*Crotalaria Leguminosæ, Crotalaria Elegans.*—This is a numerous genus, many of the species beautiful, the seeds are contained in inflated pods, which rattle when shaken, grow readily in any tolerably good soil and abound in this country.

*Crotons or Codiæum.*—Among first class foliaged plants, the crotons now hold a prominent position since the introduction of many brilliant hued varieties from the South Sea Islands.

The old Indian Croton is common in gardens with its variegated laurel like leaves or curiously twisted yellow striped ones, these are not to be compared with Croton Vitchi, C. Maximum, C. Irregulare, C. Hillianum, C. Elegans, C. Undulatum, now become fashionable, though by no means common. Some of these have bright golden yellow leaves with rich variegation, other rich crimson tints on the underpart of the leaf, and are indispensable to every good collection of foliage plants, do well at Bangalore.

*Cuphea, Lythraceæ.*—This genus of plants is rather pretty; the flowers being purple, scarlet and red, are grown from seed and by cuttings in tolerable light soil.

*Cyclamen Primulaceæ, Cyclamen Persicum.*—This is a bulbous species, thriving in a light vegetable mould, and may be cultivated by seed or its tubers.

*Cynoglossum, Boraginaceæ.*—These are pretty little annuals, natives of Europe, the colour of the flowers mostly blue, purple, white and purple, grow in any common soil.

*Cyprus Vine.*—Vide *Ipomœa quamoclit.*

*Cytisus Leguminosæ, Cytisus Argenteus.*—These species are mostly hardy trees or shrubs found all over Europe, the trees mostly bearing flowers of a yellow colour, with a few exceptions of white and purple, they are readily increased by seed, layers or buds.

*Dahlia, Compositæ.*—The habit of the Dahlia of late years has been considerably improved, and instead of having plants 8 or 10 feet high as used to be, the majority are not over 4 feet high, some even 1 to 2 feet only. The graceful habit of some, when laden with blooms from the base to the summit is most pleasing. The Dwarf kinds are termed Lillyput Bouquet or Pompon. It is a plant of the simplest culture. The tubers should be potted at the end of May, and when the plants have attained about a foot in height, be shifted to the garden beds or into very large pots. The soil should be moderately good, but made as retentive of moisture as possible, anything short of clay will suit them at the time of planting, neat straight sticks about 3 feet long should be inserted in the ground, and to these the young plants be tied. Water freely in dry weather. Side shoots or laterals should be carefully tied to stout sticks about 2 feet high, no lateral should be removed, as they produce the best flowers, and tend considerably to decrease the apparent height of the main plant. In November, the Dahlia winters, when the stems have entirely died, the roots should be carefully taken up so as *not to divide the tubers from the crown or stem* in which the life of the plant lies, be thoroughly dried and packed in dry earth till the next growing season.

The method by which favourite sorts may be increased is as follows :—The old tubers are to be placed in a large flower pot of good leaf-mould, and old manure, leaving the crowns only exposed. The shoots which quickly rise from the tubers are cut or clipped off, when about two or three inches in length and put into fresh pots, or in a bed, where they must be carefully watered, and shaded, until they have struck and taken root, when they will grow vigorously. Tubers that have no eyes near the crown should be rejected. If grown from seed, the plant should be removed when about four or six inches high, and if placed in the ground, a space of two feet at least between each plant allowed ; and as the plant arrives at maturity, it must be supported by strong sticks. When the stalk has become dry, the tubers may be removed and kept in a room either upon sand or pounded charcoal.

*Dahlia Imperialis.*—A new Dahlia 12 to 14 feet high, with large spreading panicles 4 feet across, bearing scores of white bell-shaped flowers, each little less in size than those of a common white lily and equally pure in colour, the large pyramidal inflorescence is like that of a yucca, but more spreading. The bell-shaped flowers are different in shape from the flat disc like single Dahlia, still it is a Dahlia to all intents and purposes, and comes from Mexico, is raised from seed or division of the tubers like a common Dahlia.

*Daisy.*—Vide *Bellis.*

*Datura, Huberi.*—Ornamental Annuals with large double and semi-double flowers, some very sweet scented. Sow the seed in the early rains in rich soil, and plant out the seedlings when they have grown four to six leaves, separately in mixed borders, as they grow large and bushy, the colours are tints of yellow, purple and white.

*Daubentonia Leguminosæ, Daubentonia Punicea.*—Handsome plants brought from South America closely allied to the Piscidia, grow well in a sandy loam.

*Delphinium, Ranunculaceæ, D. Ajacis.*—The Lark spur is grown very commonly by the Natives after the rains, colour a deep blue on a spiral stem; the flower takes its name from the resemblance to the Dolphin. There are many species all of which are easily grown from seed, the Natives are in the habit of sowing the seed under peach and orange trees, when grown in beds and the flowers of one colour, they have a showy and pretty appearance, a space of six inches should be allowed between each plant.

*Dianthus Sileuaceæ, Dianthus Barbatus.*—From Dios divine, and Anthos a flower. D. Barbatus the Sweet William, easily cultivated by seed and slips, blossoms almost throughout the year, and requires only a good garden soil.

*Dianthus Caryophyllus.*—The Clove Pink or carnation, grows wild in various parts of England. This has long been a favourite flower, and is now almost acclimated. It seldom ripen its seeds, and two varieties are only to be met with in Deccan. The dark crimson is not so full a flower as the variegated crimson and white; they both possess equal perfume and fragrance, but the latter when carefully grown, is certainly the most beautiful. A full grown carnation should neither have its petals too crowded nor too thin, but regularly disposed, so that all its beauties may be observed at once. The stem or foot stalk seldom exceeds eighteen inches, and this should be carefully supported. Is propagated by layers and pipings; also by seed when procurable. The plants must always be sheltered from heavy rains, and also from the hot winds; yet kept in an airy situation. If placed under cover for any length of time, they run up to thin stalks, seldom throwing out blossoms. The time for taking cuttings is when the plant is in blossom; and this may be done either at the commencement of the rains, or in the cold weather. When the plants appear to be about to blossom, all the buds save a couple should be carefully removed, as well as any small shoots on the foot stalk between the leaves. When layers are required, they must be removed from the stem with a knife or scissors, and should not be longer than two or three joints. Cut off all the lower superfluous leaves smooth, then throw the layers into water, for a couple of hours. Plant them in baskets at about six inches apart, which have been filled with old rich vegetable loam; water so as to settle the earth round the stems, and place in a shady spot, not under trees, if in the rainy season. In about six weeks they will have struck, and may be removed into pots. Do this carefully not disturbing the earth round the young roots, which are very tender, and replace in the shade again until sufficiently strong to bear exposure to the sun. The variegated have only two colours, and when stripped are called Flakes, but if spotted, Picotees. Ants (black, red and white,) are very destructive to the roots. An old plant of Flakes or Picotees, will occasionally loose both stripes and spots during the hot season, and become quite white when in flower, but resume during the rains their original colours of deep, red and white. The colour thus changing may be justly attributed to the dry hot weather, as it has been remarked in England, that sometimes fine double running flowers have returned to their whole or original colour during very dry or warm summers.

*Dianthus Chinensis.*—Common in all gardens of various colours, and some mixed, they flower all the year round, and give seed immediately as it fades, and which will spring up again if sown.

The double-flowered varieties are much esteemed; the colours are white, red, crimson, red and white.

*Didiscus Umbelliferæ, Didiscus Cœruleus.*—These plants are from Australia, and are grown from seed in a light loamy soil, and the plants either reared in pots or in flower beds.

*Dillwynia Leguminosæ, Dillwynia Glycinifolia.*—Elegant shrubs when in flower, generally of a scarlet and orange colour, from New South Wales and New Holland. They should be grown in pots in a light loamy soil, and regularly watered.

*Diplacus Scrophularicæ, Diplacus Puniceus.*—The Monkey flower, a pretty genus of plants, with flowers yellow or scarlet, they are grown in a rich sandy loam, and may be propagated by cuttings, they are natives of California.

*Dodecatheon Primulaceæ, Dodecatheon Meadia.*—Ornamental plants when in flower, colours lilac, purple and white, grown in a light soil, and cultivated by dividing the roots.

*Dolichos Leguminosæ, Dolichos Lignosus.*—These are twining plants, natives of India, and grow in any good soil.

*Dracocephalum Labiatæ, Dracocephalum Altamise.*—Many of these species are well known, amongst which is the D. Canariense, the balm of Gilead, with pretty blue flowers, the scent only lies in the leaves, and the plant seldom exceeds eighteen inches in height, the other species have large splendid blue flowers, and easily reared from seed, the plants are best grown in pots.

*Dracœna, Perennial.*—A very handsome ornamental foliaged class of perennial plants, of which D. Terminalis is Indian, with deep green long pointed leaves, which at one season of the year assume a rich crimson or deep pink hue, they are propagated by divison of the Rhizomes or roots, and like a moist shady place associated with ferns and arads.

*Echium Boraginaceæ, Echium Grandiflorum, Erinus Scrophulariaceæ, Erinus Alpinus.*—This is a little plant with purple flowers, and adapted for rock work in Europe, requiring little soil.

*Erodium Geraniaceæ, Erodium Gruinum.*—So named from Gernnos, a crane. They are mostly all from the Cape of Good Hope. Most of the flowers are devoid of odour, and those which are particularly so, are the most beautiful, whereas those again whose petals are the least showy, diffuse towards the evening and during the night, a most powerful perfume; this is particularly the case with such as have white petals spotted with red. The almost innumerable varieties now produced in England have originated by hybridization, and to enumerate them all here is unnecessary. "The flowers of all the kinds are borne in umbels on a peduncle, which in the stemless kinds arises from the centre of the source of the leaves, and in the shrubby kinds from the axil of almost all of the upper leaves. The number of the flowers borne in an umbel is various in different kinds, and greatest in those of the horse-leafed group." The commonest sorts cultivated in gardens are the deep scarlet, light, pink, and ivy leafed. The latter has a strong perfume, and scents the fingers if only slightly touched. The ordinary mode of propagation is by cuttings and seeds. Almost all the varieties produce seed, which will immediately grow if sown, and should be transplanted as soon as two or three perfect leaves are formed. The cuttings grow most readily, and should be taken off at the joints when the wood is assuming a brown appearance, and beginning to ripen. The fibrous rooted herbaceous sorts may be multiplied by dividing the roots. As all the species are rapid growers, they require pruning, and to be occasionally changed into fresh pots. They require a light rich soil of loam, and old well rotted stable manure, or else leaf, mould and sand; the cuttings when put down must be removed for a time to a shady spot, and the earth kept continually moist. I must particularly caution against cutting the plants during the rains, as the whole plant suffers by the ends of the shoots decaying; neither should they be exposed during the hot winds, especially the soft velvet-leafed varieties.

*Eryngium Umbelliferæ, Eryngium Giganteum.*—This is an extensive genus of plants, some of which are ornamental and well adapted for the flower border, the colours are blue, light blue, white, light white, and green, they thrive best in a sandy soil.

*Erysimum Cruciferæ, Erysimum Perowskianum.*—This is the only one of a numerous genus at all ornamental, it thrives in any soil, the flowers are dark orange colour.

*Eschscholtzia, Papaveraceæ.*—This is a very beautiful little flower, of a deep yellow orange colour, very delicate. It blossoms only in the cold weather, and requires care in transplanting, not more than one plant in a pot, which should be deep, the root being long and tapering; grown from seed.

*Eucharidium, Onagraceæ.*—This is a small plant bearing a purple flower, and will thrive in a good garden soil.

*Eucharis, Amazonica.*—With large sweet scented waxy white flowers, like a daphue, and fine large shiny deep green foliage, amply repays attention bestowed upon it, requires the same treatment in most respects as the Caladium, but its period of rest is shorter, does not lose its leaves, and while wintering, requires to be more often watered than the Caladium; increased by off-sets.

*Euphorbia Euphorbiaceæ, Euphorbia Variegata.*—This is a variable and very extensive genus of plants, all of which abound in a milky juice, E. Variegata will be raised from seed in any common garden soil.

*Evening Primrose.*—Vide *Godetia* and *Œnothera*.

*Everlasting Flower*, vide *Gnaphalium, Entoca Hydrophyllaceæ, Entoca Multiflora.*—This genus of plants is pretty, and may be sown in flower borders, but not too close together, their colours are blue, pink and violet.

*Fennel Flower.*—Vide *Nigella*.

*Ferns*—May be raised from seed or by division of the roots. They are indispensable to every collection and garden, and are easily grown if attention is paid to perfect drainage with plenty of moisture and shade, they are rather impatient of the shade when kept under high leaved trees, preferring a place rather where the shade is cast over them with air overhead. Some very good fern houses are now erected in the Lall Baugh at Bangalore.

*Raising Ferns from seed.*—Procure some bricks or stones, bricks would be best as they have an even surface, and are also porous, rendering them capable of holding water. These would be best, if found covered with Moss which has naturally grown on them. If not thus covered it can be very easily done. The Moss must not be thick; it can be clipped with a pair of scissors, if thick, and well washed before using, to get rid of any seed that may have fallen into it. These bricks should be placed into the pot or pan, so that their upper surface may be level with the soil used to steady them and to fill up the pot. Sow the spores in the Moss, and with a pepper dredge, dust over the Moss very lightly with burnt soil, and then with a very fine rosed water can wash down the soil and spores into the Moss. Place the pot into a saucer of water which must be kept full. Place a bell glass over, those which have a hole in near the top, we prefer as they prevent damping, affording an escape to the great evaporation which takes place; they can be left alone for a week without disturbance. There will be no necessity for surface watering until the seedlings appear; even then it is not advisable, if soaking the pot up to the rim can be quickly done. The pots should not see the sun until the seedlings are well up, even then, shade is necessary. The soil used should be previously burnt, otherwise numberless seedlings will appear, which will choke those wanted and be a cause of mischief in the operation of weeding.

*Flax.*—Vide *Linum.*

*Forget Me Not.*—Vide *Myosotis.*

*Fox Glove.*—Vide *Digitalis.*

*Francoa Francoaceæ, Francoa Appendiculata.*—These are beautiful plants when in flower, and may be planted out in the open garden, then can only be cultivated by seed.

*Fritillaria Liliaceæ, Fritillaria Imperialis.*—These are bulbous rooted plants, with very showy flowers, growing well in any light garden soil, the colours are various. They are increased by off-sets.

*Fuschias.*—Fuschias do fairly at Bangalore, grown artificially under partial shade, and the plants renewed yearly. Cuttings strike readily under glass in December and January. The young plants being carefully moved through the hot weather and repotted in June, will flower well through the rains, they thrive best in the open air where they get the shade of the house thrown over them after midday, and plenty of watering in dry weather. They will increase also from layers, but take a long time to root. Double Fuschias are now quite common in Bangalore, and a number of good single varieties, leaf mould, old rotten cowdung and sand is a good compost for them with perfect drainage. A great Fuschia grower in England advocates burnt earth exclusively for Fuschias.

*Gaillardia Compositæ, Gaillardia Picta.*—These plants are chiefly from North America, grow in any garden soil, and may be increased by dividing the roots, common everywhere, the scent of some of the species are unpleasant.

*Galega Leguminosæ, Galega Orientalis.*—These are tolerably ornamental plants, and as they form a bush of small size, they require room when planted out, the colours are mostly blue and white.

*Gardenia Rubiaceæ, Cape Jasmine.*—This is a handsome genus of plants, with flowers highly scented, readily grown by cuttings, they thrive in any garden soil, and only require a moderate share of water to flower abundantly, their colours are pink, white and pale yellow, most of which are natives of India.

*Garland Flower.*—Vide *Hedychium*.

*Gazania, Splendens.*—This plant so much used in beds in the London Parks, is perfectly hardy and easily propagated by cuttings. In the rainy season it runs more to leaf than flower, spreading over the ground, but in the hot weather from February to June it makes a great show for carpet gardening; the flowers then crop up in great numbers, while in the early morning the leaves become half erect, and show their pretty frosted under half, giving the bed a fine silvery tint.

*Gentiana, Gentianaceæ.*—This is an extensive genus of plants, some of which are very pretty, colours, green, blue, purple and white, and are found wild on the mountains of India, they should be grown in a light loamy soil, mixed with vegetable mould, the whole of the species possess a bitter tonic principle.

*Geranium.*—The term scarlet geranium applied to the whole class of zonale or horseshoe geraniums, is very confusing and obsolete. The whole family have a zone on the leaf, though sometimes but faintly developed, and are of many tints beside scarlet, every shade of pink up to white and crimson, modern growers divide them into :

Large flowering zonale Geraniums.
*Nosegay.*—Geraniums.
*Tricolor.*

*Bicolor.*

*Gold and Bronze.*

*Silver and Bronze.*

*Scarlet Tom Thumb.*

The tricolor and bicolor kind will not thrive well at Bangalore, numbers of the best kinds have been imported from England in wardian cases, and many pounds sterling spent in seed of the hybridized kinds, but they all lose their bright colours and degenerate to the green zonale, the only one that really keeps its colour is a gold and bronze seedling raised by General Haines there three years ago, which at times preserves its true tints, and has been extensively propagated. Mrs. Pollock, Italia Unita Bullian, &c., have been failures.

Avoiding then going further into the culture of the tricolor and bicolor class, it will be safe only to cultivate the large flowering and Nosegay and Scarlet T. Thumb kinds, these do very well at Bangalore, and may be raised from seed almost all the year round, and by cuttings from July to February. Plants raised from seed, are the most compact and shapely, the old plants lose their leaves and run much to wood, the cuttings the same, though in a less degree, but a collection of 8 months old seedlings are excellent specimens, the seed should get a soaking shower to start them, and after that be kept out of heavy rain while very young, and partially protected during midday sun till they have 6 to 8 leaves which then protect them effectively, geraniums, however, as a rule, like shade cast over them during part of the day instead of exposure to the sun from morning till night.

In the cold weather bandicoots often attack geraniums, and in the rains the large grub, or lava of the cockchaper destroy plants left in the ground, so much so, that very few survive through the monsoon, if in the beds, people may see a fine healthy plant of geranium suddenly droop, on examining under the roots, one of these grubs or more, will be found gnawing away the soft wood. To avoid thus the geranium should be kept in pots from March till November, when the grub pest is over. A nosegay geranium is a zonale, the petals being long and narrow and the three front ones wide apart from the two at the back, while in the scarlet zonales the flowers are round and the petals all close to each other. There are many very brilliant large flowering nosegay kinds, and they are somewhat hardier in habit than the other.

The double geraniums are very hardy, and of a coarser habit than the single, and are getting common here, but as yet only of two tints of scarlet.

*Gesnera*—is a class now sub-divided into Tydea, Gesnera, Nagœlia, Encodonca, Plectopoma, all much alike, with beautiful velvet leaves and bright flowers, treat them as recommended for Gloxinias, so never dry them off, only gradually withhold water as they decline for a month or so, still keep them occasionally watered, so that the roots never quite dry up or shrivel. They are difficult to get from Europe on account of their liability to dry up, and people importing them must expect many casualties. The best time to get them is in January, overland and pot them, directly they arrive.

*Geum Rosaceæ, Geum Coccineum.*—This is an ornamental genus of plants, the G. Coccineum being extremely handsome, but as these plants are mostly the produce of North America and Russia, are not likely to be easily raised in this country, they require a light loamy soil, and are increased by dividing the roots or by seed.

*Gilia Polemoniaceæ, Gilia Achilliæfolia.*—These are beautiful annuals and of easy cultivation, may be grown either in the flower garden or in pots, during and after the rains, easily propagated by seed in any light soil.

*Gladiolus.*—This beautiful tribe of plants should be largely planted, because they are perfectly hardy and easily grown; are gorgeously beautiful, their handsome spikes of flowers when cut and placed in water will expand and last a long time, in pots they are very effective—inexpensive kinds can be supplied by hundreds, for planting among shrubberies and around bushes. The luxuriant combination of colour in some varieties is extremely charming. There are two distinct classes of Gladiolus, Gandavensis and Ramosus. Gandavensis flowering in August, September and October—Ramosus in July and August. The best and safest time for planting is from the end of May. A succession till July. The soil should be a rich sandy compost, the pots large, twelve to sixteen inches in diameter—the drainage good. Large bulbs should be planted from three or four inches deep, smaller bulbs two inches. In dry weather, copious watering is necessary. At first expose the pots to full sunshine till noon only. When the leaves turn yellow in November, let the bulbs thoroughly dry, then store them in dry earth or sand till next growing season at the end of May. Of the Gandavensis section of Gladiolus, G. Bowienses and Brenchleyiensis, are the most showy.

*Glaucium Papaveraceæ, Glaucium Persicum.*—These are very handsome plants, and showy, either in borders or patches, they require a moderate good soil, the plants not too near each other, and the seed sown at the end of the rains. They are natives of the south of Europe and Persia. The colours red, orange, yellow and purple.

*Globe Amaranth.*—Vide *Gomphrena*.

*Gloriosa, Superba, Liliaceæ, Hind. Butchnag, from Gloriosus, Magnificent.*—This beautiful lily is a creeper, and blossoms at the commencement of the rains; it is found in the beds of ravines and edges of rivers. The flowers are of a white, yellow and orange colour, the petals long and fringed. It lasts about eight days, undergoing various changes during that time. The root is a strong poison.

*Gloxinia.*—Well suited for pot gardening, grouped together in a mass, no flowers are more showy or brilliant, of all the intermediate colours from white to purple and carmine, &c., may be raised from seed or imported roots or by division of leaves. There are two kinds, one with erect flowers and the other drooping, they thrive during the rainy season. To raise them from seed, fill the pots or pans half full of crocks, (broken tiles) over which place a layer of moss, and then fill up the pot with fine sand and leaf-mould, press the soil down firmly in the pot, and water it freely, when settled, sow the seed on the surface, and do not cover it at all with mould, it requires no such covering. Place a bell-glass or pane of glass over the pot, and keep it in a shady place watering the surface gently daily, in a fortnight or ten days the seed will germinate when the plants have formed three or four leaves, prick them off into small pots, and if properly supplied with heat and moisture, the plants will form good roots by the cold season, they must then be allowed to winter, care being taken that rats do not get at the roots which they particularly like.

Propagation by leaf is simple, almost every part of the leaf will form plants, providing a portion of the midrib is retained in the cutting. Divide the leaves transversely, place them in pots of sand covered with a bell-glass and plunge in heat, in a short time collosities will form at the base of the cuttings as soon as they have sufficiently started into growth, re-pot them in sand and leaf-mould. Gloxinias do well in small pots. At the end of the rains when the plants begin to show signs of going to rest, gradually diminish the quantity of water, but not so as to let them become quite dormant, some people dry them off altogether; this is not so good a plan, for in drying off the plants and storing them so, many shrivel and die. In May, shake the earth from the roots, trim the leaves, plant them afresh in good soil, consisting of leaf-mould, sandy loam and well-rotted cowdung, water sparingly till the plants appear to start into free growth, then water more freely.

*Glycine Leguminosæ, Glycine Sinensis*—Takes its name from Glykys, sweet, the roots and leaves of most of the species being so, the colour of the flowers which hang in racemes from the axila of the leaves are violet, yellow or purple, grown in any good soil.

*Gnaphalium Compositæ, Gnaphalium Eximium.*—These flowers possess the quality of retaining their colour long after being gathered. The stalk is covered with a whitish down, they are very hardy, both the annual and biennial, the colours are yellow, purple, crimson, yellow and white, in North America, Africa and Egypt, and grow from two to three feet in height.

*Godetia Onagraceæ, Evening Primrose, Godetia Œnothera.*—This is a very pretty single-petalled white flower, blossoming only in the evening and towards morning, turns to a pink when it closes and withers. A fresh succession of flowers continues many weeks, even during the hot season. Is propagated by seed, either in pots or beds. The seed may be sown in the rains, soil should be rich.

*Gomphrena Amaranthaceæ.*—Globe Amaranth annual; common in most gardens. The Native women wear the flowers in their hair. It resembles red clover, native name Jafferce Goondee.

*Goodia Leguminosæ, Goodia Latifolia.*—This genus of plants are all natives of New Holland, colour of the flowers yellow, they never attain any great height, they may be raised from seed or cuttings in a loamy soil.

*Gypsophila Silenaceæ, Gypsophila Elegans.*—This is a genus of small creeping plants, flowers of various colours, and will grow in any common soil.

*Hebenstreita, Selaginaceæ.*—This is a genus of under-shrubs, the flowers white, grown in common garden ground.

*Hedychium Scitamineæ, Garland Flower, Hedychium Coronarium, Zingeberaceæ*—Has large fine white waxy flowers, which appear in abundance towards the end of the rains, and are deliciously scented; easily propagated by division of the roots.

*Helenium Compositæ, Helenium Mexicanum.*—Most of the species are well adapted for borders, they are tallish growing plants, and all the yellow coloured flowers grow in any common soil. Natives of North America chiefly.

*Helianthemum Cistaceæ.*—Sun Rose, small shrubs generally used for planting on rock work, soil common garden.

*Helichrysum Compositæ, Helichrysum Macranthum.*—Many of this genus are much admired for their very lasting and brilliant colours, they grow well in a rich soil, and are easily cultivated by cuttings taken off at the joint, some species seed freely, and are found very abundant at the Cape of Good Hope.

*Heliophila Cruciferæ.*—A genus of pretty annuals, natives of the Cape of Good Hope, colours, purple, blue, violet and white, raised by seed in pots, and may afterwards be placed out in borders.

*Heliotrope.*—In addition to the common Heliotrope, Bangalore gardens now have the dark purple, very sweet scented kind, which is easily multiplied by layers.

*Heliotropium Boraginaceæ.*—A shrubby plant, with lilac coloured flowers.

*Hibiscus, Malvaceæ.*—These are all showy flowering plants, and thrive well in any garden soil; they are easily propagated by cutting or layers.

*Hovea, Leguminosæ.*—This is an elegant genus of plants when in flower, natives of New Holland and Swan River, very ornamental, and thrive in a mixture of sand, loam and peat.

*Hoya, Carnosa, Asclepiadaceæ, Wax Plants.*—This plant is well adapted for covering trellis work; it grows in gardens or pots, the flowers are of a whitish pink colour resembling wax.

*Humea Compositæ, Humea Elegans.*—This plant is a native of New South Wales, grows to the height of five or six feet, colour of the flower red, and well adapted for borders, it requires a good soil.

*Hydrangea.*—The common Hydrangea will flower fairly at Bangalore, the plants being renewed yearly. Hydrangea, variegated leaved, will also do for one season, and is very ornamental, the best way is to get yearly young plants from Ootacamund to last the season and be then discarded.

*Hypericum, Hypericaceæ, St. John's Wort.*—These shrubs and herbaceous plants, all bear yellow flowers, with one exception, the Cochin-Chinese, they are inhabitants of all parts of the world, and grown by seed in any good garden soil.

*Iberis, Cruciferæ.*—Candy Tuft, grows wild in England; named Iberis from Iberia or Spain, easily grown from seed, the colours pink and white, and blossoms towards the close of the rains.

*Indian Shot.*—Vide *Canna Indica.*

*Indigofera Leguminosæ, Indigofera Tinctoria, Indigo.*—Some of these plants are very beautiful, natives of India, and worthy of a place in any garden; the colours being purple, red or pink.

*Ipomœa Convolvulaceæ, Ipomœa Coccinea.*—Vide *Convolvulus.*

*Ipomœa Bonanox, Muricata,* (Hairy), Rubro Cerulea (blue and pink), Tyrianthina, (bright violet), Violacea (violet blue) Splendens (pale red), Tuberosa (yellow species).

*Ipomœa Quamoclit Cyprus Vine, Crimson Quamoclit,* flowers in the cold weather, of a most beautiful bright crimson colour, tube long, slender; in gardens, pretty common.

*Ipomopsis, Convolvulaceæ.*—This genus of twining plants requires the same treatment as the Ipomea, and is applied to the same uses.

*Iresine or Achyzanthes.*—We have now four kinds of Iresine, I. Herbsti and I. Aureoreticulata, the older varieties I. Lindeni and I. Acuminata, the newer kinds, these are all beautiful foliage plants, most easily increased from cuttings, requiring to be grown in a shady spot with abundance of water and richest soil, they even like two-thirds of the soil to be manure, the proper treatment of them insures their retaining their rich colours in foliage, whereas exposed to the sun and stinted of water they run up lanky, go to seed, and lose their leaves, which become a dull colour, they look their best in the morning and evening, when the sun's rays shine through the leaves, should be grouped with ferns, and the large light green Colocasia. Near a fountain they grow remarkably well, and they are one of the few plants that will do well under cover, in dark parts of a verandah, fernery, or nooks under trees, still like all other plants they prefer some share of light, just the morning and evening sun, or to be in the open when the shade of the house or a tree is cast over them most of the day.

*Iris Iridaceæ, Iris Xiphoides.*—Iris, named from Iris, the eye, alluding to the beauty of the colours of the flower. There are the fibrous rooted and tuberous rooted kinds; species numerous, hybrids, the tuberous rooted are said to be the most difficult to cultivate, though most of the species thrive well in India, they require merely a good rich soil.

*Isotoma Lobeliaceæ, Isotoma Axillaris.*—This is a beautiful elegant plant, the flowers of which, look like a large Lilac Jessamine, and are cultivated like the Lobelia.

*Ixia Chinensis and Capensis Iridaceæ.*—These beautiful flowers vary in colour and form, they are mostly from the Cape of Good Hope, and require the same cultivation as plants of the Lily tribe, and are propagated by dividing the bulbs.

*Ixora Banducha Cinchonaceæ.*—Jungle Geranium, Hind, Buckolee. A spreading shrub, smaller than I. Coccinea, but equally common in flower almost during the whole year, of a pale crimson colour; there is also a white variety, blossoms during the rains.

*Jasminum Grandiflorum, Hind, Chumbalee, or Latee Iai.*—This species is very much prized by the Natives; the large white flowers having a most powerful scent, and being in blossom throughout the year, are used as garlands on all festive occasions. Is propagated and grown as the former.

*Jasminum Jasminaceæ, Jasminum Odoratissimum.*—The yellow Jasmine, an elegant shrub, with small shining leaves, flowers bearing a sweet scent, a native of Madura introduced into India.

*Jasminum Officinale.*—Common white, with a much more powerful scent; used generally for covering trellis work by Europeans. The Natives grow it in bushes, and use the flowers at most of their festivals. Is propagated by layers; the plant does not require any particular care, further than watering.

*Jerusalem Sage.*—Vide *Phlomis.*

*Jungle Geranium.*—Vide *Ixora.*

*Kaulfussia Compositæ, Kaulfussia Amelloides.*—This is a small annual plant, with bright blue flowers, the florets of which curl back after they have been expanded a short time, it requires a light soil, and the seed may be sown at the end of the rains.

*Kennedya Leguminosæ.*—A genus of beautiful plants, with lilac and crimson coloured flowers, with short keels, whilst the K. Coccinea have long ones, they are propagated by seed in any good soil.

*Lantana Verbenaceæ, Lantana Sellowi.*—These are large shrubs producing pink, yellow, orange coloured heads of flowers, they blossom at all seasons, and are found in most gardens, the leaves have the scent of black currants, the berries are eaten, may easily be propagated by seed or suckers.

*Lark Spur.*—Vide *Delphinium.*

*Lasthenia Compositæ.*—These plants are natives of California, flowers yellow, and adapted for borders.

*Lathyrus Leguminosæ, Lathyrus Odoratus, Sweet Pea.*—The English Sweet Pea seed, rarely flowers in the Deccan and Southern India, but acclimatised seed from Nagpore and northwards will do fairly, sown in September or October.

*Lavatera Malvaceæ, Lavatera Salvitellensis.*—These annuals are common, but showy flowers in the garden, colours, pink, light blue, and they will thrive in any soil, and are increased by seed and cuttings of the ripened shoots.

*Lead Wort.*—Vide *Plumbago.*

*Ledum Cistus, Ericaceæ.*—Cultivated the same as Lavender.

*Leonotis Leonurus, Labiatæ, Scarlet Dandelion.*—A beautiful small scarlet flower. Native of the Cape, and now common in all gardens; blossoms throughout the year, and is very difficult to get rid of when once sown, any soil seems to suit it.

*Leptosiphon, Polemoniaceæ.*—These are pretty annuals, allied to the Gilia, and propagated in the same manner, the colours are white, blue and purple.

*Leucadendron, Proteaceæ.*—These are a handsome genus of shrubs, growing to a large size, with heads of yellow flowers and silky leaves, and may be cultivated in any good garden soil.

*Leucospermum, Proteaceæ.*—An interesting genus of plants, with entire downy or hairy leaves, and terminal heads of yellow flowers. They require the same culture as the Protea.

*Limnanthes, Limnanthaceæ.*—These flowers are from California, and are of a yellow colour, with a border of white, and are slightly fragrant, they are readily grown from seed as other annuals.

*Linaria, Scrophulariaceæ, Toad Flax.*—These are common plants, and may be easily raised from seed; colours, mostly purple, blue and yellow.

*Linum Austriacum.*—Some of these flowers are pretty, and may be placed in a border, the flax is too well known to need any description here.

*Linum Linaceæ.*—Flax.

*Lisianthus Gentianaceæ, Lisianthus Russellianus.*—This is a handsome plant, with purple flowers, the other species are white and yellow, the seed should be sown in a light vegetable mould, in pots, and transplanted when about three inches high, the flowers are large and handsome, and continue perfect for many days.

*Loasa, Loasaceæ.*—This is an interesting genus of plants, some of the species possessing the properties of Nettles, the flowers are red, white and yellow, they are grown from seed, and any common soil suits them.

*Lobelia.*—No plant in the flower garden is more useful than the Lobelia, especially when we have such a deficiency of good blue flowers. There are three kinds adapted to Southern Indian culture. The Lobelia Erinus, L. Ramosa, and L. Cardinalis. The two first are only propagated here by seed. L. Erinus, flowers in the cold season, and well into the hot weather, it then gives out a good mass of rich blue flowers, is sown in July and August, and the seedlings transplanted twice, as they crowd the pots, before a final move to the beds. It forms a capital inner edging to Gold Feather. Should be grown in very rich soil, and while young, be partially shaded from midday sun. L. Ramosa is a taller kind, propagated from seed, and treated like the L. Erinus, but makes a beautiful mass of blue in pots, is much earlier than the other kind, its flowers are also much bigger. Lobelia Cardinalis is a perennial, raised from seed, and also by division of the roots, it will flower profusely twice a year so treated, kept in a very shady place in large pots, with a great deal of manure in the soil and plenty of water. Its flowers are the brightest scarlet, the flower spike being sometimes three feet in height crowded with fine blossoms.

It has been very much improved in size and habit of flower of late. Bull's hybrid. L. Cardinalis, Queen Victoria, with very dark leaves, has been introduced here. Young plants put out in June or May, will flower in August, these when the bloom is over, may be cut down, the roots divided and re-potted, and will flower in February and March. In this way a succession of plants of L. Cardinalis may be had in flower all the year round.

*Lobelia Radicans.*—An annual creeping glabrous plant, a native of China. Flowers of a pink colour. In gardens it spreads over the soil rooting at every branch, and is well adapted for borders to parterres.

*Lophospermum Scrophulariaceæ, Lophospermum Scandens.*— Beautiful climbing plants, with large purple or rose coloured bell-shaped flowers, this plant is of fast growth, and well adapted for covering trellis work, easily grown from seed at the commencement of the rains, and lasts throughout the year, the soil should be rich and light.

*Lotus Leguminosæ, Lotus Jacobæus.*—These plants are tolerably ornamental, closely allied to the Cytisus Argenteus, and grow in a similar manner.

*Love Lies Bleeding.*—Vide *Amaranthus.*

*Lupinus Leguminosæ, Lupinus Bicolor.*—These flowers blossom during the latter end of the cold season, and should never be sown until the rains are over. Some of the species are very delicate, but the small blue, white lupin, rose lupin and Egyptian, flower freely, some of the species are very common in Egypt, and grown for food; the seed being ground into flour. Is propagated by seed, and should be sown in pots; and if in beds, about one foot apart.

*Lychnis Silenaceæ, Lychnis Corsica.*—There are three sorts, scarlet, white and fulgens. The first is an extremely showy flower, and ornamental either in a border or pot. It seldom exceeds eighteen inches in height, and after flowering if cut down, will shoot out and blossom again. The seed should be sown either in or after the rains, moderate care is all that is necessary.

*Lythrum, Lythraceæ.*—This is a common plant, native of Great Britain, it thrives in any common soil, and easily cultivated from seed.

*Madia Compositæ, Madia Elegans.*—This is a plant of no particular beauty, the flowers of which are yellow, and may be grown easily from seed in any common soil.

*Magnolia, Magnoliaceæ.*—This a very extensive genus of elegant and showy plants, when in flower, both as trees and shrubs, they thrive well in any good garden soil, and flower during the rains.

*Malope, Malvaceæ.*—These are very beautiful annual plants, and grown readily from seed at the commencement of the rains, tho colour of flowers, purple and violet, the plant grows to the height of seven or eight feet, and is better adapted for a shrubby than the flower garden.

*Malva Malvaceæ, Malva Miniata.*—This is an extensive genus of plants of easy culture, and every variety of colour, easily propagated by seed, cuttings, or dividing the suckers.

*Marigold.*—Vide *Tagetes.*

*Martynia, Pedaliaceæ.*—These are handsome plants, common in India, the leaves are covered with a glutinous soft substance, the flowers are red, and pale purple, the capsule of the seeds is hard, with a hooked bill at the end. The plant thrives luxuriantly in any light rich soil.

*Marvel of Peru.*—Vide *Mirabilis.*

*Mask Flower.*—Vide *Alonsoa.*

*Maurandya Perennial.*—Is an elegant little creeper, with pretty leaves and flowers in three colours, white, pink and purple, should be sown easily in the rains, the young plants re-potted singly and put to trellises, prefers a half shady spot where it can get plenty of rain, does not do well immediately under trees, should be cut down in the early hot season, and will spring up again as fresh as ever.

*Mignonette.*—Vide *Roseda.*

*Mimosa, Leguminosæ.*—Of this genus of plants, many are to be found all over the country, the leaves of some of the species are remarkable for being sensitive to the touch. The pink and yellow flowers of one of the small shrubby kinds are particularly beautiful in the rains, readily grown from seed in any soil.

*Mimulus, Scrophulariaceæ.*—Monkey Flower.

*Mimulus, Cardinalis.*—These plants are well suited for flower borders, the colours are chiefly blue, red and yellow, easily grown from seed in any garden soil, it takes its name from *mimo* an ape, the seed bearing some resemblance to the face of a monkey.

*Mirabilis Jalapa Nyctaginaceæ.*—Native name, Gool Bajee or Abbas. This plant is very beautiful, though very common, and known as the Marvel of Peru. The flowers are of various colours, red, white and yellow, also variegated red and white, yellow and white. The root when dried is prepared for medicinal use. It becomes in a short time quite a weed in the garden. Is propagated by seed and in any soil.

*Monkey Flower.*—Vide *Diplacus* and *Mimulus.*

*Monstera Deliciosa.*—A very remarkable looking parasite found in the Mysore jungles. It has great perforated leaves of a very singular nature, and though treated here generally as a creeping parasite, it is much used in Europe as a lawn plant easily propagated by cuttings and layers.

*Morina Dipsacaceæ, Morina Elegans.*—This is Native of Persia, the colours red and white, grown from seed as most other annuals.

*Mountain Sorrell.*—Vide *Oxyura.*

*Myosotis, Boraginaceæ.*—The Forget Me Not.

*Myosotis, Palustris.*—This plant is common in England, and is grown easily here by seed in a light soil, which should be thinly sown in pots, or by division of the roots, or cuttings.

*Nasturtium.*—This old fashioned plant has been very greatly improved of late, from a straggling coarse trailing kitchen garden plant, it has been got into a dwarf compact habit, producing masses of brilliant flowers of rich scarlet, crimson, orange, golden yellow, straw colour, blush rose, spotted yellow, &c.

The best kinds for bedding are the Tom Thumb and compactum varieties, these are quite hardy, and only require sowing in moderately light soil as they become little bushes, and are liable to be blown out of the ground by the high winds so prevalent here, a few twigs should be inserted about them to steady and protect them. They will do fairly in the rainy season, but best in the cold weather. A large kind of Nasturtium Lobbianium has some magnificent varieties with very large vivid scarlet flowers and dark leaves, but of a more spreading habit and require plenty of space, these may be raised from seed and then multiplied to any extent by cuttings struck in sand. Of the Lobbianum varieties, Crown Prince Etna, Vesuvius are the favourites, or the Dwarf, Tom Thumb varieties, the following are recommended, Scarlet King of Tom Thumbs, Golden King of Tom Thumbs, King Theodore, Improved Scarlet and Golden Compactum, Compactum luteum,

Trentham rose, Bluish rose, Beauty. For masses of a good yellow, Golden King rivals, Calccoloria floribunda.

*Nelumbium Nymphæaceæ, Nelumbium Speciosum.*—Large water Lily, grows wild in tanks, in all parts of India.

*Nemesia Scrophulariaceæ, Nemesia Floribunda.*—These plants may be cultivated from seed in any rich light soil, the colour of the flowers is purple.

*Nemophila Hydrophyllaceæ, Nemophila Aurita.*—These plants are all annuals, and require a great deal of moisture, growing and flowering in shady situations, the colours are white and purple, blue and dark purple, they are natives of California and North America.

*Nicotiana, Tobacco.*—Some of the Tobacco tribe have enormous leaves, and are handsome plants for leaf gardening.

*Nicotiana, Wigandioides*—and grandiflora, are best for this purpose.

*Nigella, Ranunculaceæ, N. Sativa.*—Fennel Flower.

*Nigella Hispanica.*—Some of the flowers are pretty, and only require to be sown in open ground at the commencement of the rains, the colours are chiefly pale, blue and yellow.

*Night Blowing Cereus.*—Vide Cereus.

*Nolana Nolanaceæ, Nolana Grandiflora.*—Trailing annual plants with white, yellow and blue flowers, easily raised from seed in any garden soil.

*Nonea Boraginaceæ, Nonea Rosea.*—These are plants of no great beauty, and may be raised in common garden soil.

*Nuttallia Malvaceæ, Nuttallia Grandiflora.*—A genus of pretty plants, when in blossom resembling the poppy; they should be grown in a light rich soil of vegetable mould, the colour of the flowers, is pink, purple, red and purple.

*Nymphæa, Esculenta.*—This species has a tuberous root, which is eaten and held in esteem by the natives.

*Nymphæa Nymphæaceæ, Nymphæa Alba.*—Found in tanks and grown as the rest of the species.

*Nymphœa Rubra, Hind. Kummul, Red Flowering Lotus.*—In tanks, flowers about the close of the rains, of a dark crimson colour.

*Nymphœa, Stellata.*—This plant is common in ponds and tanks. The flowers are blue.

*Œnothera, Drummondii Nana.*—Improved Evening Primrose, a trailing plant, with large sulphur coloured flowers, open from 4 o'clock in the afternoon, till noon the next day, is a great stand by in the hot season when few other flowers are left, often throws out 50 to 100 blossoms at that time of year, will not do well in the rainy season, but should be sown in November, one plant in good soil will cover a large space, three or four grouped together make a fine bed of yellow.

*Orchid-Growing.*—In Bengal orchid houses are constructed after the plan of the Native pan or betel inclosures. Walls and flat roof of stout posts and bamboos form the basis for a light frame work, or trellis on which coarse grass is thinly fastened. Roof and sides equally. The grass being so disposed as to cut of all direct solar rays, without inducing any appreciable darkness. Orchids, though impatient of direct exposure to the sun, nevertheless delight in abundance of light. In such a house, they should be staged in pots which have plenty of holes in their sides to admit the air, and escape of water. The potting material is lumpy charcoal and pieces of brick in about equal parts. As regards watering from November till February, no water as a rule should be given them. In March, the flowering season, a little only is given to the plants as the flower buds get fairly set, the ground however, may be watered freely night and morning. When the flowering season is over, an abundance of water at night and the whole house syringed, the floor saturated three times a day to keep a humid atmosphere. When the rains set in they get an abundance of water naturally.

This appears a better plan of treating orchids in a dry climate like this, than sticking them with mud and cowdung on the branches of trees.

Ornamental foliage for bedding Ribands, &c., &c., Frosted foliage, Cineraria, Maritima, Centaurea, Ragusina, Centaurea Gymnocarpa, Salvia, Argentea, all raised from seed. Stachy's Lanata Gazarania Splendens, from division of the roots. Golden foliage, Golden Feather, Pyrethrum from seed and division of the roots, if from seed, sow it in the dry, cold and hot weather, as the seedlings are impatient of damp. As seedlings, they must be kept much in the shade, and no manure mixed in the soil which should be very sandy.

Crimson foliage, Amaranthus Elegantissimus, from seed. Dells Deep Crimson Beet, Iresine Herbstii and Lindeni, Coleus, Alternanthera sessilis.

Bronze, pink and copper coloured foliage, Coleus, Alternanthera, Amœna, Telianthera, Dells Black Beet, Gold Feather and Dells Beet, are excellent contrasts.

Variegated foliage, Vinca Elegantissima, Aureoreticulata Perennial, propagated by layers, Iresine Aureoreticulata by cuttings, Coleus, Assistatia, beautiful white and green foliage plant from the Neilgherries, by layers, variegated grass, two kinds.

*Orobus Leguminosæ, Orobus Fischeri, Bitter Vetch.*—Readily cultivated from seed in any good soil, colours various.

*Oxalis, Oxalidaceæ.*—Wood Sorrel.

*Oxalis Rosea.*—Tuberous rooted plants from the Cape of Good Hope, and are easily cultivated at the commencement of the rains; the small tubers should be allowed to remain in the pots in which they have grown, and be carefully removed into fresh earth after the rains have set in, and if well attended to, will readily spring up and produce abundance of rose coloured flowers.

*Oxylobium Leguminosæ, Oxylobium Cordifolium.*—These are ornamental plants, easy of culture in any common soil, the colours are yellow, orange and scarlet.

*Oxyuru, Polygonaceæ.*—Mountain Sorrel.

*Oxyuru Chrysanthemoides.*—Native of Britain and North America, cultivated in any garden soil.

*Pansies.*—Pansies are delicate plants at Bangalore, heavy rain generally kills them if left uncovered. May be sown in June and again in October, must be potted in rich soil, and shaded during midday; put under cover always when there is heavy rain, will grow from cuttings, but are easiest raised from seed. They are too delicate here for the border.

*Papaver Papaveraceæ, Papaver Croceum.*—This species which is almost always variegated, is sown only as a border flower, for its large and full handsome appearance. The scent is anything but agreeable. The seed should be sown where the plants are to remain, and six inches the least space allowed between each plant. They do not bear transplanting. The common cultivated species from the capsule of which opium is procured is of various colours, and when sown in beds has a very pleasing effect. The seed (kus kus) is usually used by Natives in confectionary, having the taste of sweet almonds. Is propagated by seed only.

*Passiflora, Passifloraceæ, Passion Flower, Passiflora Alata.*—These are ornamental climbers, are common in most parts of India, the species are numerous, being of easy culture. Some of them are fruit bearing as the Pedulis and Laurifolia, the latter is known from its dark shining leaves. There are several wild varieties.

*Patersonia Iridaceæ, Patersonia Glauca.*—These plants are natives of New Holland, the cultivation of which is by division of the fibrous roots similar to the Iris.

*Pelargonium, Geraniaceæ.*—See *Geranium.*

*Pentstemon Scrophulariaceæ, Pentstemon Digitalis.*—These are herbaceous plants, and are cultivated as the Chelone, the flowers are of every variety of colour.

*Petrea Verbenaceæ.*—This is a climbing plant, with dark shining green leaves, and beautiful lilac or purple flowers hanging in racemes. It is a native of South America, and only requires to be regularly watered, and grown in a good garden soil, to cause it to extend itself over an immense space, its long slender whip like shoots should be lopped down, to make it throw out branches, at the end of which the flowers appear in most elegant festoons towards the close of the cold season. It is easily propagated by layers.

*Petunias.*—The large flowering hybrid kinds like grandiflora, inimitable maculata or blotched, are not hardy, and very liable to damp off when exposed to rain and during wet weather, in the cold weather also they do not thrive. The only time they really do fairly at Bangalore, is when sown in the cold season, and flowering in the early hot weather. The consequence is, really good Petunias are scarce here, while the common old purple and white varieties are mere weeds and not worth growing.

*Phacelia Hydrophyllaceæ.*—Hardy plants, flourishing in any common soil; the flowers are curious from the manner in which they slowly unroll themselves, some are perennials, and others biennials, the flowers are chiefly pink and blue coloured, propagated from seed.

*Pheasant's Eye.*—Vide *Adonis.*

*Phlomis Labiatæ, Phlomis Russelliana, Jerusalem Sage.*—These are perennial and shrubby plants, with coarse hairy leaves resembling the common sage; the flowers are purple, red, yellow, &c., growing readily from seed in any common soil.

*Phlox Drummondii*—This is one of the brightest and most useful of our garden annuals whether for pots or beds, and is very hardy, it will do fairly sown in the early part of the rainy season, though the flowers get a good deal knocked about by heavy rain, but best sown anywhere in October and November after the rains. It then flowers well through the hot season and makes the garden glow with its rich scarlet, crimson, pink, purple and white colours, besides giving out in the morning and evening a very nice scent.

*Phlox Perennial*—Is very hardy, and flowers all the year round, is propagated by cuttings and grown in large pots, in full sunshine.

*Pinks.*—Picotees and Carnations will flower here if the plants are brought down from the Neilgherries and carefully grown, kept out of heavy rain Carnation seed will come up well, and fine large plants can be so raised, but these never flower.

Indian and Japan pinks do very well indeed, sown at the end of October, they flower well through the cold and early hot season, in beds and pots, and are very gay and desirable, of these the Hedwig kinds single and double are the best.

*Platylobium Leguminosæ, Platylobium Triangulare.*—These are free flowering shrubs, with pretty orange, yellow or red coloured flowers, and are readily grown from seed in any tolerable garden soil.

*Platystemon Ranunculaceæ, Platystemon Californicum.*—These are annuals with cream coloured flowers, natives of Carlifornia, and said to grow best in sandy loam.

*Plumbago, Plumbaginaceæ.*—The Lead Wort, (White) P. Zeylanica, (Red) P. Rosea, (Blue) P. Capensis. The White Plumbago is common; so are the other varieties. The red and blue, blossom throughout the year; but the latter, which is the handsomest of the whole, and introduced from the Cape, is by far the most esteemed. Is propagated by layers.

*Podalyria Leguminosæ, Podalyria Genistoides.*—These are pretty shrubs with silky leaves, and should be grown in a light garden soil, their colours are mostly white, purple, blue or red, and should be raised from seed.

*Podolepis Compositæ, Podolepis Gracilis.*—The stems of these plants are covered with scales, the flowers are white, yellow and pink, these plants are adapted for borders, and may be raised from seed.

*Podotheca Compositæ, Podotheca Capitata.*—A yellow flowering plant of no great beauty, readily cultivated from seed.

*Polygala Polygalaceæ, Polygala Speciosa.*—All the species of this genus are very handsome, showy flowers, they are natives of the Cape, some parts of Europe and America; their colours are chiefly pink, scarlet, red or white, they are readily grown from seed, and should be raised in a light soil.

*Polygonum, Persicaria, Polygonaceæ.*—This is a very extensive genus of plants, the Dwarf Persicaria, a garden plant, is of easy culture, also the red and white, the P. Hydropiper, a water plant, has beautiful pink flowers.

*Poppies.*—The Double Marseilles Poppies are very gay and easily grown, sown broadcast in a bed, in good soil, in the rainy season, but they take up a great deal of room, and are very short lived. The large coarse opium poppy is not deserving of place in a flower garden.

*Portulaca.*—There are not less than eight distinct colours and kinds of Portulaca, the double ones are very elegant like satin rosettes, the cultivation is most easy, sown at the end of the cold weather either in beds or pots, in very rich sandy soil, the surface being manure dust in which the seed should be sprinkled without further covering, mats should be put over the beds for two or three days to exclude light, and retain an even temperature. If sown too thickly, the young seedlings may be thinned out and transplanted, shading them after the move for a couple of days. A succession of Portulaca may be grown up to July, after which the heavy rain and colder weather stops their growth till February. A large bed of Portulaca properly grown, is a beautiful sight in the morning, in fact, few flowers can match it in brilliancy and variety of colour. Care should be taken before sowing the seed, that the beds or pots are perfectly level or the seed will be washed down to the lowest part, and with seed sown in a bed, the edges should be a little raised to prevent heavy rain washing the seed and fine mould away altogether.

*Potentilla Rosaceæ, Potentilla Atrosanguinea.*—These are herbaceous plants, and handsome when in flower, they grow in any garden soil, the colours are various, and easily raised from seed or by dividing the roots, the shrubby species grow from two to three feet high.

*Primula, Primulaceæ.*—The Primrose. This genus of plants includes the Auricula, Polyanthus and the Primrose. They all form in Europe ornamental border flowers; but will not succeed in South India.

*Protea, Proteaceæ.*—These plants are natives of the Cape, and would be found difficult to cultivate from their fleshy roots, the soil best suited for their growth, is light loam mixed with sand, they require great attention, as they suffer either from a want or excess of water.

*Pyrethrum, Gold Feather.*—Gold Feather is an excellent edging for borders and very useful, as contrast foliage in masses with Dells Black Beet or Lobelia Erinas. Is easily reproduced by division of the roots. To grow it from seed is less easy, as the seedlings are very apt to damp off in wet weather, the best time for sowing the seed is in the beginning of the dry hot weather, the seed should be sprinkled on the surface of very sandy soil in broad pans and be thinly covered with sand, on no account let any manure be mixed with the soil in which it is sown. Cover the pans with mats till the seed germinates and afterwards shade the seedlings from bright sun, they will require a good deal of attention in this respect till they are half grown and ready to transplant into other pots before final move to the border. During the rains, the beetle grub is very active, eating away their roots, it is therefore a risk to plant young seedlings in the ground before November when the grub season is over. The old plants are hardy, and do not seem to be so much attacked. In the very hot months, April and May, it is desirable to lift the old plants to a shady moist place till the rains set in, otherwise a good many will die, making great gaps in the lines. The Gold Feather, flowers the second rainy season, and is then best divided, it no longer retains its compact dwarf habit.

*Quaking Grass.*—Vide *Briza.*

*Quisqualis Combretaceæ, Q. Indica.*—The Chinese Honey Suckle, or Rangoon Creeper. Flowers, scarlet outside, yellowish, white within, hangs in large clusters, very useful in covering walls or trellis work, the scent at night is unpleasant to some persons being sickly. It is a very common plant in the gardens of the Deccan, and may be raised from seed or layers.

*Reseda Resedaceæ, Reseda Odorata, Mignonette.*—There are many species of this genus, most of which are natives of the South of Europe and Egypt. This sweet scented little plant may be cultivated throughout the year, only requiring moderate care in watering, and when the blossoms have passed their maturity, cut down the shoots, when fresh ones will spring up. If you require the seed, observe as soon as the capsules are full, to pick off the branches and let them dry; otherwise, if let remain on the plant they drop out and are lost. It loses much of its fragrance, if grown in too rich a soil. Is propagated by seed, either in pots or beds; each plant should be about from four to five inches apart.

*Rhexia Melastomaceæ, Rhexia Virginica.*— This is a genus of shrubby plants, handsome when in flower, they require a good soil, and may be propagated by seed or dividing the roots, colours are purple, pink and white.

*Rhodanthe, Compositæ.*—This plant is a native of the Swan River, and is said to be as beautiful an annual as has been introduced into the English collections, it grows to a large size; and is covered with innumerable blossoms of rose and yellow colour when grown from seed, the plants require to be continually shifted into larger pots, and the blossom buds at first pinched off, the shifting may be repeated five or six times, until the plants have acquired a shrubby character, when the flowers will all expand and continue in succession for some time.

*Roses.*—Roses do very well indeed at Bangalore, and of late a good number of excellent kinds have been introduced and are become plentiful. A volume might be written on rose treatment, but to be brief, and confining, remarks to treatment of roses in pots: it is desirable to state, as a rule, that roses will never flourish in a soil naturally wet or retaining sour water, perfect drainage must be secured. The soil should be rather stiff or tenacious, enriched with manure cowdung, well rotted stable manure and burnt earth. Old night soil that has been long mixed with earth or ashes is also very good. Roses must be periodically pruned, and once a year have manure to the roots, and this is best done in the early rains when the roots are in full action, and every shower should place an abundant supply of food within their reach.

Pruning, the extraordinary vigour and beauty of some plants on which goats had been browsing, gave the ancients the first idea of pruning roses, three ends are sought in pruning to maintain the plant in full health and vigour, to induce it to assume a fine form advantageous to development of its blossoms, and to secure an abundance of good flowers. If we leave a rose tree unpruned for a year, a number of buds will burst forth producing masses of blossoms fit for nothing. This can be seen after the rains on unpruned Rose Edward trees, they send forth long coarse unripened stems, bearing heads of buds twenty and thirty in number, not one of which will be a perfect bloom, all such immatured shoots should be eradicated. If an unpruned tree is allowed to go on so for two or three more years, it becomes greatly enfeebled, the flowers more and more degenerate, and the ends of the yearling shoots will die back for want of nourishment. The more vigorous in habit a plant is, the more shoots should be thinned out, and the *less should those which are left be shortened.*

Manure water is beneficial when not given too frequently nor in a very concentrated form, it imparts a freshness and dark hue to the leaves and increases the vigour of the plant.

When roses are in full leaf they enjoy plenty of water, during their period of rest they require much less. As the buds first break, it is good to syringe them occasionally.

Roses are impatient of shade and confined places, where they do not get plenty of air and light. They are reproduced by cuttings, layers and budding, the new kinds are easiest budded on the common Rose Edward Stock.

With budded plants, be careful to remove all suckers which are usually apt to arise in great abundance, and soon starve the plant, if not destroyed.

# LIST OF ROSES GROWN IN THE LAL BAGH, BANGALORE.

1. *Edward.
2. Persian.
3. Cashmere.
4. *Geant de Bataille.
5. *Devoniensis.
6. *Boothia.
7. *Lamarque.
8. Yellow.
9. Emma.
10. *Clara Sylvain.
11. *Brennus.
12. *Brennus single.
13. *Victoria.
14. *Eugene Beauharnais.
15. *Crimson China.
16. *Large Crimson China.
17. Arch Duke Charles.
18. Saffrano.
19. *Cabbage.
20. Pink Cluster.
21. White Cluster.
22. *Copper Rose.
23. *Copper Tea.
24. White Tea.
25. Thornless Cluster.
26. New Cluster.
27. Neilgherry Cluster.
28. Fairy Queen.
29. *Devoniensis, No. 2.
30. *Souvenir de la Malmaison.
31. Scarlet Cluster.
32. Common China.
33. Mycrophylla.
34. President Porcher.
35. La Tendresse.
36. Christiana Neilson.
37. Prince Humbert.
38. *Madame Masson.
39. La France.
40. President Willermoz.
41. Reine de Medes.
42. *Elli Morel.
43. Mrs. John Berners.
44. Madame Rowland.
45. *Tournefort.
46. Archimedes.
47. Madame Adele Hazzard.
48. Alba Carnea.
49. Madam Annie Wood.
50. Louis de Savoy.
51. *Melanie Willermoz.
52. *Reine de Portugal.
53. *Mareschal Niel.
54. Countess of Mecklenburg.
55. *Coquette des Alpes.
56. *Boule de Niege.
57. *Charles Turner.
58. Abbe Veneir.
59. Imperatrice Charlotte.
60. Mrs. Ward.
61. Thyra Hammerich.
62. Reine Blanche.
63. Souvenir de Porteau.
64. Madame Jacqueer.
65. Berthie Baron.
66. Montplaisir.
67. Marie Duebee.
68. Victor le Behan.
69. Nardy Freres.
70. Dupay Jamain.
71. Gloire des Mousseuses.

\* Those marked with an asterisk are specially recommended.

*Rosa Rubiginosa, Rosaceæ.*—Sweet Briar, native name, gul nusreen. This species of rose which was once scarce in the Deccan, is now to be met with in many gardens, it sometimes blossoms, if budded on the Persian Rose Stock.

The general mode of propagation is by layers, but a much quicker and easier method is to bud it on the stock of a rose.

*Rudbeckia Compositæ, Rudbeckia Fulgida.*—This is a showy genus of plants, and will grow in any common soil, they attain a large size, and are therefore more adapted for a shrubbery; the colours chiefly yellow, and orange; propagated by seed or by dividing the roots.

*Russelia, Scrophulariaceæ.*—This plant with rush-like branches, bears a deep scarlet trumpet-shaped flower, hanging in long axillary peduncles down the stalk: it blossoms during the greater part of the year, and is highly ornamental, growing luxuriantly in a rich soil. It is propagated by layers or cuttings.

*Salpiglossis, Scrophulariaceæ.*—This genus of showy plants require much care in their cultivation, the situation in which they are grown should be sheltered and partially shaded, for if exposed to the sun they become withered and die suddenly, the colours are purple, red, white and variegated. When grown in pots, it should be frequently shifted into pots, only a little larger than the previous ones, so as to make the plants bushy, the soil should be loam, mixed with sand.

*Salvia Labiatæ, Salvia Coccinea.*—This is a very extensive genus, consisting chiefly of extremely showy flowering plants of every variety of colour, and therefore well worthy of cultivation, the plants may all be grown from seed in any good garden soil at the commencement or after the rains.

*Sanvitalia Compositæ, Sanvitalia Procumbens.*—A pretty compact plant, and from its nature adapted to cover a small patch or bed in the flower garden. Colour yellow, and raised from seed.

*Saponaria Silenaceæ, Saponaria Procumbens.*—This is a pretty genus of rose coloured, pink or yellow flowers, and from its trailing habit, best suited for covering rock work, cultivated from seed.

*Scabiosa Dipsacaceæ, Scabiosa Elegans.*—These plants with the scent of honey are well adapted for ornamenting the flower garden, they are propagated by seed, and grow readily in any good soil, the seed may be sown in pots at the close and the plants removed, when a few inches high.

*Salvia, Herbaceous, Perennial.*—Of this very brilliant coloured, profusely flowering genus, four kinds are easily reared at Bangalore, Salvia Patens, with large, very rich cobalt blue flowers, is raised from seed during the rains, but most successfully in October; flowers twice a year. In the hot season it dies down to the root, making a fresh start in the early rains, prefers a half-shady moist situation, must be kept in large sized pots, in rich soil, well drained.

*Salvia Splendens*—is a very handsome perennial, with large scarlet flowers, Calyx and Corolla both scarlet, grows readily from cuttings taken in the rains and cold season: thrives in large pots in shade and in shady places in the ground under trees, must have very rich soil and abundance of water. Salvia Coccinea, has flowers of the same rich scarlet colour but smaller than S. Spendens, grows readily from seed in moist rich soil in the rainy season.

*Salvia Japonica* has large rough leaves, throws up long spikes of lavender blue flowers, individually smaller than any of the three kinds above mentioned, is grown from seed in the rains and perfectly hardy, but like the other Salvias, prefers shade, moisture and rich soil.

*Schizanthus Scrophulariaceæ, Schizanthus Grahami.*—This is a genus of pretty showy annuals, colours of the flowers are crimson, white and variegated, and should be grown and treated as the Scabius.

*Schizopetalon Cruciferæ, Schizopetalon Walkeri.*—This is a singular plant, with curiously cut petals and a strong tapering root, and should be grown and potted like the Ecshscholtzia.

*Scutellaria, Labiatæ.*—These plants are handsome when in flower, and are adapted for the front of borders, the colours are purple, yellow, red or blue, the flowers resembling the Antirrhinum, and may be grown from seed in any good garden soil.

*Scyphanthus, Loasaceæ.*—These are pretty little yellow flowers, and require the same treatment as the Loasa.

*Sedum Crassulaceæ, Sedum Cœruleum.*—A species of succulent plants with various coloured flowers, all of which should be grown separately in pots in a light sandy soil, mixed with brick rubbish; they are propagated by seed, these plants are well adapted for rock work.

*Senecio Jacobæa, Compositæ, Purple Rag Wort.*—This belongs to an extensive genus of plants, and is a native of the Cape of Good Hope, it is easily raised from seed like other species of groundsels in common garden soil.

*Serruria, Proteaceæ.*—This genus of plants require the same treatment as the Protea.

*Silene Silenaceæ, Silene Compacta, Catch Fly.*—These are elegant flowering plants of easy culture from seed, the flowers are of various colours, and require only the same treatment as the other species of Lychnis.

*Siphocampylus, Lobeliaceæ.*—These are small pretty shrubs, growing well in a light sandy soil, and are propagated by seed and cuttings.

*Snakes' Head Lily.*—Vide *Amaryllis Frittilaria.*

*Snap Dragon* or *Antirrhinum.*—The Snap Dragon will only do well at Bangalore when kept out of rain, generally exposure to one heavy downpour will kill a young plant, requires large sized pots well drained, the Snap Dragon will flower well in the cold season and through the hot season.

The new series of Dwarf Antirrhinums are very pretty, as also the miniature kind called Linaria, this is much hardier here, stands the rain, whether in pots or flower beds. White ants seem particularly destructive to Snap Dragons.

*Solanum.*—This is a large tribe of ornamental leaved shrubs, and plants much used in England for leaf gardening, Solanum Warccywicksi, S. Robustum, S. Marginatum, S. Laciniatum are desirable, and grow easily from seed.

Weatherills hybrid Solanums or Currant Tomato, are very pretty, little pot plants covered with large berries of the size of a cherry, bright orange, and well suited for table decoration, raised from seed.

*Sollya Pittosporaceæ, Sollya Heterophylla.*—These are ornamental little shrubs with bright blue bell flowers, should be grown in a loamy soil, and are propagated by seed or cuttings.

*Sparaxis, Irideæ.*—This is a pretty species of Irideæ, and is cultivated by dividing the roots.

*Spatalla, Proteaceæ.*—This genus are all Cape plants, and require the same treatment as other Proteaceæ.

*Sphnogyne Compositæ.*—This is a genus of small shrubs, bearing mostly all yellow flowers, cuttings root freely in a loamy soil.

*Stachys Labiatæ.*—Stachys Lavata, handsome woolly frosted foliage plants, propagated by cuttings, very useful for broad edging to borders, or riband lines, does not flower in the Deccan.

*Stapelia, Asclepiadaceæ.*—This is an extensive genus of plants, with curiously marked flowers like a toad's back, they are star-shaped, and grow from the roots; these plants being succulent, are apt to drop off if grown in too rich or moist a soil, they give seed, and may be cultivated from it, but more readily from slips shaded partially, and watered sparingly.

*Statice, Plumbaginaceæ, Sea Lavender.*—Many of these species bear pretty purple, white and blue flowers, and are much cultivated at Home, the S. Arborea is a very handsome shrub, and requires a large space for its spreading roots, is propagated by seed in good garden soil.

*Stenactis Compositæ.*—This is a showy purple flower, and well adapted for borders; it is a native of California and propagated by cuttings or dividing the roots.

*Stocks.*—German ten weeks and intermediate stocks are annuals suited to Bangalore gardening, and should be sown late in October and November, in pots or nursery beds in rich soil, be transplanted twice, while small seedlings before removal to the garden beds. They require moderate protection from heavy rain and fierce sun as seedlings, and are attacked by blight and caterpillars while young. When two-thirds grown, they are all the better for plenty of sun. The soil round the roots should be repeatedly broken up, and a little manure on such occasions added before a copious watering. Wall flower stocks are ten weeks stocks with leaves like wall flowers, but stock flowers. Wall flowers do not succeed at Bangalore.

*Swainsonia Leguminosæ, Swainsonia Galegifolia.*—This is a pretty species of shrub, with purple, red and white flowers, grown from seed in good garden soil.

*Sweet Briar.*—Vide *Rosa Rubiginosa.*

*Sweet Pea.*—Vide *Lathyrus.*

*Sweet Sultan.*—Vide *Centaurea.*

*Sweet William.*—Vide *Dianthus.*

*Stevia Compositæ, Stevia Purpurea.*—These are pretty small flowering plants, natives of New Spain and Mexico, propagated by seed, cuttings and division of the roots in any good garden soil.

*Stipa, Graminaceæ.*—A beautiful species of grass, grown chiefly in gardens for the sake of the beautifully feathered heads.

*Streptocarpus, Bignoniaceæ.*—This is a handsome plant from the Cape of Good Hope, produces abundance of pale, purple flowers, it requires a good garden soil, and is increased by seed.

*Sun Rose.*—Vide *Helianthemum.*

*Sutherlandia Leguminosæ, Sutherlandia Grandiflora.*—This is a pretty shrub with scarlet flowers, native of the Cape, and is readily increased by seed in any good garden soil.

*Tabernæmontana, Apocynaceæ.*—A genus of interesting plants, mostly bearing white, sweet-scented flowers. A mixture of loam, peat, and sand suits them best; and young plants may be obtained from cuttings, planted in sand, under a glass, in a moist heat.

*Tacsonia.*—Tacsonia, a sub-tribe of Passion Flower, with brilliant scarlet, crimson and rose-coloured flowers, should be sown in pots in rich soil early in June, the pots exposed to the sun during the forenoon only, and no rain must be allowed to reach the young seedlings; if so, they are almost certain to die; when the seedlings have grown about six or eight inches high, transplant singly, still keeping from rain. In October they may be shifted to large pots, and in the cold season will flower profusely if kept in a sunny spot, sheltered from cold cutting wind. During the second hot season, they should again be sheltered from the afternoon sun, and in June re-potted in the largest sized pots, they will attain in the following monsoon to the size of large creepers, and no more than ordinary care need be taken of them.

The finest kinds are Tacsonia Ignea, and Tacsonea Vans Volxemi.

*Tagetes Compositæ, Tagetes Lucida African Marigold.*—This is common in all gardens, and readily grown from seed.

*Telekia Compositæ.*—This plant bears a yellow flower, and grows in any common garden soil.

*Thistle.*—Vide *Argemone.*

*Thorn Apple.*—Vide *Datura.*

*Tiger Lily.*—Vide *Tigridia.*

*Trumpet Flower.*—Vide *Bignonia.*

*Thunbergia Acanthaceæ, Thunbergia Alata.*—These climbing plants bear flowers of various colours. The T. Grandiflora hangs in beautiful blue racemes, and is adapted for covering trellis work. The species are grown from seed in any good soil.

*Tigridia Iridaceæ, Tigridia Conchiflora, Tiger Flower.*—These beautiful species are grown like other lilies, the flowers open in the morning, and are of a short duration; a second blossom appears on the same stem about the third day after the first has withered.

*Tobacco.*—Vide *Nicotiana.*

*Trailing Plants.*—Bangalore is very rich in large creepers. The Bougainvillea, Bignonia Venusta, Beaumontia Jerdoni, Jacquemontia, Thunbergia Calonyction, Ipomœa Leari, Ipomœa Horsfalli, and a great variety of Passion Flowers are common and easily increased by layers, Antigonon, Leptotus, a very fine Mexican Creeper with abundance of beautiful rose-coloured flowers, is a recent introduction and does well, expected to rival the Bongainvillea and Bignonia Venusta. Hexacentris Mysoriensis is another beautiful creeper, only requiring to be grown in shade to succeed well. In the early rains some of the large creeping Cacti are very beautiful and of the simplest culture.

*Tweedia Asclepiadaceæ, Tweedia Cœrulea.*—These plants bear blue flowers, and succeed well in a sandy peat soil, and are readily grown from seed. .

*Valerian.*—Vide *Centranthus.*

*Veratrum Melanthaceæ, Veratrum Nigrum.*—This genus takes its name from the dark colour of its roots. The flowers are mostly white, dark, purple and green. It is cultivated in a rich garden soil by seed or dividing the roots, which contain powerful medicinal properties.

*Verbascum Scrophulariaceæ, Verbascum Formosum.*—These plants producing abundance of yellow and orange coloured flowers are well suited for a shrubbery. They are propagated by seed or division of the roots.

*Verbena.*—To raise Verbena from seed it must be sown in June and July, but the quickest way of multiplying established varieties is by layers in the months of March and April. With a good supply of water the common kinds of Verbena will flourish throughout the hot months and until the heavy rains in July, either potted or in beds, but when the heavy rains set in, they will die off, unless they are brought under cover, even when thus protected, they no longer grow freely, and many casualties must be expected. The soil should be fresh red earth well manured. The new Auricula or eyed varieties of Verbenas are more delicate, and will only do well in large pots sheltered from midday sun and heavy rain.

*Veronica Scrophulariaceæ.*—They are common pretty annuals, with blue flowers, cultivated in any good garden soil by seed or division of the roots.

*Victoria Regia, Nymphœaceæ.*—" This beatiful Water Lily has been successfully raised in the Botanical Garden at Calcutta from seed sent by Dr. Wallick from England on the 9th of September 1851. It was received and sown in the garden on the 6th of November following, where it lay in a dormant state until the 23rd of April 1853. On the 13th of May same year, the seedling had made a healthy growth, and was transferred on that date to the mound prepared for it in the tank. The largest leaf when planted out was little more than three inches in diameter. The total number of leaves produced up to the 5th of September were forty-four, fifteen of which were on the plant in different stages of development, when the first flower had made its appearance on the surface of the water, and the largest leaf produced up to that time measured four feet 5½ inches in diameter. The first flower bud appeared partly above the water on the morning of the 6th September, and by sunset the same evening, had partly expanded the flower which closed up the next morning, and finally opened again at sunset the same evening." Journal of the Agri-Horticultural Society, Cal. Vol. 8., 1853.

*Vinca Apocynaceœ, Vinca Rosea.*—The Periwinkle.—These are trailing plants, and well known in English gardens. They produce seed, but are more generally propagated by runners which take root easily; they require a good deal of moisture.

*Viola Violaceœ, Viola Odorata.*—These sweet scented little plants, have become quite acclimated in the Deccan, they are best grown in pots and require to be moderately shaded, the morning sun being sufficient for them: the plants must be protected from the hot winds, and divided out into small bunches when transplanted. The white Violet is not known in the southern part of India, but in England, the finest are generally found in calcareous soils; in India the Violet seldom blossoms if grown in garden beds.

*Viola Tricolor.*—See *Pansies.*

*Viscaria, Silenaceœ.*—This genus of plants, have all glutinous stems, and are propagated from seed, requiring the same culture as the Lychrus.

*Wall Flower.*—Vide *Cheiranthus.*

*Water Lily.*—Vide *Nymphœa.*

*Water Lily.*—Vide *Nelumbium.*

*Wax Flower.*—Vide *Tabernœmontana.*

*Wax Plant.*—Vide *Hoya Carnosa.*

*Whitlavia, Whitlavia Grandiflora.*—A hardy annual with bell-shaped flowers growing up the centre stalk, resembling small Gloxinia blossoms, to be sown towards the end of the rains and allowed to flower in pots. In some, the flowers are rich purple, in others pure white.

*Wigandia.*—A class of grand ornamental foliage plants with

handsome flowers, about the size and somewhat of the shape of the Solanum but in form of spikes, the leaves are from two to three feet long and more than one foot broad, the plant has an erect habit, and grows to seven feet in height. It is propagated by seeds which are very minute, and should be repeatedly shifted and sheltered, till they become large enough to remove to the garden bed.

*Wood Sorrel.*—Vide *Oxalis.*

*Zinnia Compositæ, Zinnia Elegans, Alba.*—Crocea and various others, may be all sown at the commencement of the rains, either separately or in beds. The flowers are pretty and ornamental, and require very little care: the seed as it falls, springs up immediately, and from its profusion, almost becomes a weed in the garden.

# FOREST TREES, FRUITS, AND FLOWERING SHRUBS.

ABROMA AUGUSTA. *Byttneriaceæ.* NAT. B. OOLUT-KUMBUL.—A shrub with soft velvety branches, flowers in the rains, of a dark purple colour, capsule five-angled; the fibres of the bark are strong, and white, well adapted for making cordage though not so strong as hemp.

ABRUS PRECATORIUS. *Leguminosæ.* NAT. B. SWETA KOONCH. TAM. CONDUMUNNIE.—A common twining plant with a woody stem, bears small red berries, with a black spot on the top, or more rarely black, with a white eye; the seeds are used as weights by jewellers, under the name of vahl, or rutee; the root is employed as stick liquorice, being mucilaginous and sweet.

ACACIA ARABICA. *Mimoseæ.* NAT. H. BABULA. TAM. KAROO-VELUM.—Common in the Deccan, thrives equally well in black or red soil, growing rapidly and requiring no water; the flowers are yellow and the tree on the whole ornamental, the seeds and pods in the hot season are of great value to the shepherd, as they are readily eaten by goats and sheep. It abounds in gum.

Another species, found also in the Deccan, called *Ramkanta*, which grows tall and erect with a Cypress like appearance, differs in form and the colour of its legumes from the Arabica, it is extremely ornamental, but the Natives have an objection to the tree from some superstitious motive, an ill omen being attached to it; the wood of both species is hard, and used for cart wheels, ploughs, &c.

ACACIA CATECHU. NAT. KHADIRA OR KHUERA. TAM. PODEEL-MAUN.—A small armed tree, flowers in the rains, colour white, in long axillary spikes, furnishes the Terra japonica.

ACACIA SPECIOSA.—A tree of rapid growth, flowers white, very fragrant, with long stamens, the wood is strong and serviceable.

ACACIA STIPULATA.—The unarmed acacia, flowers of a pink colour, very handsome.

ACHRAS SAPOTA. *Sapotaceæ.*—This tree has been introduced from Goa, it yields a fruit the size of a quince, the flesh of which of a yellow colour, has an agreeable smell, and pleasant taste. The fruit is generally brought to Bombay for sale in December from Goa.

ADANSONIA DIGITATA. *Bombaceæ.* BAOBAB OR MONKEY BREAD-TREE.—A large tree said to be found in Senegal and Abyssinia. It is the largest known tree, with the trunk of an immense size close to the ground, (the diameter of which is sometimes as much as thirty feet) but fast tapering and of little height in proportion, seldom exceeding seventy-three feet, somewhat resembling a cone. Flowers, large and white, appear in May and June. On the sea coast the fishermen use the fruit as floats for their nets. The tree lives to a great age, whence it has been called "arbre de mille ans"; and Humboldt speaks of it as "the oldest organic monument of our planet." The roots are of an extraordinary length; a tree only twelve feet high has been known to have a tap root many feet long. The foliage is sometimes so abundant as to conceal the vast proportions of the trunk, and the branches spread out drooping at the extremities to such a degree as entirely to conceal it; the whole forms a nearly hemispherical mass of verdure from 140 to 150 feet in diameter, and sixty or seventy feet high. The pulp of the fruit is slightly acid and agreeable, and frequently eaten: while the juice expressed from it, mixed with sugar, constitutes a drink which is valued as a specific in putrid and pestilential fevers. The trunk of the tree is subject to a particular disease owing to the attack of a species of fungus which vegetates in the woody part, and which, without changing its colour or appearance, destroys life and renders the part so attacked as soft as the pith of trees in general. Such trunks are hollowed (by the Africans) into chambers, and within them are suspended the dead bodies of those who are refused the honor of burial. There they become mummies, perfectly dry and well preserved, and are known by the name of Guiriots.

ADENANTHERA PAVONINA. *Mimoseæ*. NAT. RANJUNA. TAM. MANSENI KOTTA.—Redwood. An unarmed tree; flower small, and white; the seeds are of a bright scarlet colour, worn as beads, also used as weights; the wood yields a dye used by Brahmins.

ÆGLE MARMELOS. *Aurantiaceæ*.—NAT. BEL. T. MAREDOO. —The Bengal Quince. A thorny tree with ternate leaves, fruit smooth, resembling an orange with a yellow hard rind, the pulp is used by the natives in chronic diarrhœa; it has also an aperient quality and is said to be very nutritious, the rind, which is astringent, is used in dyeing yellow.

AGLAIA ODORATA.—*Aurantiaceæ*.—A shrub with ternate and pinnate leaves, and very small yellow flowers in axillary racemes.

AGATHIS AUSTRALIS. *Coniferæ*.—The New Zealand pine. A most stately pine, lately introduced from the Cape into the Horticultural Society's Garden, Bombay, by A. N. Shaw, Esq.

AGATHIS LORANTHIFOLIA.—Dammar pine of the Eastern Isles.

AGATI GRANDIFLORA. *Leguminosæ*. NAT. BUCKA OR BOKPHOOL. —This is a tree of rapid growth, generally cultivated for its large red or white flowers and pods, the *legumes* are from twelve to eighteen inches long, and as well as the flowers, are much used for food by the Natives: there are several species with a variety of variegated and red flowers.

AGAVE MEXICANA. ORDER *Bromeliaceæ*.—This plant resembles the Aloe; the centre scape rises to the height of 18 or 20 feet, flowers in the rains, while the seed germinates in the capsules before they drop off. It grows in almost any soil, requires little care, and yields in Mexico, the celebrated liquor called "Pulque," which is thus procured.

"When the Indian becomes aware that the plant is about to flower he cuts out the heart, covers it over with the side leaves, and all the juice which should have gone to the stem of the flower, runs into the empty bason thus formed, into which the Indian, thrice a day and during several months in succession inserts a kind of syphon and applying his mouth to the other end draws off the liquor into a gourd by suction, first it is sweet and scentless, but easily fermented. It is said to be the most wholesome drink in the world, and remarkably agreeable, when one has overcome the first shock of its rancid odour. A very strong brandy is distilled from Pulque, which has the advantage of producing intoxication in an infinitely shorter period."

AILANTUS EXCELSA. *Rutaceæ.* NAT. ARALU. TAM. PERUMARUTTOO.—A large tree with pinnate leaves from two to four feet long; leaflets coarsely toothed; flowers in terminal panicles, appear in January and February. The wood is used for sword handles, &c.

AILANTUS MALABARICA.—This is a handsome tree with long pinnate leaves, flowers small, white, in terminal racemes, appear in February and March.

ALLAMANDA CATHARTICA. *Apocynaceæ.*—A scandent milky shrub, with large yellow flowers, which blossom in succession throughout the year. A native of South America: common in gardens.

ALANGIUM DECAPETALUM. *Alangiaceæ.* NAT. ANKOOL.—A small tree with whitish flowers; the petals vary on the same tree from six or eight to ten. The fruit is astringent, but eaten by the Natives.

ALEURITES TRILOBA. *Euphorbiaceæ.* NAT. AKHROOT.—Belgaum Walnut. This tree has been introduced into India from the Society Islands; it grows to a large size, the leaves are frequently three or five lobed, from five to eight inches long and nearly as broad, and are generally covered with a mealy substance, giving the tree a peculiar appearance; the flowers are small, white, in terminal panicles. Fruit, roundish, two celled, each containing a nut resembling in flavor the filbert; the Natives say the fruit when fresh is unwholesome and requires to be kept for one year before it may be eaten, the kernels yield more than 50 per cent. of a fine clear oil.

ALEXANDRIAN LAUREL.—Vide *Calophyllum Inophyllum.*

ALIGATOR PEAR.—Vide *Laurus Persea.*

ALMOND PERSIAN.—Vide *Amygdalus Communis*.

ALMOND INDIAN.—Vide *Terminalia Catappa*.

ALOE COMMON.—Vide *Aloe Perfoliata*.

ALOE PERFOLIATA. *Hind*. KOOUR. *Liliaceæ*.—Is so' generally known as to need no description. It is chiefly planted to form hedge-rows, and makes an excellent fence. It flowers in the rains, and the stem grows to the height of ten or twelve feet. The leaves make a good common cordage, or rope, used for drawing mats, &c.

ALTHÆA ROSEA.—*Malvaceæ*.—This plant grows wild all over the country, and is used for medicinal purposes as at home.

AMOMUM ZINGIBER. *Scitamineæ*.—Grows in all parts of India: it is generally cultivated in gardens, being sown about the commencement of the rains, and taken up in eight or nine months, though sometimes left in the ground for the following year. For mode of culture, see Vegetable list.

AMOMUM NUTANS.—*Scitamineæ*.—I believe this to be the only species found in the gardens, of the Deccan. It never bears fruit, but is perhaps one of the most beautiful flowers we possess. It multiplies very fast by the roots, and in a short time takes up a large space, throwing out long branches with drooping panicles of flowers, appearing more like wax. Colours pink and white. It is a native of some of the Eastern Islands, and has never been known to give seed. The only flower I have ever seen approaching near it in beauty, is one of the parasites blossoming in May at Mahabuleshwar.

AMPHILOBIUM MUTISII. *Bignoniaceæ*.—A pretty climber with purple flowers, well adapted for trellis work.

AMYGDALUS COMMUNIS.—*Amygdaleæ*. *Hind*. BADAM.—This tree never bears fruit, and is only grown as an exotic; it might be used as a stock for the peach, plum, &c.

AMYGDALUS PERSICA. *Amygdaleæ*. NAT. SHUFT ALOO.—There are but three varieties of this fruit met with in the Deccan—a large round white sort, of a delicious flavor; the flat China; and a small thin-skinned description, more resembling an apricot in appearance, and much harder than the others. The peach is easily cultivated by seed or layers. A seedling will throw out blossom in the second year, and be ten or twelve feet in height: it requires to be carefully pruned, wintered, and watered. No branches should be allowed to grow on the stem closer than three feet from the ground; all spurious and misplaced shoots should be rubbed off before gaining strength to exhaust unnecessarily the juices of the tree; and all distorted leaves, the work of insects, of parasitic plants,—mildew, &c.—should be picked off and destroyed.

The kernels of the peach should be carefully removed from the shell, and in no ways injured if required for planting: they should be sown in small beds at the commencement of the rains, about eighteen inches apart, and as soon as they are fit for removal, a good sized ball of earth must be taken up with the roots, to prevent the root fibres from receiving injury. All the buds around the stem had better be rubbed off by the hand, as far as requisite, and a proper shape be given to the tree, by cutting out all the superfluous spurs and their branches. The time for opening the roots of the peach is after the close of the rains: remove the earth with care, so as not to injure the roots, for the space of three feet round the stem; pull off all the leaves, and cease to water the tree until the blossom buds appear; then cover up the roots with good loam mixed with old rotten manure; water freely every third or fourth day until the fruit begins to ripen, when you must be guided by circumstances. It is necessary sometimes to thin the fruit, and also to put the peaches in bags, as they begin to ripen, otherwise the birds will destroy them.

Peaches first come in about February, and with care may be continued until the rains commence, after which the excess of moisture received by the leaves and roots causes the fruit to swell and burst.

AMYRIS HEPTAPHYLLA. *Amyridaceæ.* NAT. KARUN-PHUL.— A shrub with alternate pinnate leaves, and small yellow flowers; the leaves when bruised have the smell of Anise.

AMYRIS COMMIPHORA.—The wood and resinous juice of all these species have a strong balsamic smell.

ANACARDIUM OCCIDENTALE. *Terebinthaceæ.* NAT. HIJIILEE. BADAM.—This tree grows to a large size in many parts of the Deccan, and is found in Native as well as European gardens. It is very ornamental when in leaf, bearing sweet-smelling flowers, succeeded by a pear-shaped fruit of a yellow and red colour, which is eaten by the poorer class. The nut hangs at the end of the fruit outside; and is of a kidney shape. Between a double shell, covering the kernel, is a very acid juice, which, if applied to the skin, or inadvertently to the lips, immediately raises a blister. The juice is sometimes used for marking linen, as it is impossible to wash it out. The milky juice from the tree also stains linen a dark brown colour. The kernel, when roasted, is very sweet and pleasant, but is considered rather astringent. In the West Indies, the fruit or apple is bruised, and a juice expressed from it and fermented, which produces a sort of wine; and if distilled, a spirit is obtained from it, which makes excellent punch. The gum that exudes from this tree is valuable, from its resemblance to Gum Arabic.

ANONA SQUAMOSA. *Anonaceæ.* NAT. SHETA-PHUL.—Custard Apple. Very generally cultivated all over India, and grows wild in many parts of the Deccan. It has on some occasions of famine proved the staff of life to the poorer classes. The tree when cultivated and pruned, during the hot season produces fruit afterwards of double the usual size.

ANONA CHERIMOLIA.—A succulent fruit of a dark purple colour containing a soft sweet mucilage, and is much esteemed by the Peruvians.

ANONA RETICULATA. NAT. RAM-PHUL. BULLOCK'S HEART.—This tree grows to a lage size. The fruit is so called from its fancied resemblance to the heart of the animal. The colour is a dark brownish red. When ripe, it is a soft, sweetish, pulpy fruit, but has not the fine flavor of the custard apple. It is ripe from November to June, but not much esteemed by Europeans.

ANONA MURICATA. SOURSOP.—This tree is a native of the West Indies. It grows to about the same size as the Bullock's Heart. The fruit is of a greenish colour when ripe, and has a rough thorny appearance: the flavour is very peculiar, differing from the other species of the Anonaceæ: the scent resembles that of black currants; the seeds are similar to those of the custard-apple. The fruit ripens in March; and in the West Indies is considered very cooling in fevers. It bears only once a year.

AOONLA PLUM.—Vide *Phyllanthus Emblica.*

APPLE.—Vide *Pyrus Malus.*

APRICOT.—Vide *Prunus Armeniaca.*

ARACHIS HYPOGEA. *Cæsalpinieæ.* NAT. VILAITEE MOONG.—This nut has the peculiar property of thrusting its legume into the earth to ripen the seed, and is easily cultivated by offsets, which are thrown out in May or June. It is generally sold ready roasted by the Natives in the bazaars. It requires a good soil and much water. A fine, clear, sweet oil is obtainable from it.

ARECA CATECHU. *Hind.* FOOFLEE SOOPAREE. *Palmaceæ.* BETEL NUT PALM.—This beautiful tree is commonly cultivated: it grows to the height of from fifteen to forty feet, and is to be found in most native gardens. The trunk is very slender, but of the same size throughout, and requires to have either matting or straw tied round it to prevent its splitting from the dry winds; when this happens it immediately decays. It flowers at all seasons; and the seed when ripe should be sown, if young plants are required, at about eighteen inches apart. These palms form a very striking appearance in gardens when mixed with the cypress alternately. The pepper vine is trained up on this palm in Malabar.

ARGYREIA CUNEATA. *Convolvulaceæ.*—Purple Convolvulus. ARGYREIA ACUTA.—White. ARGYREIA SPECIOSA. NAT. SAMUDRA SHOKA OR GOOGULEE.—This is a large and elegant creeper, flowers during the rains and cold weather, of a rose, and purple colour, common throughout the country, the leaves are covered below with a mealy down; whilst the upper surface has a dull green appearance, and is applied by the Natives to act as a discutient.

ARISTOLOCHIA INDICA. *Aristolochiaceæ.* ARISTOLOCHIA BRACTEATA. ARISTOLOCHIA ACUMINATA.—A twining shrubby plant; leaves alternate, simple, stalked, scolloped flowers axillary, solitary, and of a dark colour. The root is very bitter.

ARNOTTO.—Vide *Bixa Orellana.*

ARROW-ROOT.—Vide *Curcuma Angustifolia.*

ARTOCARPUS INCISA. *Urticaceæ.* BREAD FRUIT TREE.—This tree grows to a tolerably large size in Bombay, and is also to be met with in some parts of the Deccan. It bears a fruit the size of a large orange, or small pumplemose, with a muricated rind. It seldom ripens in Bombay, the fruit falling off in the cold season. Like the jack, it bears fruit both on the branches and roots, which also afford a thick milky juice, convertible into bird-lime. The fruit, cut into slices and fried, has something the flavor of a sweet potato dressed in a similar manner. It will grow from cuttings, and requires a light soil, with care, and watering at first.

ARTOCARPUS INTEGRIFOLIA. JACK TREE. NAT. KANTAL. TAM. PEELA MARUM.—This tree grows to an immense size. The wood is used for furniture, and the fruit, which issues direct from the trunk or stem, has a rough coated appearance, hanging like a large green bag; the scent is very disagreeable. It is not in much request by Europeans, although the seed when roasted resembles a chestnut in flavor. The finest fruits sometimes grow on the roots, and will be found from the cracking of the earth above them. When this fruit tree is grown in Native gardens and the stem is forked, they generally place a large stone between the branches: the reason for this I am unacquainted with. The wood is in much request by Cabinet makers from its resemblance to mahogany: from its viscid juice bird-lime is prepared.

ASCLEPIAS CURASSAVICA. *Apocynaceæ.*—An erect growing plant, with linear, lanceolate leaves; flowers terminal, of a reddish orange colour. The root dried and pounded is used as an emetic.

ASCLEPIAS GIGANTIA. RED VAR. MUDAR. NAT. AUK. TAM. YERCUM.—This plant and the following species grow wild all over India; from the wood, charcoal is made for gunpowder; the bark yields a fine strong silky fibre, which is used for fishing-lines, &c., it also yields a milky juice from which madarine is prepared. The juice when inspissated and boiled furnishes a substance closely resembling gutta percha. The follicles, when ripe, contain a fine silky down which may be spun and converted into cloth; the leaves warmed and moistened with oil are used by the Natives as a discutient.

ASCLEPIAS HAMILTONII.—A shrub much resembling the former, but differing in the segments of the corolla not being reflexed.

ASTRAPÆA WALLICHII. *Byttneriaceæ.*—A shrub; leaves angularly lobed, very soft to the touch; flowers in large compact umbels, scarlet with yellow anthers; having rather an unpleasant scent.

ASYSTASIA FORMOSA. *Acanthaceæ.*—This plant is a native of India, and abounds on the Coromandel Coast; the flowers are purple, and it is readily grown from seed.

AVERHOA CARAMBOLA. *Oxalidaceæ.* TAM. TAMARTUN PULLUM.— The Kurmul, or Kumruk. A tree common in gardens—flowers in short racemes, variegated with white and purple; fruit acutely angled and acid, much used for tarts and pickles, there are two kinds, the acid and sweet.

AVERHOA BILIMBI. NAT. BELUMBOO. TAM. BILIMBIE PULLUM. —This fruit is pleasant tasted, but rather too acid, it is commonly made into pickles or preserves.

AZALEA INDICA. AZALEA AURANTIACA.—This is a beautiful genus of plants, admired for its white, orange, purple, scarlet, and variegated flowers, which it produces in great abundance, grows freely from seed, and requiring a light soil. Each plant should be grown separately in pots.

BALANITES ÆGYPTIACA. *Olacineæ.* NAT. HINGENBET.—A small thorny tree with alternate bi-foliate leaves, and greenish white flowers; fruit about the size of an egg, covered with a smooth dry cortex; flourishes in black soil.

BALSAMODENDRON GILEADENSE. *Burseræ.*—Vide *Dracocephalum.*

BAMBUSA ARUNDINACEA. *Graminaceæ. Hind.* BAS.—The Bamboo grows in all parts of the Deccan, both in the hills and jungles, and therefore needs little description. There are two varieties, male and female. A product, called Tabasheer, is found in the hollow joints of the latter, and sold at a high price among the Natives. These trees when in clumps are very handsome, but make a great litter when the leaves begin to fall after the rains. Nothing, however, can be more beautiful than the foliage when in fresh leaf. The young shoots, just as they strike out of the ground, are made into pickle, and also boiled and eaten by the poorer classes. The seed is sometimes boiled with meat and spice, and formed into a broth or soup. There is also a species in Bengal bearing a pear-shaped fruit—the Bambusa Melocanna.

BARLERIA PURPUREA.—*Acanthaceæ.* BARLERIA CRISTATA.—A shrubby spreading plant, with opposite, sub-rotund nearly sessile leaves; spines in axillary pairs longer than the leaves; flowers solitary, large, of a beautiful pink colour.

BARRINGTONIA ACUTANGULAR. *Myrtaceæ.* NAT. HIJJUL. TAM. RADAMI.—A large tree, flowers in pendulous racemes of a dark scarlet colour, fragrant; fruit oblong, four-sided sharp angles.

BASELLA ALBA. *Chenopodiaceæ.* NAT. SUFFET-POOL.—A twining succulent plant with smooth fleshy leaves; grows very rapidly from seed, and is eaten as spinage.

BASELLA RUBRA. NAT. POOTIKA. MALABAR NIGHTSHADE.—A succulent plant of the same species, only with red leaves, and is used as the former; grows in any garden soil from seed, but requires sticks for it to climb upon.

BASSIA LATIFOLIA. *Sapotaceæ.* NAT. MOULA. TAM. IPEI.—This tree is very common; deciduous in the cold season. An intoxicating spirit is distilled from the flowers, which have a very disagreeable scent; the seeds yield an oil which is used to adulterate ghee.

BASSIA LONGIFOLIA. *Sapotaceæ.* NAT. MOOA. TAM. ELOOPIE.—This is a large tree like the former; the wood is used for the construction of carts, planks, &c., and a fatty oil is obtained from the seeds.

BASTARD CEDAR.—Vide *Cedrela Toona.*

BATATAS PANICULATA. *Convolvulaceæ.*—Beautiful dark purple flowers.

BATATAS PENTAPHYLLA.—Stems twining, very hairy, flowers in the rains, cream coloured.

BAUHINIA ACUMINATA. *Cæsalpinieæ.* NAT. KANCHUN.—A shrub with white flowers.

BAUHINIA ANGUINA. NAT. NAG-POOT.—An extensive and rambling shrub, with flexuous compressed stems and small white flowers. The Bauhinias are highly ornamental, and may be known by their curious doubled lobed leaves.

BAUHINIA PURPUREA. NAT. DEB-KANCHUN.—A tree with fragrant flowers of a deep rose colour; flowers at the commencement of the rains.

BAUHINIA VARIEGATA. NAT. KANA-RAJ.—A tree with white and variegated flowers, which appear in April and May.

BAUHINIA VAHLII. NAT. CHAMBOOLEE.—An immense scandent shrub; leaves about a foot in breadth, with rounded lobes; legumes pendulous, from twelve to twenty inches long, covered with a brown velvet down.

BEAUMONTIA GRANDIFLORA. *Apocynaceæ.*—A gigantic climbing shrub; flowers in February, and is very showy. Native of Nepaul.

BETEL NUT PALM.—Vide *Arecha Catechu.*

BEGONIA RENIFORMIS. *Begoniaceæ.* NAT. HOOWURJO.—An herbaceous succulent plant; flowers of a pale pink colour, and fragrant.

BERBERIS ASIATICA. *Berberidaceæ.* THE BERBERRY. *Hind.* HUDING-NIOONG-MARI.—This tree is found in the hills of Nepaul, and most probably on the Neilgherries. I met with it first in Deyrah Dhoon. There is a large and small blue fruited sort, as well as the red. I have never seen it in the Deccan. The trees have blossomed in Botanical Gardens at Calcutta.

BERBERRY—See *Berberis Asiatica.*

Bergera Konigii. *Aurantiaceæ.* Nat. Bursunga. Tam. Karaway-pillay.—The Koodia Neem, commonly known as Currypak, is common throughout the country. It grows to a tree of tolerable dimensions with pinnate leaves; strongly scented; flowers in February and March; fruit of a deep purple colour, the leaves are used for flavouring curries, &c., by the Natives.

Bhere Fruit.—Vide *Zizyphus Jujuba.*

Bignonia Undulata. *Bignoniaceæ.* Bignonia Grandiflora, &c.—A tree with drooping branches like the weeping willow; leaves covered with micaceous scales; flowers in lateral racemes, very large, orange-coloured, and scentless.

Bilimbi.—Vide *Averrhoa Carambola.*

Bixa Orellana. *Bixaceæ.* Arnotto. Nat. Kistee.—A tall shrubby plant with large, heart-shaped, soft velvet leaves on long footstalks; flowers large, in loose terminal panicles, of a pale peach colour. The capsule prickly. The red pulp which covers the seed is used by the Natives as a dye, the bark for cordage, and the seeds for colouring butter.

Blackberry.—Vide *Rubus Lasiocarpus.*

Blighia Sapida. *Sapindaceæ.* Nat. Akhee.—Native of Guinea. Has pinnate leaves, and the habit of a Sapindus; fruit, size and shape of a pear, of a red colour, much esteemed in Guinea and the West Indies.

Bombax Ceiba.—This is a large tree, which in South America and the West Indies is used for canoes.

Bombax Malabaricum. *Bombaceæ.* Nat. Saur.—A large tree, trunk-armed with prickles, leaves deciduous in the cold season; flowers in February and March, large, of a bright red colour and vase-shaped, which in the morning contains a limpid sweet fluid, drunk by the Natives; the wood is white, soft, and of little use.

Borassus Flabelliformis. *Palmaceæ.* Brab or Tar Tree.—This tree, the loftiest of its tribe, needs no description: it yields the juice known by the name of Palmyra toddy. The fruit is also eaten.

BOSWELLIA GLABRA. *Bursereæ.* NAT. SALAEE. TAM. MO-RÆDA.—A small tree; leaves pinnate, deciduous; flowers terminal, small, white with a red nectary, anthers yellow; yields the gum salai.

BOSWELLIA THURIFERA. NAT. DUP-SALAEE.—A tree with leaves pinnate as the last; grows on the hills of the Deccan, and both furnish the gum Olibanum.

BRAB TREE.—Vide *Borassus Flabelliformis.*

BREAD FRUIT TREE.—Vide *Artocarpus Incisa.*

BRIEDELIA. *Euphorbiaceæ.* BRIEDELIA SPINOSA.—A tree with a pretty large trunk, branches armed with strong thorns, leaves alternate, bifarious; flowers small, of a greenish yellow, berry the size of a pea, the bark strongly astringent.

BROUSSONETIA PAPYRIFERA. *Urticaceæ.*—From the bark of this tree a kind of paper is made, the juice is also used as glue in gilding leather or paper, the bark furnishes a beautiful strong white fibre. The plant is a native of Japan, and the young shoots are used for basket work, &c.

BRUGMANSIA SUAVEOLENS. *Solanaceæ.*—This is a South American plant, forming a bush from six to eight feet in height, and when in blossom has a very splendid appearance, from its numerous long white pendulous trumpet-shaped flowers, one foot or more in length. It blossoms in succession three or more times during the year, and is easily cultivated from cuttings; it may be grown in any good garden soil, but if reared in pots, they must be of the largest size, and plenty of water is required, when the buds make their appearance during the cold season.

BRYONIA GRANDIS. *Cucurbitaceæ.* NAT. KOONDOORIE. TAM. COVAY.—Small sized variety of the gourd species.

BUCHANANIA LATIFOLIA. *Terebinthaceæ.* NAT. PYALA OR CHAROONGA. TAM. MORÆDA.—This is a jungle tree, flowering after the rains. It bears fruit about the size of a small cherry, in long bunches, colour of a darkish purple: the kernels, or seeds, which are covered with a double shell, after being prepared by the Natives, are sold in the bazaar four or five pounds for a rupee: they possess the flavor of almonds, and are used as such by the Native confectioners. A very fine oil might be expressed from the seed. The method of preparing them by the Bheels is this: the fruit when ripe in May is gathered, then soaked in water to soften the outer pulp, when it is washed and rubbed off by the hands: the little nut is then dried in the sun, and afterwards broken between a common chuckee or stone-wheel, such as is used for grinding wheat: the kernels are then sifted and winnowed.

BULLOCK'S HEART.—Vide *Anona Reticulata.*

BUTEA FRONDOSA. *Leguminosæ.* NAT. PULAS.—A large tree called the Bastard Teak, flowers in March, of a beautiful deep red, shaded with orange, downy, they are used to dye with: the wood is esteemed for its toughness, and a gum like kino and also lac is obtained from it.

BUTEA PARVIFLORA.—A scandent shrub, flowers small and white.

CADABA INDICA. *Capparidaceæ.*—The Indian Cadaba, a straggling shrub, flowers in terminal racemes, of a dingy white, nearly throughout the year, very common about Mussulman burial grounds.

CÆSALPINIA SAPPAN. *Cæsalpiniaæ.*—This genus as a whole is of considerable importance, but the species in point of beauty have little to recommend them; they all grow well in sand, peat, and open loam mixed. *C. Sappan* yields the sappan wood of India.

CÆSALPINIA SEPIARIA. NAT. CHILLOOR.—A scandent strong armed shrub; flowers yellow, generally used to fence round fields.

CALAMUS DRACO. *Palmaceæ.*—Dragon's Blood. This plant is a native of Sumatra, and is little known in the Peninsula of India. The plants when young are elegant, and resemble small palm trees, after which they become scandent and overrun any neighbouring trees.

CALAMUS ROTANG. NAT. BEN BENT.—This plant has been introduced from the Moluccas, and is the well-known Rattan plant.

CALAMUS RUDENTUM. NAT. MOTIE BETE.—This is a larger species, and is found in some of the gardens of the Deccan.

CALONYCTION ROXBURGHII. *Convolvulaceæ.* NAT. CHANDNEE. NAT. MURICATUM.—Flowers, bluish purple.

CALOPHYLLUM INOPHYLLUM. *Guttiferæ.* NAT. PINNAY.—The Alexandrian Laurel. A very handsome tree with dark green shining leaves, flowers white and fragrant, fruit round, smooth, size of a large marble, the kernels yield a fixed oil, known as "pinnay oil" used as an application in Rheumatic affections, also for burning in lamps.

CALYPTRANTHES CARYOPHYLLIFOLIA. *Myrtaceæ.* NAT. JAMOON. TAM. NAWEL.—These are large growing timber trees, the wood is light, and chiefly used for making grain measures, the bark is astringent, and is used in a decoction by the Natives for dysentery.

CALYPTRANTHES JAMBOLANA. NAT. JAMOON. TAM. TURKOLUM.—This is a large and handsome tree, flowers in February and March, and thrives in any good soil. The fruit of the best sort is as large as a common blue plum, which it resembles in appearance; it has a rough astringent flavor, and should be soaked in salt and water before it is eaten. The fresh stone if planted grows immediately.

CAPE OR BRAZIL GOOSEBERRY.—Vide *Physalis Peruviana.*

CAPRIFOLIUM SEMPERVIRENS. *Caprifoliaceæ.*—The Lonicera or Trumpet Honey-suckle named after Adam Loniceir, a German Botanist. Common all over England. Grows in hedges, thickets, and clefts of rocks; flower yellow, or white with deep, red streaks, and remarkable for its odour. Lonicera Sempervirens, a native of North America, with flowers, scarlet outside and yellowish white within—very useful in covering walls; the scent at night is unpleasant to some persons, being sickly. Lonicera Chinensis is common in some gardens of the Deccan. Is propagated by slips and layers in any good garden soil.

CARDAMOM.—Vide *Amomum Nutans.*

CARDIOSPERMUM HALICACABUM. *Sapindaceæ.* NAT. SHIBJOOL. TAM. MOODA-COTTON.—The heart-pea or balloon vine; annual climbing plant, with an inflated membranous capsule—hence its name.

CAREYA ARBOREA. *Myrtaceæ.* TAM. KUMBEE.—A large tree, leaves deciduous in the cold season; bears an oblong fruit, size of an egg; has a very peculiar scent, no use is made of it.

CARISSA CARANDAS. *Apocynaceæ.* NAT. KURUNDA. T. WAKA.—The Wild Black Carandas. A large thorny bush. Grows wild in most parts of the Deccan, bearing a dark blue coloured berry when ripe, and sold in the bazaar. There is also a cultivated sort in gardens. The fruit of the latter when ripe is sometimes eaten by Europeans, but in the green state is made into tarts, jellies and pickles: the jelly is considered inferior to none made of other Indian fruits. The wild sort is gathered and sold by the Natives for the same purpose.

CARTHAMUS TINCTORIUS. *Compositæ.* NAT. KOOSUM. TAM. SENDOORKUM.—This plant known as safflower or bastard saffron, yields a fine yellow dye, and from the seed a clear oil is obtained, generally cultivated in fields at the latter end of the monsoon.

CARYOPHYLLUS AROMATICUS. *Myrtaceæ.*—This tree is a native of the Molucca Islands and chiefly cultivated at Amboyna, it is extremely handsome, and of luxuriant foliage, the whole tree and leaves are strongly aromatic. The Clove tree is propagated by seed or layers, the plant thrives best in a strong compact soil of a clayey nature, and arrives at maturity eight or nine years after sowing. The seeds should be sown about six inches apart, in beds with plantain leaves or mats suspended two or three feet from the ground to shelter the young plants from the sun, for if not protected from it when young, they droop and die. When the plants are five or six months old, they should be transplanted at a space of fifteen or sixteen feet asunder, and will bear about the sixth year.

CARYOTA URENS. *Palmaceæ.* NAT. BHERLEE-MAHAR. TAM. TEROOGA.—An ornamental palm with clusters of dark red succulent berries which are very acrid. It yields toddy, and an inferior sort of sago is obtained from the trunk.

CASHEW-NUT.—Vide *Anacardium Occidentale.*

CASSIA ALATA.—A stunted shrub, pretty only when in flower. The leaves are useful in Ringworm.

CASSIA AURICULATA. NAT. TURWUR. TAM. AVARAY.—A very common shrub, grows abundantly in all parts of the Deccan, with pretty yellow flowers, the bark is used for tanning, and the stems to make Native tooth-brushes.

CASSIA FISTULA. *Cæsalpinieæ.* NAT. AMULDAS. TAM. KONNEKAI.—Native of the country, and is perhaps, when in blossom, one of the most beautiful of the common jungle plants or trees. It grows from ten to thirty feet, and has a dark green leaf with long pods when ripe hanging from the branches. They contain a sweet pulpy juice, which is mildly cathartic, and well known to Native practitioners. The pods vary in length from a foot to a foot and a half.

CASSIA LANCEOLATA.—The leaves of this plant are used as Senna.

CASTOR OIL PLANT.—Vide *Ricinus Communis.*

CASUARINA MURICATA. *Myrtaceæ.* TINIAN PINE. NAT. HURI.—This is commonly called the fir tree in India, from its general resemblance. It is grown in all parts of the Deccan, and has a very handsome appearance amongst other trees. It has been introduced about twenty or twenty-five years, and will grow to the height of forty feet. The small cones abound with seed, and should, if required, be gathered just before ripening ; you have only to place them in the sun, when the seed will fall out, and may be planted immediately in baskets, boxes, or beds of good loam.

CEDRELA TOONA. *Cedrelaceæ.* HIND. TOOMA.—The Bastard Cedar. This tree grows in the ravines of the Concan. Its timber resembles mahogany, and is used very extensively in Bengal for furniture. The flowers are used in Mysore and other parts of India to form a beautiful red dye, with which cotton is coloured. The bark is very astringent, and is used by the Natives in cases of fever. It is called Bastard Cedar from an aromatic resin exuding from it resembling the American Cedar. Flowers white, very numerous, but small, smelling like honey.

CERDERA FRUTICOSA. *Apocynaceæ.*—A large shrub, native of salt marshes, the fruit is a deadly poison, it is the "ordeal tree" of Madagascar.

CERBERA THEVETIA.—A large shrub with leaves like the

Oleander, and bell-shaped yellow flowers; common, easily propagated by cuttings.

CHERRY.—Vide *Prunus Cerasus.*

CHICKRASSIA TABULARIS. *Cedrelaceæ.*—This is a magnificent tree formerly called the Swietenia Chickrassa.

CHINA BOX.—Vide *Murraya Exotica.*

CHLOROXYLON SWIETENIA. *Cedrelaceæ.* NAT. BILLU KURRA.—Satin wood tree. This tree grows abundantly in the jungles of Goozerat and the Deccan, the wood seldom exceeding fifteen inches in breadth, it is of a light yellow colour, close grained and takes a good polish, well adapted for picture frames and light furniture; it is apt however to lose its colour by age, if not protected by varnish.

CHONEMORPHA MACROPHYLLA. *Apocynaceæ.*—Takes its name from *Chone* a funnel and *Morpha* form; a very handsome climbing shrub, with large white flowers, well adapted for a screen or covering a wall.

CHRYSOBALANUS ICACO. *Rosaceæ.*—The cocoa plum-tree of the West Indies lately introduced.

CHRYSOPHYLLUM ACUMINATUM. *Sapotaceæ.* STAR APPLE. NAT. PEETAKARA.—This tree grows to a large size, thirty feet or more, the branches round, and leaves having a ferruginous down upon them when young. The flower is of a pale yellow, and the fruit ripens in October, about the size of a large crab apple: the pulp is of a yellowish colour and firm inside, the outer rind being of a dark brown. It requires no particular soil. There are several trees in the Residency Garden at Hyderabad.

CICCA DISTICHA. *Euphorbiaceæ.* NAT. URFALAYOORIE. TAM. ARNELIE PULLUM.—Country Gooseberry. A small tree, leaves pinnate, from one to two feet long, scattered about the ends of the branches. Flowers small, of a reddish colour. Fruit round, size of a gooseberry: it has an acid flavour.

CINNAMOM.—Vide *Laurus Cinnamomum.*

CISSUS QUADRANGULARIS. *Ampelideæ.* NAT. HARJORA. TAM.

PERUNDIECODIE.—Stems four angled, winged and jointed; it has all the properties of a parasite; the stems are succulent, and beaten up into a paste, are given by the natives for asthma.

CITRUS AURANTIUM. *Aurantiaceæ.* NAT. NARINGEE.—This tree is now extensively cultivated all over the Deccan. The finest sorts are the Cintra, Cowlah, and a small sweet orange which grows on a tree more like a creeper. The principal method of culture is by budding, the stocks generally being either seedlings or cuttings from the sweet lime. The best Cintra, with a thin close rind, is produced upon the seedling stock, and it is said that the fruit grown upon the sweet lime stock is generally loose and soft: this is very perceptible with some of the oranges. The best time for budding is in the cold season.

CITRUS DECUMANA. SHADDOCK OR PUMPLEMOSE.—This is the largest of the orange tribe, and is universally cultivated in gardens: the varieties are red and white—the former preferred by some persons. The tree grows to a large size in a rich soil, and requires much pruning: the best time for doing this is when the crop of fruit is off. Fruit as fine as any seen has been produced at Ellichpoor from the seed of a pumplemose brought from Bombay. The tree, when planted, should have a space of twelve feet all round it: the blossom is used for flavoring sweetmeats.

CITRUS LIMONUM. LEMON OR LIME.—There are so many varieties that they can hardly be described separately, being unnecessary. The large and small yield abundance of acid juice, and the tree is easily cultivated by layers, which soon throw out root fibres. The lime, which is of the smaller description does not bear fruit so quickly as the larger sort, but if carefully pruned, and watered, will continue fruiting all the year round, and be very productive. *Sweet Lime, Meeta Neemboo.*—This is a sweet variety, and grows to the size of a large orange. It is easily propagated by seed. The juice of the fruit is very grateful to persons with fever, although rather tasteless. It will grow also from cuttings. The young shoots make a very good stock for orange grafts.

CITRUS MEDICA. Citron.—This fruit grows to a large size, the outer rind very rough and covered with excrescences, and when ripe of a deep yellow colour and fragrant; used to form a preserve, and the juice is made into lemonade. Is propagated by cuttings, layers, or seed.

CITRUS MONOPHYLLA.—Wild along the Ghauts.

CITRUS TRIFOLIA.—China, about the size of a marble.

CLEARING NUT.—Vide *Strychnos Potatorum.*

CLOVE TREE.—Vide *Caryophyllus Aromaticus.*

CLOVE TREE, WILD.—Vide *Caryophyllus Aromaticus.*

COCOANUT. *Palmaceæ.*—The cocoanut tree belongs to this elegant genus. The species grow upwards of fifty feet high, and are cultivated best in a mixture of loam and peat, or light sandy loam, in a warm moist atmosphere. They succeed well in our collections if they have plenty of heat and are not too much exposed to the sun, as in their native countries they thrive best in the shade.

COCCULUS CORDIFOLIUS. *Menispermaceæ.*—The heart leaved Cocculus. Native name Goolwail. A twining shrub with scabrous corky bark, and broad cordate leaves. The flowers are mostly whitish green and the berries scarlet of the different species. This plant possesses febrifuge properties.

COCHLOSPERMUM GOSSYPIUM. *Ternstromiaceæ.*—A large tree, leaves lobed, deciduous; flowers, terminal, large, bright yellow. Appear in March and April, when the tree is destitute of leaves. Capsules large, containing a silky cotton, used merely for stuffing pillows, a gum called kuteera is procured from it, which is sometimes substituted for Tragacanth.

COCHLOSPERMUM SERRATIFOLIUM.—A tree resembling the gossypium, but with the lobes of the leaves serrated.

COFFEA ARABICA. *Rubiaceæ.*—In gardens of the Deccan, this plant seldom exceeds nine or ten feet in height, plants are easily raised from fresh seed in a nursery bed where they may remain until they are one or two feet high, when they should be carefully removed to the situation where they are to remain for good, and placed at about twelve feet apart, they will thrive well in almost any good light soil; but require a certain amount of protection from the sun, the most favourable situation for a plantation is the side of a hill exposed to the east, as the plants suffer much from hot winds, the shade of plantain trees offers a good protection to them. In the neighbourhood of Aurungabad, there are some coffee trees which have borne fruit in abundance in a garden enclosed on all sides, and which even in dry weather is moist from being shaded by a number of high cocoanut and sooparie trees, and the whole further protected by surrounding buildings, from the dry winds during the greater part of the year.

CONOCARPUS LATIFOLIA. *Combretaceæ.* NAT. DOURA. TAM. SIRIMAUM.—A large erect growing tree common in the Kennery Jungles, but is of a stunted growth on the hills of the Deccan; the fruit is small, scaly, and cone-shaped.

COOKIA PUNCTATA. *Aurantiaceæ.*—The Wampee tree. This bears a rough skinned fruit in April and May, which grows in clusters, containing a sweetish acid juice, resembling black currant in flavor. It grows to a large tree, and has very dark green shining leaves. Rather ornamental, and requires very little care.

CORAL PLANT.—Vide *Jatropha Multifida.*

CORAL TREE.—Vide *Erythrina Indica.*

CORDIA ANGUSTIFOLIA. *Cordiaceæ.* NAT. GOONDNEE.—Tree from thirty to forty feet high, the wood is very tough, used for carriage poles, &c., fruit the size of a large pea, round and smooth, the pulp yellow, and gelatinous, the tree is common throughout the Deccan.

CORDIA MYXA. NAT. LUSOORA. TAM. VIDI-MARAM.—This is a common tree throughout the Concan, the Natives eat and pickle the fruit, the wood soft, and of little use, except for burning.

CORNUS CAPITATA. *Caprifoliaceæ.* NAT. BHUMOWRA.—This genus of plants consists of large trees and shrubs, the bark of the C. florida and sericea are said to be most excellent tonics.

CRATÆVA RELIGIOSA. NAT. BEL KA PAAT.—This tree is generally found near tombs and temples, the leaves are somewhat aromatic.

CRATÆVA TAPIA. *Capparidaceæ.* NAT. VARANA. TAM. MAVILINGHUM.—A middle sized tree bearing showy greenish white flowers, the juice of the bark is astringent and prescribed by the Natives in intermittent fever, a decoction of the bark is also used for a similar purpose.

CROSSANDRA AXILLARIS. *Acanthaceæ.*—Axil-flowered Crossandra.

CROTON SEBIFERUM. *Euphrobiaceæ.* NAT. PIPPALYANG. This tree is not very common, and is only to be met with in a few gardens. It is an ornamental tree, and bears flowers and fruit for a great part of the year together. The fruit is of a pear shape, yellow and red, which when ripe opens and displays two or three black seeds enveloped partially with a fatty-looking substance. It is this from which the Chinese extract the tallow and make into candles.

CROTON TIGLIUM. NAT. JUMALGOTA.—A small tree, leaves alternate, ovate, cordate, from three to five inches long and two or three broad; yields the croton oil.

CROTON VARIEGATUM. *Euphorbiaceæ.*—An ornamental shrub commonly called the laurel, the leaves are variegated; there is also a willow leaf variety equally ornamental and handsome; the plants thrive best in large pots or tubs, and are easily propagated by cuttings. The willow leaf variety thrives best in a situation shaded from the noonday sun.

CUCUMIS MELO.—Vide *Melon.*

CUCUMIS SATIVUS. *Cucurbitaceæ.*—Vide *Cucumber.*

CUPRESSUS GLAUCA. *Ooniferæ.* NAT. SURUS.—This is a tall, elegant, and graceful tree, well adapted for border walks in a garden, being always green, and a favorite with the Natives. It grows easily, and is generally planted alternately with Areca. Slips, if taken off before the commencement of the rains, and planted in beds shaded from the sun, take root; each slip should be six inches apart, and if common care is used, one-fourth of the plants will strike and grow. After that they may be put out in nursery beds, at the distance of one foot from each other, until required for transplanting, to where they are to remain.

CURCUMA ANGUSTIFOLIA. *Scitamineæ.*—Arrow-root. This root grows wild in all the hilly parts of the Deccan, and is used by the Natives for food. The West Indian Arrow-root produces the most farinaceous matter. The tubers should be planted in a good rich soil, about one foot apart, just before the rainy season; and taken up as soon as the leaves are dry. Rats, porcupines, and wild hogs, are very destructive to it, both when first planted, and also when ripe. Such tubers as are required for seed should be kept in a dry place in sand.

CUSCUTA REFLEXA. *Convolvulaceæ.* NAT. HULDI-ALGUSI-LUTA Species.—A parasite with filiform twining succulent stems, leafless, smooth, yellow; flowers white.

CUSTARD APPLE.—Vide *Anona Squamosa.*

CYCAS CIRCINALIS. *Cycadaceæ.*—A very handsome tree, in appearance resembling the Palm tribe, but related to the Coniferæ: common from Tellicherry to the foot of the Ghauts.

CYMBIDIUM ALOIFOLIUM. *Orchidaceæ.*—This is a beautiful plant, when in flower, of a purple and yellow colour, and blossoms in April, native of India.

DALBERGIA SISSOO.—*Leguminosæ.* NAT. SHEESHUM.—This is a most useful tree, growing in the jungles; the wood is used principally, from its strength and natural bend, for native hackeries: when it can be procured long and straight, it makes good shafts for buggies.

DALBERGIA ARBOREA. NAT. KURUNJEE. TAM. POONGA-MARUM. —A large tree with light green foliage, deciduous at the end of the cold season, the wood is light and firm and serves for common purposes, the seeds yield an useful oil.

DALBERGIA LATIFOLIA. NAT. SWETA-SHALA.—This is a large tree with a thick stem, the centre and large branches of which furnish to the manufacturer, the timber generally called blackwood, it is close-grained and admits of a fine polish and is therefore particularly adapted for furniture.

DATE.—Vide *Phœnix Dactylifera*.

DELIMA SARMENTOSA. *Dilleniaceæ.*—A shrub with small white flowers in panicles.

DENDROBIUM PIERARDI. *Orchidaceæ.*—A parasite; caulescent, stems leafless, from six to twelve inches long, round jointed; flowers, several towards the top of the stem, of a light rose-colour.

DENDROBIUM ALBUM. *Orchidaceæ.*—A parasitic flower in white racemes.

DEUTZIA SCABRA. *Philadelphaceæ.*—Very ornamental plants, producing white flowers, not so large as the snowdrop, but many together, in numerous clusters on the young branches; the foliage is dark green. They thrive in any garden soil, and may be propagated with facility by cuttings or layers.

DESMODIUM LATIFOLIUM. *Leguminosæ.*—A shrubby plant, bearing handsome purple flowers.

DESMODIUM. RECURVATUM—Jungle grass. Flowers in the rains, colour purple and white.

DESMODIUM GYRANS.—Flowers pale yellow tinged with blue, the lateral leaflets have the power of singular motions.

DILLENIA SPECIOSA. *Dilleniaceæ.* NAT. MOOTA KURMUL.—A large tree; flowers white and yellow, nine inches in diameter; fruit size of a cocoanut. The thick fleshy leaflets of the calyx have an agreeable acid taste, and are eaten by the Natives.

DIOSPYROS GLUTINOSA. *Ebenaceæ.* NAT. GAUB. TAM. PANICHEKAI.—A small tree, bearing a rusty coloured fruit abounding in a glutinous astringent juice, obnoxious to insects and is used by book binders, and also for soaking fishing nets in.

DIOSPYROS EBENUM.—The Ebony tree. Yielding a heavy black wood, grows abundantly in Ceylon and many parts of the Deccan.

DIOSPYROS SAPOTA.—Vide *Achras Sapota*.

DOMBEYA PALMATA. *Byttneriaceæ.*—A shrub; leaves palmate, resembling the common castor oil plant; flowers, in large terminal corymbs, rose-coloured, appear in September and October.

DOMBEYA ANGULATA.—A shrub; leaves cordate, acuminate and serrate; old ones three or five angled; flowers in corymbs, of a pretty rose-colour.

DOMBEYA TOMENTOSA.—A small tree with rose-coloured flowers, but smaller than the above two species.

DRACOCEPHALUM. *D. Moldavicum.*—An unpretending annual, bears small blue and white flowers. To be at all effective the plants must be grown crowded in patches. Sow in October.

DURANTA ELLISIA. *Verbenaceæ.*—This is a beautiful large shrub with light blue pendulous flowers, it blossoms almost throughout the year, readily grown from cuttings, the flowers are scentless.

DURANTA PLUMIERI.—This is a large shrub like the former, with handsome drooping blue flowers having the scent of almonds, the clusters of seed berries which are numerous; when ripe have a very pretty appearance from their dark orange colour, they do not appear to germinate readily.

DURIO ZIBETHINUS. *Bombaceæ.*—This is a large tree, the Durian of the Malays, and is found mostly in the islands of the Indian Archipelago; the fruit has a very strong fœtid scent, and in consequence is not at first relished by Europeans; the seed of this fruit, like that of the Jack is the part eaten. The tree has lately been introduced into the Company's Gardens on the Madras side.

EARTH NUT.—Vide *Arachis Hypogea.*

ECHITES ACUMINATA. *Apocynaceæ.*—A climbing shrub with white flowers and habit as the last.

ECHITES PANICULATA. *Apocynaceæ.*—A climbing shrub with large yellow showy flowers.

ELÆOCARPUS OBLONGUS. *Elæocarpaceæ.* NAT. KASSOW.—This is a handsome tree, flowers in May, petals beautifully fringed, the foliage is frequently tinged with red giving an autumnal appearance to the tree.

ELÆOCARPUS GANITRUS. NAT. ROODRAKYA.—This tree is a native of Java, the seeds are about the size of common marbles, and are worn as necklaces by Brahmins and Faqueers, they are commonly called *Utrasum* beads.

ELATE SYLVESTRIS. *Palmaceæ.* NAT. KAJOOREE.—Wild date. Common throughout the Deccan.

ELÆAGNUS DULCIS. *Elæagnaceæ.* NAT. SHOOSHUNA.—This tree or shrub is usually covered with leprous scales; leaves alternative or opposite, entire, without stipules. Flowers axillary—often fragrant. The fruit is about the size of a small olive, oblong. It is eaten by the Persians.

ELEAGNUS CONFERTA. NAT. AMGOOLEE.—A scandent shrub, with silver-coloured leaves beneath. The fruit is red when ripe, and eaten by the Natives.

EMBELIA PETRANDRA. *Myrsinaceæ.* NAT. AMBUT.—A scandent shrub with alternate polished leaves; flowers in the cold season; fruit red, size of a currant.

EMBELIA RIBES.—Another of the species; a scandent shrub like the former, only with rough tuberous knobs on the stem; both are confined to the higher ranges of mountains.

ENTADA PURSÆTHA. *Mimosa.* NAT. GRADUL.—An immense climbing shrub forming elegant festoons, legumes from one to three feet long, four or five inches broad, formed of a series of joints, each containing one seed: they are roasted and eaten.

ERIOBOTRYA JAPONICA. *Pomaceæ.*—The Loquat. This tree is now introduced all over the Deccan, and bears fruit twice in the year. It is highly esteemed both for desserts and preserves. It is a native of Japan, but grows in great perfection in New South Wales. The finest fruit is produced at the second crop, at the end of the cold season, and requires protection day and night; from birds in the former, and flying foxes in the latter. The fruit is of a yellow colour, with thin skin, a sweet acid pulp, one or two seeds in the centre—sometimes more. The seeds grow easily. Proper attention does not seem to have been given to this fruit, as it appears to be capable of great improvement.

ERINOCARPUS NIMMONII. *Tiliaceæ.*—Jungle Bendy. A middle sized tree; flowers yellow in terminal panicles, appear in September and October. Fruit triangular, covered with bristles; angles somewhat winged, as a pleasing scent.

EROIDENDRON ANFRACTUOSUM. *Bombaceæ.*—This is a large tree growing in many parts of the Deccan, flowers drooping, dingy white, blossoms in the cold season, the capsules when ripe contain a fine silky cotton like substance.

ERYTHRINA INDICA. *Leguminosæ.* NAT. PANGRA.—Indian coral tree; trunk and branches armed with prickles. Flowers in March and April, in terminal horizontal racemes, of a bright scarlet colour. This tree is used as a prop for vines; grows well by cuttings of any size. There is also a white blossoming Erythrina.

ERYTHRINA SUBLOBATA. T. BADADOOMOO.—A tree, frequently of great size, branches spreading and numerous, trunk without prickles, the wood commonly used for making light boxes, scabbards, &c., and is generally called moochee-wood.

ERYTHRINA SUBEROSA.—This tree is less common than the Indica, the trunk covered with deeply cracked corky bark, deciduous in the cold season, flowers in February and March.

EUGENIA ACRIS. *Myrtaceæ.* NAT. SUNG.—A small tree; grows in Bombay, the leaves have a pleasant smell when bruised.

EUGENIA JAMBOSA. NAT. GOOLAB JAMB.—This tree bears a light whitish yellow fruit, pear shaped, with smooth skin, having a rose flavour: it is commonly cultivated in gardens on the coast. Hyderabad is the only part of the Deccan where it is known to flourish; many attempts have been made without success to rear it elsewhere. It is easily propagated by seed, and grows luxuriantly in a good garden soil. The red coloured species having the same flavour, is called the Jambo Malacca.

EUGENIA MALACCENSIS.—Cultivated as the former.

EUPHORBIA NERIFOLIA. *Euphorbiaceæ.* NAT. SHIJ. TAM. ELAKULLIE.—Grows all over the rocky parts of the Deccan. It has a whitish dead appearance except during the rains, and forms a capital fence round fields, &c.

EUPHORBIA ANTIQUORUM. NAT. SAYORD.—A leafless curious

looking shrub, with spreading triangular branches from a four angled stem, armed with double spines : common.

EUPHORBIA LIGULARIA. NAT. MUNSA-SHIJ.—With twisted five angled stems: common.

EUPHORBIA TIRUCALLI. NAT. LUNKA-SHIJ. TAM. KALLI.—This plant is much used for making hedges, and from its continual green appearance is well adapted for the purpose. It grows best either upon a bank, or wall of large stones laid loosely for the purpose, having a good cover of earth upon it. Any cuttings will grow, and the plant if by itself will attain the height of twenty feet or more. The wood makes the best charcoal for gunpowder. A parasite of a yellow thread-like appearance, and leafless, (the Cassytha Filiformis) is very destructive to it, and will totally destroy a tree or a whole hedge in a short time, if not removed.

EUPHORBIA TITHYMALOIDES.—The Slipper Plant. This is a thick deep-green leafed plant: it grows about three feet high, but if kept trimmed may be used for a border to a flower parterre, for which purpose it is admirably adapted. It suffers nothing by cutting, and if occasionally watered is always green. It grows well from slips; bears a small pink flower, and can be kept at any height. It is sometimes called buckthorn.

EXILE TREE.—Vide *Thevetia Nerifolia.*

FALSA.—Vide *Grewia Asiatica.*

FERONIA ELEPHANTUM. *Aurantiaceæ.*—Elephant Apple. This is a large handsome tree, with pinnate leaves; bears a grey-coloured edible fruit, the size of an orange, which contains a sweetish pulp, eaten with sugar, and sometimes made into chatnees. The scent is very unpleasant when dry. The cortex of the fruit is used by firework-makers. An excellent pure gum is procured from the tree.

FICUS CARICA. *Urticaceæ.* NAT. UNJEER. TAM. SIMIE ATTIE.—This tree bears fruit almost the whole year round. There are two varieties, the white and the blue, cultivated in all the Native gardens, the young trees producing the finest fruit. The Italians, as the fruit begins to ripen, prick each with a pin, putting a drop of sweet oil on the spot:—it is said that this causes an increase in the size of the fruit. The trees may be grown by layers and suckers at the commencement of the rains, and during the cold season. Cuttings strike easily in the course of six weeks. The finest fruit that I have seen grown has been on young trees of two years old, near which dead animal matter had been buried. The trees should be pruned annually, and the best way is to cut down the old branches that have borne fruit, leaving one or two buds that promise to throw out healthy shoots. The fruit when ripening must be protected from birds, either by nets or bags.

FICUS INDICA. NAT. BUR. TAM. ALAVEREI.—Banian, or Indian Fig-tree. Common all over India, growing to an immense size, from the branches of which stems descend and on reaching the earth take root: a glutinous juice is extracted by incision, from which bird-lime is prepared.

FICUS RACEMOSA. NAT. GULLAR KE CHAWL. TAM. ATTIE.— A large tree common throughout the country, the milky juice of this tree is considered a valuable external application in ringworm.

FICUS RELIGIOSA. NAT. PIPUL. TAM. ARASUM.—This tree is equally common with the last, and is generally planted about Hindoo temples. The roots are most destructive to buildings, for if once they establish themselves amongst the crevices, there is no getting rid of them.

FICUS GLOMERATA. NAT. OOMBUR.—A large tree with fruit like the common fig, grows in clusters along the branches, flavour insipid, but eaten by the poorer classes. This tree thrives best near a watercourse, or on the banks of rivers.

FICUS ELASTICA.—Indian rubber tree. Common in gardens, with handsome large glossy leaves, from the large branches stems descend as in many of the Indian species of Ficus.

FIR TREE.—Vide *Casuarina Muricata.*

FLACOURTIA SAPIDA. *Flacourtiaceæ.* THE PANEOLA PLUM. NAT. BINCHA. T. PUDDA-KANAEW.—This fruit tree is generally cultivated about Calcutta, and grows to the size of a common plum: it resembles a gooseberry in appearance, the skin thin and shining and of a purple appearance. The tree is not common on this side of India, and only one or two are to be found in Bombay. The fruit here is not so large as in Calcutta, where it is common during the rains; it contains from ten to twelve seeds, and is both palatable and wholesome, and well worthy of more general cultivation. The tree grows to a large size.

FRAGARIA. *Rosaceæ*. THE STRAWBERRY.—This plant multiplies itself from runners and suckers; the old plant, after it has ceased bearing, throwing them out. As soon as the rains have set in, these runners may be removed into a nursery bed, for their being more easily looked after, and should have the space of nine or ten inches allowed between them: they will throw out other runners, the whole of which may be separated and transplanted at the proper season.

They thrive best in a light soil with good old stable and vegetable manure at first, and as soon as they show a disposition to flower, may have old goats' or sheep's manure added around each plant, a couple of double handsful being sufficient.

In no part of the Deccan, should the plants be put out for fruiting before the close of the rains, the latter part of September being quite early enough. Suckers which I planted for experiment at the commencement of August, grew to a good size, and did nothing for ten or twelve weeks but throw out suckers, which were continually removed, and after all fruited badly: the finest and most prolific crop were got from suckers put out in the beginning of October. Some strawberries were gathered in November from the plants put out in August, but they were so few as in no way to induce me to try the experiment again. Varieties can only be procured from seed; and to procure the seed, select the finest ripe fruit, rub it on a sheet of paper, and dry it. When the rains commence, soak the seed in water, reject all that float, the remainder sow in baskets in a light loam, when they will be fit to remove in about six weeks, and should be put in other baskets four or five inches apart, and taken care of until ready to be transplanted into beds, where they are to remain. As these plants throw out suckers very fast, they must be constantly looked after, and removed unless you have a scarcity of plants. They will commence bearing in six months from the time of sowing the seed.

You may as soon as the rains have ceased, put your suckers that have rooted into square beds, each not less than one foot apart, five in a row : this will give you twenty-five in each bed—as many as can be easily looked after and gathered without trampling on the bed and thereby injuring the plants. When the earth is of a clayey consistence, I have seen the strawberry cultivated on ridges. Some think this is a good plan, but I prefer the beds: however, it can be easily tried. It is sometimes necessary, in consequence of flooding the beds, to put tiles under the fruit to keep it clean, but it also attracts the notice of the birds : if straw or grass be used, then the chances are that white ants destroy your plants. This it is that makes some persons prefer the ridge system of growing, as they say the fruit is cleaner in consequence : all I know is, that fine fruit may be grown either way; and if on ridges, the same distance must be allowed between the plants as in beds—and even in the latter the plants may be put on raised cones of earth. The common vegetable manure is all that is required at first until near flowering, when a handful or two of goats' or sheep's dung should be put round the plant, opening the earth and scraping it together. Water during the evening and very early in the morning.

GARCINIA PURPUREA. *Guttiferæ*. WILD MANGOSTEEN. NAT. KOKUM-BRINDAO.—A very elegant tree, of a conical form, branches drooping, leaves dark green ; fruit round and smooth, size of a crab apple, when ripe of a purple colour throughout the inside ; and of an agreeable flavour, it is much used at Goa for jellies and syrup, the tree grows to the height of thirty feet and is found in the Concan, and along the Malabar Coast.

GARCINIA MANGOSTANA.—The Mangosteen. This tree has been introduced from Singapore into Bombay, but the fruit has never been brought to any perfection: probably if grafted on the Brindoa, which is common in the Concan, (and several trees are found in Bombay,) it might be much improved. I have been informed by a friend, that the Mangosteen ripens (and is equal to the Penang fruit) in the Company's spice gardens on the hills near Courtallum.

GARCINIA GAMBOGIA.—This tree grows to a large size, the fruit furrowed, acid, and pleasant, size of a small orange, is common throughout the Malabar Coast.

GARUGA PINNATA. *Burseraceæ*. NAT. KOORUK.—A tree, leaves pinnate, deciduous; flowers of a yellowish white, in panicles covered with a mealy kind of white substance; fruit size of a small plum, used for pickling.

GINGER.—Vide *Amomum Zingiber*.

GMELINA ARBOREA. *Verbenaceæ*. NAT. SEWUN.—A large tree; leaves petioled, cordate and pointed; flowers in April and May, large, yellow, tinged with brown. The wood of the tree is used for making the cylinders of drums, &c.

GMELINA ASIATICA. S. BIDDARI. TAM. NEELACOMUL.—A shrub; with small scolloped leaves and large yellow flowers armed with thorns, and forms an excellent hedge.

GMELINA PARVIFLORA. TAM. GOOMADI.—A shrub like the former, having dark orange coloured flowers.

GOSSYPIUM RELIGIOSUM. *Malvaceæ*.—This shrub produces a brownish coloured cotton, commonly called Nankeen cotton, it is more generally cultivated in gardens as an exotic, on account of the colour of its wood.

GOSSYPIUM NIGRUM.—This is an ornamental tall growing shrub generally cultivated in gardens on account of its dark red flowers;—from the staple of the wood being short although fine, it is not of much value.

GOSSYPIUM ALBUM. NAT. KAPAS OR ROOI.—The common cotton plant. This plant is generally cultivated at the commencement of the rains in the black soil throughout the Deccan: the plant attains the height of from eighteen inches to four and a half feet, according to the soil and culture.

GRAPES.—Vide *Vitis Vinifera*.

Grewia Asiatica. *Tiliaceæ.* Nat. Phulsi.—This shrub is generally cultivated in most fruit gardens; it bears a dark purple berry, when ripe, containing one or two small stones. The fruit is generally made into sherbet by pouring boiling water on it, and when cool, adding sugar to the taste. The plants are generally cut down almost to the ground in November, and even the leaves are burnt round the stalks, after which the roots are opened and manured, and watered occasionally, when new shoots spring out, and the fruit is borne near the axilla of each leaf; when of a dark purple, they are ripe and fit for use, grown readily from the seed.

Grewia Hirsuta. T. Javelliki.—A shrubby plant; fruit hairy, common in the jungles.

Guava.—Vide *Psidium Pybiferum.*

Guazuma Tomentosa. *Byttneriaceæ.*—Rather a common tree, with small yellow axillary and terminal flowers, capsule woody, tubercled, about the size of a small plum.

Guettarda Speciosa. *Rubiaceæ.* Nat. Paneer-ka-pool.—A small tree, with large white fragrant flowers, in blossom throughout the year: the tree is sacred both to Siva and Vishnoo.

Heritiera Littoralis. *Sterculiaceæ.* Nat. Soondree.—A small tree, with alternate entire leaves, and flowers in axillary panicles.

Hibiscus Mutabilis. *Malvaceæ.*—The Changeable Rose. A large shrub bearing white flowers in the morning, and changing to red in the course of the day: easily propagated by cuttings.

Hibiscus Rosa-Sinensis.—The Shoe flower. A large shrub with several varieties of single and double flowers of various colours.

Hibiscus Tiliaceus.—Lime-tree leaved ditto.
,, Phœniceus.—Purple ditto.
,, Lampas.—Three pointed ditto.
,, Populneus. Nat. Parspipal.—Poplar leaved. This is a large handsome tree with dark green shining leaves, the flowers yellow, shaped like a tulip, capsules when ripe, hard and

downy, and on being cut through a yellow pigment exudes, having the appearance of gamboge: propagated easily by seed, and the tree is well adapted from its ornamental appearance for avenues, or the road side.

HIPTAGE MADABLOTA. *Malpighiaceæ*. NAT. BOKNEE OR UTI-MOOKTA.—Delight of the Woods. A large climbing shrub, with very beautiful white and yellow flowers in terminal racemes; petals fringed; four white, one yellow;—one of the stamens much longer than the rest; fruit unequally three winged. The bark is a good sub-aromatic bitter.

HOG PLUM.—Vide *Spondias Mangifera*.

HORSE RADISH TREE.—Vide *Moringa Pterygosperma*.

HOVENIA DULCIS. *Rhamnaceæ*.—This tree was originally brought from China, the fruit is a capsule, which contains a sweet juice and is said to have the flavour of the Bergamot pear.

HOYA CARNOSA. *Apocynaceæ*.—Wax-plant. This plant is common in gardens both in Bombay and the Deccan; the flowers are of a whitish pink colour, resembling wax. It grows well in the garden or in pots, and is particularly well suited for covering trellis work; it seems to prefer a northern aspect and blossoms generally in February or March; and as one set of flowers fall off, others appear shortly after on the same stem, and in this manner a succession of flowers continue three or four times.

HURA CREPITANS. *Euphorbiaceæ*.—The Sand-box tree; a small armed tree of rapid growth. The fruit resembles a small orange without the peel, and when ripe, its numerous valves burst with an elastic jerk.

HYDROCOTYLE ASIATICA. *Umbelliferæ*.—An herbaceous plant, grows in moist shady places, flowers green, and of an uninteresting nature.

INGA DULCIS. *Mimosa*. TAM. KOROOKAPULLY.—A large and handsome tree, with drooping branches armed with short straight thorns. Pods curiously twisted, filled with a sweet pulp, which forms a nourishing food. This is the best hedge plant in South India.

Ipomœa Tuberosa. *Convolvulaceæ.* Malabar Creeper.—An immense climbing plant, with woody stem ; common in gardens ; a native of Tropical America ; leaves palmated, seven parted. Flowers yellow and showy, appear in October and November. It is in general use for covering old walls, trellises, &c., and for which purpose, from its exceeding rapid growth, it is well adapted.

Jack Tree.—Vide *Artocarpus Integrifolia.*

Jamoon.—Vide *Eugenia Jambosa.*

Jatropha Manihot. *Euphorbiaceæ.* Tam. Maravullie. Nat. Shuftaloo.—The Tapioca plant. This is a shrub with palmate leaves, resembling the castor oil plant ; it is of easy culture. The juice fresh from the roots is highly poisonous ; but the root when roasted or boiled, may be eaten with safety : it yields also tapioca, a nutritious flour, and grows well in any good soil or situation.

Jatropha Curcas. Nat. Bag-Bherenda. Tam. Caat-amunak.—The angular leaved physic nut. This plant is principally used as a hedge from its easy growth, it flowers in the rains ; the seeds are administered as a purgative, but are very uncertain in their operation.

Jatropha Multifida Coral Plant.—This shrub is common in almost all the gardens ; where it is known by its resemblance to the substance from which it is named. The seed is sometimes eaten by children, but is of a deleterious nature, and an emetic should be immediately administered. I have known several instances of this occurring. The inspissated juice forms a substance like caoutchouc.

Juniperus Communis. *Coniferæ.*—A handsome shrub with bark of a dark brown colour which peels off in little flakes, cultivated in the Botanical Garden at Calcutta.

Juniperus Chinensis.—This low spreading shrub has also been brought from China and cultivated in the same gardens as the above.

Justicia Picta. *Acanthaceæ.*—This is a very ornamental and

handsome variegated shrub, bearing red flowers, having green leaves with large white spots fringed with green, and some varieties with red and dark red spots. The leaves are used for the decoration of the dessert after dinner, and other ornamental purposes: few leaves can be found on which some grotesque resemblance to the human countenance may not be fancied or traced.

JUSTICIA ECBOLIUM. *Acanthaceæ.* NAT. OODOO-JATEE.—A shrubby plant with azure coloured flowers.

JUSTICIA PANICULATA. NAT. CREYAT.—This plant grows wild in the Southern parts of India, and is highly prized as an excellent stomachic; and is said to form the basis of the famous French bitter tincture termed Drogue Amére.

JUSTICIA NASUTA. NAT. KABUTER KE JAR KE JURR.—A shrubby plant with white flowers in axillary and terminal panicles; grows spreading along the ground. The leaves are bruised and used by the Natives for curing ringworm.

JUSTICIA COCCINEA.—This is a species bearing a small pink flower. The leaves are of a reddish colour underneath. It is said by the Natives that the root is an antidote to the bite of a snake, and that it is the root sought after by them when bitten by the cobra.

JUSTICIA GENDARUSSA. NAT. KALI-SHUMBALI.—A handsome shrubby plant with bark of a dark purple hue very smooth, and in some varieties green, flowers during the rains, it grows readily by cuttings or slips: the leaves when rubbed have a strong and not unpleasant smell; they are roasted and given by the Natives in chronic rheumatism.

KLEINHOVIA HOSPITA. *Byttneriaceæ.*—A tree with alternate broad cordate leaves and small pink flowers in terminal panicles; capsule pear shape and inflated.

KUMRUCK.—Vide *Averhoa Carambola.*

KURUNDA.—Vide *Carissa Carandas.*

LAGERSTRŒMIA ALBA. *Lythraceæ.* LAGERSTRŒMIA INDICA. NAT. HENNA OR TELINGA-CHINA.—This is the white flowering species of the China mendic. A common shrub in gardens, and used for border hedges, it bears a small reddish flower and grows easily from cuttings at the commencement and during the rains.

LAGERSTRŒMIA REGINŒ. NAT. URJOONA.—A small tree with opposite oblong leaves; flowers in May in large terminal panicles of a dark blue or purple colour, exceedingly showy.

LAGERSTRŒMIA LANCEOLATA. NAT. BODAH OR BONDAGA.—An erect tree with oblong lanceolate leaves, flowers small, white, appearing in April and May, the whole of the species may be propagated by seed or cuttings in any garden soil.

LAUREL.—Vide *Croton Variegatum*.

LAURUS CAMPHORIFERA. *Lauraceæ*. NAT. CAFOOR.—Camphor tree of China introduced into Bombay, it is a large tree with ascending branches, bark of the stem somewhat rough, but on the inner surface is smooth and mucous. The tree does not blossom until it has attained a considerable size, the fruit is a purple berry the size of a pea, it is composed of a soft pulpy substance having the flavour of cloves and camphor: the camphor is obtained by incision in the bark whence it exudes, a tree seldom produces more than three pounds.

LAURUS CINNAMOMUM. NAT. DAR-CHEENI.—This tree is rare in the Deccan, and is only to be found in private gardens; where it is most probably introduced from Ceylon, where it blossoms in January and February, the seeds ripen in about four months, the berry is oval about the size of a pea and when first gathered the taste resembles that of the Juniper berry, and when dry, if boiled, yields a substance which when cold becomes solid like wax, and may be made into candles; propagated by seeds, shoots, or layers; soil a sandy loam mixed with decayed vegetable matter.

LAURUS PERSEA. *Lauraceæ*.—This tree grows to a large size and requires much water. The wood is very brittle. It bears fruit during the rains, the size of a baking pear, but to describe it more accurately would be to say that it is from six to eight inches long, and in the thickest part about three inches in diameter. It is called Subaltern's butter. The outside has a dark green skin, rather thin; and inside a soft whitish pulp, which may easily be divided with a spoon. The seed is about the size of a pigeon's egg, and will grow if planted immediately. The flavour of the pulp is sweet and creamy, and perhaps the name of Subaltern's butter is derived from this particular taste and appearance. The Natives do not seem fond of it.

LAVANDULA VERA. *Lamiatceæ.* NAT. SITAKEPUNGERIE.—This plant never blossoms in the Deccan, as far as I can discover, but grows to great perfection on the Neilgherry Hills. The bush here has a strong aromatic scent, but seldom survives more than two years. Is propagated by cuttings and layers, in a good rich soil—it grows best in pots.

LEAD WORT. *Plumbaginaceæ.* PLUMBAGO. RED COLOURED. BLUE. WHITE.—The white flowered grows wild.

LEMON.—Vide *Citrus Limonum.*

LEONURUS TATARICUS. *Stachydeæ.*—Tartarian Motherwort.—This is a shrubby plant grown from seed and cultivated in some gardens.

LIME, SWEET. MEETA NEEMBO.—This is a sweet variety, and grows to the size of a large orange. It is easily propagated by seed. The juice of the fruit is very grateful to persons with fever, although rather tasteless. It will grow also from cuttings. The young shoots make a very good stock for orange grafts.

LIMONIA PENTAPHYLLA. *Aurantiaceæ.* NAT. ASH-SHOURA.—The five leaved Limonia bears a smooth roundish red fruit about the size of a marble, eaten but not held in any estimation; easily propagated by seed.

LIMONIA ACIDISSIMA.—A shrub with pinnate leaves, and winged petioles; fruit small, size of a pea; an article of commerce, used as a tonic.

LIQUORICE PLANT.—Vide *Abrus Precatorius.*

LIRIODENDRON. *Magnoliaceæ.*—The tulip tree.—This tree is highly ornamental growing to a large size and well adapted for a plantation or lining an avenue, the flowers are large and of a yellow and red colour which appear in the rains, it is easily raised from seed. The bark is a strong tonic and is said to be equal to the Peruvian. The wood is fine grained and smooth, used by Coach makers and Carpenters.

LITCHI.—Vide *Scytalia Litchi.*

LONICERA LESCHENAULTIA. *Caprifoliaceæ.*—T. Moullee-quedi. —A twining villous shrub, native of the Neilgherries, is found in many gardens of the Deccan where it grows in great luxuriance, it is easily propagated by cuttings or layers.

LOQUAT.—Vide *Eriobotrya Japonica.*

LOTUL.—Vide *Osyris Wightiana.*

LUCERN.—Vide *Medicago Sativa.*

LYCOPERSICUM. ESCULENTUM. TOMATA OR LOVE APPLE.—The produce of South America—a genus of the same family as potatoes. There are two sorts, single and double : may be sown immediately the rains commence, in beds; afterwards transplanted in rows, two feet apart, and trailed upon sticks of a strong description. If the soil is good, they will grow to seven or eight feet in height. The double, which are the finest, if sown in June, ripen in October. The lower branches should be pruned, and a succession of crops may be kept up until April. The small single tomata, with a slight protection from the dry winds, will continue until the rains.

MACLURA TINCTORIA. *Urticaceæ.*—This tree grows to the height of thirty or forty feet, from the wood Fustic, a yellow dye is obtained.

MALABAR NIGHT-SHADE.—Vide *Basella Rubra.*

MALABAR CREEPER.—Vide *Ipomœa Tuberosa.*

MALPIGHIA COCCIFERA. *Malpighiaceæ.*—A small stunted shrub, with leaves resembling the box; common in gardens.

MANGIFERA INDICA. *Terebinthdceæ.* NAT. AMB. OR AMBA.— Is a highly esteemed fruit, and may be procured twice in the year, but I have never met with any trees bearing two crops in the Deccan, only in Bombay. Propagation may easily be effected by seed and cuttings, &c., but the process is slow, as a tree thus raised will not bear fruit before the fifth or sixth year, whereas those that are grafted produce in the second or third, although it is injurious to the tree to let it bear so early, and I therefore recommend that the blossoms should be removed. Young grafts will sometime, indeed very often, blossom the first season they are removed, and if allowed to bear fruit, it checks them for a length of time after. A mango graft may be applied at any time of the year: the stock must be kept continually moist by watering. When the graft and stock have become united, the former must be partially divided by a notch with a sharp knife: this may be done after six weeks have elapsed from the time of its first being united: a second cutting may be effected a fortnight later, and the complete removal from the parent tree at the expiration of nine or ten weeks. After this, remove the graft into the shade for a fortnight longer, when it may be put into the spot where it is to remain. A graft tree never attains the size of a seedling, neither will it continue to live or bear so long, and I doubt much if the seed of a graft mango would produce the same fruit, whereas a seedling often does so. The time that a seedling takes to produce fruit is the great objection to this mode of rearing trees: nevertheless a young tree of three years old might have one of its branches brought into blossom by ringing; this would enable the cultivator to judge if the tree was worth preserving or not. The finest flavoured sorts of mango grown in Western India, are the Alphonso, Raspberry, Mazagon, Doriah, and Malgrobah: this latter variety is of a greenish tinge inside when ripe, and by far the largest of the whole, being three times the size of an Alphonso; and it ripens the last.

When the graft is planted out, it requires only a moderate proportion of care, clearing the ground of all weeds, and removing any buds that shew themselves. Within the space from the ground to where the first branches are to rise from, all superfluous and weak shoots should be removed more particularly those from the centre of the tree, as also all branches that trail on the ground, unless required for grafting from. The tree is better for being pruned, and whenever the interior of the tree may contain superfluous branches, or when there is not sufficient room for the growth of the young and fruit-bearing shoots, a clear space must be provided,—and this can only be done by pruning. The best time for this operation is soon after the tree has done bearing fruit. No old and decayed wood should be allowed to remain, and great care be taken to remove on the first appearance the Borer,\* should they indicate their presence by their appearance on the bark. When trees are old and have their bark injured, it must be all cleared away, and the parts covered with the composition recommended for that purpose.

I have been favoured with the following information from a friend at Aurungabad: Take slips from the healthy branch of a mango, at least two feet long, taking care to cut it one inch above the joint at the top and the same below the joint at the bottom. The cuttings will not all be equal, as in some branches the joints are short and in others long. The thickness of the slip is to be from three quarters to three inches in diameter. Half the length of the slip is to be slightly punctured with an awl, and then inserted into the ground to that depth (half of the slip) perfectly perpendicular; and then make a knob at the top of the slip with plain cowdung. The cuttings must be well watered in such a manner as to keep up an uninterrupted moisture in the ground; and moreover the cuttings are to be well shaded, and the coverings only to be removed by degrees as the plants attain leaves and strength, and not to be transplanted on any account until the next monsoon. The slips begin to bud within a month generally, but sometimes take a much longer period. In all cases the punctures are indispensably necessary, to admit of root fibres being thrown out from them.

The tree and fruit may both be improved, if, during the cold season, the ground is dug all round the roots, and by the addition of a suitable quantity of good old manure. The seed will only grow when fresh, and seldom after six weeks. From twenty to twenty-four feet of space should be allowed between each tree if a graft: double the space is required for a seedling.

MANGO.—Vide *Mangifera Indica.*

MANGOSTEEN.—Vide *Garcinia.*

\* See Clearing Fruit Trees.

MARSH MALLOW.—*Althæa Officinalis.*

MARTYNIA DIANDRA. *Pedaliaceæ.*—An herbaceous plant with large cordate leaves, covered with a glutinous dew-like substance; flowers diandrous, much like those of the Foxglove. Capsule, with a curious double hooked bill.

MEDICAGO SATIVA. *Leguminosæ.* LUCERNE.—Cultivated in the Deccan for feeding horses, also in Goozerat, where it is coming fast into use among the Natives as green food for cattle. Propagated by seed: may be sown at any season, in beds or rows. It requires much water, and each plant should have five or six inches of space allowed to it. Cultivators generally cut it, as it begins to blossom, when fresh shoots spring up, and a succession of crops is continued in this way for several months, by manuring it occasionally.

MELIA AZEDARACH. *Meliaceæ.* NAT. BUKAIN.—A species of Neem, found in all parts of the Deccan, especially round villages.

MELIA AZADIRACHTA INDICA. NAT. NIM. T. VEPA VAYMPA. —Blue Neem tree, or Indian Lilac. This tree, like the last, is generally found near habitations; the flower much resembles the Lilac, and an oil is expressed from the fruit. The bark is used as a febrifuge; the wood is light, strong and useful.

MEMECYLON TINCTORIUM. *Memecylaceæ.* NAT. ANJUNEE.—A highly ornamental tree with deep green shining leaves; flowers in February and March, of a purple colour, with the calyx beautifully streaked on the inside; it is called the Ironwood tree. The leaves are used to stain mats of a yellow colour.

MESUA FERREA. *Guttiferæ.* NAT. NAGASAR OR NAG CHUMPA. —A tree much cultivated for its elegant blossoms with silver petals and anthers like gold; they are highly prized by the Natives; their perfume partakes of that of the rose and violet.

MICHELIA RHEEDII. *Magnoliaceæ.* NAT. PEELA CHUMPA OR GOLDEN FLOWERED CHUMPA.—This is a handsome tree with beautiful golden coloured flowers, held in high estimation by the Hindoos, the bark of the root of the tree is used medicinally in some female complaints.

MILK HEDGE.—Vide *Euphorbia Tirucalli.*

MILLINGTONIA HORTENSIS. *Bignoniaceæ.*—An elegant tree growing to the height of fifty feet, is in blossom towards the close of the rains, and the seeds ripen in March. The bark is of a soft spongy nature, the wood is white, firm, and close grained.

MIMOSA PUDICA. *Mimoseæ.* NAT. LAJUK. TAM. TOTAL-VADIE.—The Sensitive Plant. Common in gardens, and grows readily from seed, colour of the flowers pale pink.

MIMOSA ALBA.—The White Mimosa.

MIMOSA SCANDENS.—The climbing Mimosa. Nat. Gela. T. Gila tiga.

MIMOSA ADENANTHERA.—The unarmed Mimosa. Nat. Lajwanta species.

MIMUSOPS ELENGI. *Sapotaceæ.* NAT. TAINDOO OR BACUL, MULSARI.—An ornamental tree with dark green oblong alternate leaves, and white fragrant flowers; common.

MIMUSOPS HEXANDRA. NAT. RAJUN. T. PATTA.—This is a tree, common in the Deccan, and is generally planted by the Mussulmans with the Elengi; the wood is much used where strength and toughness is required; the fruit is eaten by the Natives.

MIMUSOPS KAUKI. NAT. KSHEERNI OR KIRNEE.—This tree grows to a large size, and is generally planted in groves: the fruit, which is about the size of a small olive, is of a yellow colour when ripe, after the rains, and contains a sweet clammy juice, eaten chiefly by the Natives.

MISTLETOE.—Vide *Viscum Opuntioides.*

MOMORDICA CHARANTIA. *Cucurbitaceæ.* NAT. KURILLA.—This vegetable is very commonly cultivated by the Natives at the commencement of the rains, the fruit is from ten to fourteen inches long, and from two to four in diameter; the edges are curiously notched and ridged, the flavour is bitter, and it requires to be soaked before being cooked.

Momordica Dioica. T. Angakara Gudda.—This is a smaller species and round-fruited, but differs little from the former: both are much cultivated by the Natives for their curries.

Monkey Bread Tree.—Vide *Adansonia.*

Moringa Pterygosperma. *Moringaceæ.* Nat. Mooring.—Indian Horse Radish tree.—This tree grows readily from seed, and attains a height of from fifteen to twenty feet, in its second year; the root when young and fresh scraped, has the flavour of English Horse radish; the pods when young and green are used as a vegetable both boiled and in curries; the seed when ripe yields a fine clear oil; the wood of the tree is soft and. of little use.

Moringa Concanensis.—A new species discovered in the Southern Concan.

Morus Indica. *Urticaceæ.* Nat. Toot.—Indian Mulberry. A small tree with long tapering leaves sometimes lobed, fruit dark red, used for making tarts.

Morus Alba. The White. Morus Nigra. Black.—These trees grow equally well in the Deccan; the white, growing to a very large tree, shedding its leaves before the hot season. The red mulberry bears fruit in the rains, as well as the black. Silkworms may be fed on the young fresh leaves, although the leaves of the white are preferred. Grows from seed or cuttings.

Morus Atropurpurea. Nat. Shaitoot.—Cultivated as the former.

Mulberry.—Vide *Morus Indica.*

Murraya Exotica. *Aurantiaceæ.* Nat. Bibzar or Koontie.—An ornamental shrub, with beautiful dark green leaves; flowers white, and fragrant in the evening, and commonly known by the name of China-box; it is to be found in most gardens, and is easily grown by layers or cuttings.

Murraya Paniculata.—A small tree with pinnate leaves; flowers white and fragrant, appear in December and January; fruit reddish.

Musa Sapientum. *Musaceæ.* Nat. Kilah.—The Plantain.

There are several varieties of the Banana cultivated in the Deccan,—the large red, the green, and the yellow. A small sort, which is supposed to be the real Banana of the West Indies, is perhaps the most luxuriant of the whole. The plants blossom at all seasons, and as soon as the drupe of fruit begins to ripen, which is known by some turning colour, it is cut and hung up to ripen in the house. The plant will not bear again, and may be cut down (otherwise it will perish of itself,) when the surrounding shoots grow up and blossom as the former. The plants are generally grown in beds or clusters in a good rich soil, when fine fruit is almost the sure return. In transplanting the shoots, if two or three feet high, about one half is generally cut off.

MYRISTICA MOSCHATA. *Myristicaceæ.* NAT. JAYPHUL.—This tree has been introduced from the Eastward. The fruit ripens in the rains: it is the size of a large plum, with a green covering, and upon being ripened, discovers a net-work of a dark red colour surrounding the nut, which has a most beautiful appearance: this is the spice known as mace.

" The first care of the cultivator is to select ripe nuts and to set them at the distance of a foot apart in a rich soil, merely covering them very lightly with mould. They are to be protected from the heat of the sun, occasionally weeded, and watered in dry weather every other day. The seedlings may be expected to appear in from thirty to sixty days, and when four feet high, the healthiest and most luxuriant, consisting of three or four verticles, are to be removed in the commencement of the rains to the plantation, previously cleared of trees and underwood by grubbing and burning their roots, and placed in holes dug for their reception at the distance of eighty feet from each other,—screening them from the heat of the sun, and violence of the winds. They must be watered every other day in sultry weather; manured once a year during the rains, and protected from the sun until they obtain the age of five years. The nutmeg tree is moneocious as well as dioecious but no means of discovering the sexes, before the period of inflorescence, is known. Upon an average, the nutmeg tree fruits at the age of seven years, and increases in produce till the fifteenth year, and is said to continue prolific for sixty or eighty years. Seven months in general elapse between the appearance of the blossom and the ripening of the fruit; and the produce of one bearing tree with another, under good cultivation, in the fifteenth year may be calculated at five pounds of nutmegs, and a pound and a quarter of mace. It bears all the year round, but more plentifully in some months than others, and generally yields more abundantly every other year. It is necessary that the roots of the trees during their growth should be kept well covered with mould, for they have a tendency to seek the surface. The growth of the lateral branches is to be alone encouraged, and all suckers, or dead and unproductive branches, are to be removed with the pruning knife, and the lower shoots lopped off, with the view of establishing an unimpeded circulation of air."—*Penang Gazette.*

MYRTUS COMMUNIS. *Myrtaceæ.* NAT. VILATI-MINDI.— Myrtle. Very common in all the gardens; grows well by layers, and even cuttings. This shrub requires careful pruning, and after the rains all the leaves, on which insects have deposited their larvæ must be removed, or the plant will lose its verdure and beauty by the destructiveness of the young caterpillars.

NAUCLEA CADAMBA. *Rubiaceæ.* NAT. KUDUMBA.—This tree grows to a very large size, common about villages; the fruit is eaten by the Natives, who esteem the tree as "holy."

NEPHELIUM LITCHI. *Sapindaceæ.*—This tree, originally from China, is an ever-green, and grows to a large size. The fruit is of a dark brown colour, and contains a glutinous yellow sweet sort of pulp: it is not much prized—perhaps from its inferior quality to the Chinese fruit, which is much esteemed. The fruit ripens in March and April.

NERIUM ANTIDYSENTERICUM. *Apocynaceæ.* NAT. INDURJAU. —A common shrub flowers in April and May in terminal corymbs. The bark is used as an astringent.

NERIUM OLEANDER. NAT. KARZAHRA. DOUBLE RED AND WHITE.—This grows wild on the banks of rivers, bearing both white and red flowers: the root is poisonous. There are two other varieties very commonly met with bearing double flowers both red and white, and by budding the red colour on the opposite one in several parts of the same stalk, a very pretty appearance may be given to the shrub. The yellow congener is called the Exile—introduced I believe from America. Grows easily from cuttings.

NERIUM GRANDIFLORUM. NAT. MENDASINGHI.—Double species cultivated by seed or cuttings.

NETTLE.—Vide *Urtica Interrupta*.

NICOTIANA TABACUM. *Solanaceæ*. NAT. TAMBACA. NICOTIANA PERSICA.—The well known Tobacco plant, is grown from seed and requires a rich soil, the plants should be at least two feet apart, and if the leaves are required for preservation and use, the flowers as they appear must be removed with the leading stem.

NUTMEG.—Vide *Myristicha Moschata*.

OLIBANUM.—Vide *Boswellia Thurifera*.

OLIVE. *Olea*.—The Olive is a very important genus of plants, on account of the oil, &c., which is obtained, chiefly from some of the varieties of *O. europœa*. They are also much admired for the fragrance of their flowers, which renders them worthy of a place in every collection. They grow well in loam and peat; ripened cuttings root readily in sand, under a glass. They may also be increased by grafting on the common privet.

OPUNTIA. *Cactaceæ*. THE PRICKLY PEAR OR NOPAL.—This is used as a hedge plant about gardens, and forms a strong useful fence, both against men and cattle, but harbours rats and other vermin, also snakes. The red fruit is used as a dye, and may also be eaten.

ORANGE.—Vide *Citrus Aurantium*.

ORCHIS COMMELINÆFOLIA. *Orchidaceæ*.—Root of two or more spindle-shaped succulent tubers; scape erect, about eighteen inches high: round, smooth jointed; with cylindric sheathes; about half the length of the joints. Flowers white, scentless;

appear about the middle of the rains on pasture lands in the Southern Concan. Several species are found in the hills.

ORCHIS MASCULA. *Orchidaceæ.*—The Salep plant is found on the Mahabulesh Hills. It blossoms in June, and the roots are dug up and gathered after the rains in November or December. Another variety is found in the hills and jungles near Candeish, but possessing a very bitter principle. It is dug up by the Bheels, and sold when fresh for a few pice the seer. It requires a great deal of soaking and preparation before it can be deprived of its bitter quality. When dry, it is in appearance as fine as the Persian. It requires being boiled in at least six different waters, and then dried in the sun, when it will become perfectly sweet and fit for use.

ORIGANUM MARJORAM. *Lamiaceæ.* NAT. MURWA. TAM. MAROO. —A native of India, very easily reared in beds or pots, either by slips from the roots, or seed. It is used for flavouring ragouts, sauces, &c.

OSYRIS WIGHTIANA. *Santalaceæ.*—The Lotel. A small tree with twiggy erect-growing branches; in flower and fruit most of the year. The fruit when ripe is of the size of a small sloe, of a yellow colour, with a mark on the top like a "blaeberry." It is sweet and very pleasant when tasted, and is deservedly ranked amongst the wild fruits by Col. Sykes.

OXYSTELMA ESCULENTUM. *Apocynaceæ.*—A twining perennial; deciduous, flowers in the rains, large, white, with a slight tinge of rose colour, and streaked with purple veins; texture thin and delicate.

PANAX FRAGRANS. *Araliaceæ.* NAT. GOOTI-SOONA.—A shrub, with fragrant flowers of green colour, a native of Nepal.

PANAX FRUTICOSUM.—A shrub, with large supra decompound leaves, commonly grown in gardens, and easily propagated from cuttings.

PANAX OBTUSUM.—A shrub, like the former, but not so commonly cultivated in gardens, the roots of all are said to possess medicinal qualities, and are much esteemed by the Chinese for their beneficial influence on the nerves.

PANEOLA PLUM.—Vide *Flacourtia Sapida.*

PARINARIUM EXCELSUM. *Pomaceæ.*—A large tree brought to Bombay from Goa; the fruit which ripens in December and January, resembles a coarse plum, and is held in much estimation.

PARKIA BIGLANDULOSA. *Mimoseæ.* NAT. CHENDOO PHOOL.—A very elegant tree; the flower-buds resemble balls of red velvet, legumes filled with a farinaceous edible pulp.

PARKINSONIA ACULEATA. *Cæsalpineæ.*—A small graceful tree, with pretty yellow flowers in loose pendulous racemes; grows readily from seed, and is well adapted for hedge rows, the stem from which the leaves spring is capable of being converted into a white fibre, and might be used for paper making.

PEACH.—Vide *Amygdalus Persica.*

PEAR.—Vide *Pyrus Communis.*

PEDALIUM MUREX. *Pedaliaceæ.* NAT. BURRAY-YOKEROO.—A succulent plant, with small yellow flowers which appear in the rains, the green leaves when agitated in water render it mucilaginous: this is prescribed by the Natives in dysuria, the seeds are supposed to possess similar virtues.

PENTAPETES PHŒNICEA. *Byttneriaceæ.*—An erect growing plants; flowers axillary, large, of a beautiful bright red colour, appear during the rains.

PENTAPTERA TOMENTOSA. *Combretaceæ.* NAT. USUM.—A large jungle tree with thick leathery leaves; fruit smooth, five winged; the fibre of the wood is very tough, and used for making shafts to gigs, &c.

PENTAPTERA ARGUNA. NAT. URJOONA or URJOON-SADRA.—This tree, like the former, is a common jungle tree, the bark is used internally by the Natives as a tonic and is also applied externally as a vulnerary.

PERGULARIA ODORATISSIMA. *Asclepiaceæ.*—This is a creeper with a climbing woody stem, cracked bark, flowers yellow, and very fragrant, well adapted for covering trellis work.

Peristrophe Lanceolaria. *Acanthaceæ.* Peristrophe Speciosa.—Vide *Justicia.*

Persoonia. *Proteaceæ.*—The Dele, the Embothrium, the Hakea, Banksia and Persoonia, are interesting plants introduced from the Cape and New South Wales, the species being chiefly confined to the southern hemisphere. They are handsome green shrubs, and prized by gardeners for the neatness of their appearance and beauty.

Pharbitis Hispida. *Convolvulaceæ.*—The pale blue large flowered Pharbitis.

Philadelphus Coronarius. *Philadelphaceæ.*—A handsome shrub, producing white blossoms, having the appearance and smell of orange flowers; propagated by seed or layers.

Phillyrea Paniculata. *Oleinæ.*—A small tree with oblong ovate leaves; flowers in terminal panicles, pure white, bending down the branches, and giving the tree a graceful appearance. Introduced from China.

Phœnix Dactylifera. *Palmaceæ.*—Is a fine lofty-growing tree, with a rugged trunk, and leaves from six to eight feet long. The inhabitants of Arabia, Upper Egypt, &c., chiefly live upon the fruit of it, the hard stones are even ground up as food for their camels, and of the leaves they make bags and baskets. In Barbary, the midribs are used as fences for their gardens, and they sometimes make use of the trunks in small buildings. The threads of the integuments between the fronds are made into ropes, and the rigging of smaller vessels; a juice is sometimes extracted from the tree by incisions, or scooping holes at the top, which is afterwards made into an agreeable wine.

Phœnix Farinifera. *Palmæ.*—Is a dwarf species. The fruit ripens in May, and a species of sago is procured, from the trunk, which is split and dried, and then beat in wooden mortars until the farinaceous parts are detached.

Phyllanthus Emblica. *Euphorbiaceæ.* Nat. Awla or Aunlee. —This grows to a pretty large tree and is cultivated throughout most parts of India, and is found wild throughout the Concan and Deccan; the fruit resembles the gooseberry having a sharp acid juice, and is eaten raw by the Natives, and is sometimes made into preserves; the bark is strongly astringent and is used for tanning leather.

PHYLLANTHUS LONGIFOLIUS. *Euphorbiaceæ*. NAT. HURPORORI. —A small tree, commonly cultivated for the sake of its fruit, which is the size of a large gooseberry ; it is more esteemed by the Europeans than the Emblica, and is used both as a pickle and preserve.

PHYSALIS PERUVIANA. *Solanaceæ*. NAT. TAPUREEA.—The Winter Cherry. This plant, commonly called Cape Gooseberry or Brazil Cherry, grows luxuriantly in a good soil. The seed should be sown at the commencement of the rains. The young plants when about six inches high should be set out in rows at least two feet apart from each other, sufficiently wide apart, in fact, to allow the gardener to pass easily between them. They may be grown either on sticks or on trellis, and should be carefully pruned. The young shoots bear the finest fruit, and if carefully attended to, will bear almost all the year round,—the excellence and abundance of the fruit well repaying for any extra care bestowed on the cultivation of the plant. Being of easy culture, it is hardly known to what a state of improvement this apparently worthless fruit may be brought. Produced under an improved method of cultivation, it is a most wholesome and useful fruit. I know of none more so for tarts, or even for dessert, and for making jam or preserve. After seeing the common fruit, grown without care or attention, one would scarcely credit the size of that produced under proper and careful management. The bush should every now and then be carefully pruned cutting out the old wood, as the new shoots provide the finest flavoured fruit.

PHYTOLACCA ICOSANDRA. *Phytolaccaceæ*.—An herbaceous plant ; leaves alternate, entire, without stipules; flowers racemose. A tincture from the ripe berries has the reputation of being a remedy for chronic rheumatism and syphilitic pain.

PINE-APPLE. *Bromeliaceæ*.—The plants that yield this very superior fruit is much esteemed for its sweet aromatic flavour.

It flowers in February and March and ripens its fruit in July or August. Young shoots and suckers not required should be removed from the plant as soon as they make their appearance. The proper season for planting, as will be understood from the above, is in August. Situation must be well exposed to the sun, they should be placed in rows at a distance of three feet at least, and two feet from each other. They are propagated readily during the rains by striking suckers or the green crowns from the fruit in sand. The stumps should not be thrown away but placed in a damp pit when a crop of young plants be the result.

PINUS LONGIFOLIA. *Coniferæ.* NAT. CHIR.—The long-leaved pine.—A tall erect growing shrub, with subverticelled branches and linear lanceolated leaves.—Introduced from the Cape.

PISONIA GRANDIS. *Nyctaginaceæ.* NAT. BAG-ACHEBA.—A straggling shrub, armed with strong axillary recurved thorns; flowers small in axillary terminal panicles. Forms an excellent hedge plant.

PISONIA INERMIS. NAT. KONGI-PUTRI.—Without thorns.

PLANTAIN.—Vide *Musa Sapientum*.

PLANTAIN LEAFED PALM.—Vide *Urania Speciosa*.

PLUMIERIA ACUMINATA. *Apocynaceæ.* NAT. GOBU-CHUMPA.—A small elegant tree, common: flowers white and yellow, tinged with red, very fragrant. A pure white caoutchouc is obtained from this tree.

PLUMIERIA ALBA. NAT. GULACHIN.—The White Chumpa.

POINSETTIA PULCHERRIMA. NAT. KRISHNA-CHOORA.—This is a beautiful plant, growing to the height of five or six feet, the leaves during the rains are green, and afterwards become of a bright scarlet having a most showy appearance, easily propagated by cuttings, both leaves and bark contain a milky juice which when dried and boiled possesses some of the properties of gutta-percha.

POMEGRANITE.—Vide *Punica Granatum*.

PONGAMIA GLABRA. *Leguminosæ.* NAT. KARUNJ.—A tree with foliage resembling the Bacts; flowers in April and May: oil is made from the seed.

Porana Volubilis. *Convolvulaceæ.* Nat. Bhowree.—A twining plant, flowers white, in axillary and terminal racemes; propagated by seed; requires no particular soil.

Prickly Pear.—Vide *Opuntia.*

Prunus Armeniaca. *Amygdalineæ.* Nat. Zard-alu.—The Apricot. This tree grows to a large size in gardens of the Deccan. It blossoms at the same season as the peach, from January to March; the fruit forms and attains the size of a common marble, after which it falls off, and this no care can prevent. Many efforts have been made to get buds to take both on the peach and almond stocks but without success, attempts to graft it by approach has hitherto been unsuccessful: the tree grows well on the first range of the Himaylayas bearing abundance of fruit in the months of May and June. Propagated in the same way as the peach.

Prunus Cerasus. Nat. Padam.—The Cherry. This tree is not found in any part of the Deccan; but abounds wild in the hills north of Deyrah Dhoon, producing a small common black fruit fit only for preserves, &c.

Psidium Pyriferum. *Myrtaceæ.* Nat. Jamb.—This tree grows in all parts of the Deccan. The fruit is both red and white, pear-shaped and round: it is esteemed as a dessert fruit, but the scent when too ripe is unpleasantly powerful; it makes a most excellent jelly, and also is prepared in a similar manner to damson cheese at home. The fruit sometimes is as large as a common baking pear, and I have known one weigh half a pound. They have been brought to great perfection in some gardens, and the fruit of a large size divested almost of seed: this sort generally has a very rough knotty coat, and is more spongy and less firm than the other varieties. As plants continually grown from layers in time cease to produce seed, perhaps this variety has been so procured. It is easily increased by seed, and only requires a good soil to thrive in. The trees should be pruned once a year, otherwise the branches become very straggling. Good gun stocks are made from the old wood.

Pterocarpus Marsupium. *Leguminosæ.* Nat. Beeala or Peetshala.—A tree with pinnate leaves and white flowers in terminal panicles. Gum Kino is procured from the bark and leaves.

Pumplemose.—Vide *Citrus Decumana.*

Punica Granatum. *Granateæ.* Nat. Anar.—The Pomegranate. There are two varieties of this tree, bearing white and red fruit—both sweet, and much inferior to the dried brought from Persia and Bussorah to the Bombay market. The tree grows easily from seed, and large fine juicy fruit, where the soil is good, is often produced. There is a variety which is generally sour, used by the Natives for sherbet. The dried bark of the root is made into a decoction and given for worms. By a continuation of layers from successive plants the fruit becomes almost seedless.

Pyrus Malus. *Pomaceæ.* Nat. Seb or Seo.—The two sorts of apples commonly found in most Native gardens in the Deccan, are said to have been first introduced from Persia. They are of a small description; one, sweet and luscious, grows in bunches; the other, which is larger, has a rough taste, and is better adapted for tarts. They may be propagated by layers, suckers, and even cuttings. The young plant should never be allowed to throw out branches at less than two or three feet from the ground; all the buds beneath must be rubbed off. Never plant them closer than from nine to twelve feet each other, and if there is sufficient ground, keep them separate from other trees, so that they can either be wintered or watered as required. Remove all suckers round the stem of the tree, or from the roots, [unless required for stocks,] when cut them clean off with a sharp knife. The trees may be opened immediately after the rains, if not in blossom. Pluck off all the leaves carefully, and beware, in so doing, that the blossom buds are not injured, which Native Malees, in the careless manner of stripping the leaves, are very apt to do; —then prune the tree. As soon as the blossoms appears set, put plenty of old rich manure to them, and water well every third day until the fruit is nearly ripe. If you continue watering after this, it makes the fruit mealy and insipid. When the fruit is all gathered, cease to water the trees, and as soon as the leaves turn brown and dry, which will be in the course of a month, then open the roots for two or three days, cover with manure again, and water well as before, when you may probably get a second crop in April or May.

PYRUS COMMUNIS. NAT. AMRUD.—The Pear. This tree is not common in the Deccan gardens though some trees are to be found having been brought chiefly from Bangalore; the fruit is of a tolerable large size but coarse and hard which only renders it fit for baking and stews. The same kind of fruit is found in the Upper Provinces of Bengal.

PYRUS CYDONIA. *Pomaceæ.* NAT. BEHEE.—The Quince. This tree has probably been introduced from China or Bengal, and is now to be met with in many gardens. It grows like the apple. The fruit is plentiful at Sattara, and I have met with it at Poonah. In other parts of the Deccan I have seen the tree in blossom, but the fruit did not set,—perhaps for want of proper treatment.

QUAMOCLIT PHŒNICEA. *Convolvulaceæ.*—This is a very handsome climber with flowers crimson, tube long and slender; grows readily from seed.

QUAMOCLIT VULGARIS. INDIAN FORGET-ME-NOT.—Sometimes called the star creeper, from the shape of the flower which is of a deep rosy red.

QUAMOCLIT ALBA. PURE WHITE.—Common like the former easily grown from seed.

QUERCUS SERRATA. *Amentaceæ.* NAT. SHINGRA.— These trees are only found in the hill stations, where they have been grown from seed by private individuals. At Mahabuleshwar, a few plants have been grown, more resembling a shrub than a tree.

QUINCE.—Vide *Pyrus Cydonia.*

QUISQUALIS INDICA. *Combretaceæ.*—A scandent shrub with beautiful flowers of various colours, from white to orange and deep red; has a very powerful perfume towards night. It grows from layers, or seed, but the latter are very difficult to find. It is by some called the Rangoon creeper.

RASPBERRY.—Vide *Rubus.*

REIDLEIA TILIÆFOLIA. *Byttneriaceæ.* NAT. MATHOOREE.—A small tree; the young leaves very soft and velvety; flowers small rose-coloured, in axillary and terminal corymbiform panicles, appear in November.

RHUS LUCIDA. *Terebinthaceæ.*—Shining leaved Sumach, introduced from the Cape.

RICINUS VULGARIS. *Euphorbiaceæ.* NAT. ERUNDI.—This tree is so common all over the country, that any description of its culture is unnecessary, except that if any person wishes to grow it for use, I would recommend a good soil, and sufficient space between the plants to enable them to benefit both by the sun and air.

ROSE APPLE.—Vide *Eugenia Jambosa.*

ROTTLERA TINCTORIA. *Euphorbiaceæ.* NAT. SHENDREE OR TOONG.—Monkey faced tree, from these animals rubbing their faces, with the fruit. A large tree with alternate, ovate oblong leaves, of a ferruginous colour beneath; flowers in the cold weather. Fruit size of a pea, covered with a red mealy powder, used as a dye.

RUBUS LASIOCARPUS. *Rosaceæ.* BLACKBERRY. NAT. GOWREEPHUL.—Now cultivated generally in the Deccan, and believed to have been first brought from the Mysore Hills. It grows easily from seed; a few of the ripe fruit rubbed on a sheet of paper, and dried in the sun, will enable you to forward the seed to friends at any distance. (The same with the strawberry.) The plants should never be nearer than four or five feet, and may be cut down at the commencement of the rains, when they will throw out fresh shoots, and bear fruit in abundance. As it requires little care, and only an occasional supply of water, this bramble forms a very perfect and secure hedge to a kitchen garden. The finest fruit is very inferior to a common raspberry.

RUBUS RUGOSUS.—The Raspberry. This plant never grows in the Deccan: a wild species is described by Graham as found in Mahableshwar.

RUTA GRAVEOLENS. *Rutaceæ.* NAT SATOORI.—Common Rue.

Saccharum Officinarum. *Gramineæ.*—Of all the varieties of sugar-cane cultivated, the Otaheite seems now to have the preference, although I have seen in Berar cane looking as fine. The cane if it grows to seed is considered almost useless for sugar-making. A description of the mode of culture I consider unnecessary.

Sago Palm.—Vide *Phœnix Farinifera.*

Saguerus Rumphii. *Palmæ.*—This tree is scarce, and only found in some of the gardens in Bombay, where it has been introduced from the Sumatra Islands. It is only grown as an exotic, and is a very beautiful species of palm, from its pinnate leaves. It is propagated by suckers from the roots of the old trees.

Samadera Indica. *Simarubaceæ.*—A tree common throughout the Southern Concan.

Santalum Album. *Santalaceæ.* Nat. Chunduna or Ghundasaru.—Sandal-wood. This tree grows both in gardens and the jungles. It bears a small black-berry, which if planted grows without any trouble. The wood is generally brought for sale in small logs seldom exceeding eighteen inches in length. It is unnecessary to describe its use.

Sapium Sebiferum. *Euphorbiaceæ.* Tallow Tree.—This tree is not very common, and is only to be met with in a few gardens It is an ornamental tree, and bears flowers and fruit for a great part of the year together. The fruit is of a pear-shape, yellow and red, which when ripe opens and displays two or three black seeds enveloped partially with a fatty-looking substance. This it is from which the Chinese extract the tallow and make into candles.

Sapindus Indicus. *Sapindaceæ.* Nat. Hoorooa.—A small tree, flowers irregularly, fruit round and hard: three celled with a seed in each and which are used by the Natives for intoxicating fish, the taste of the fruit is nauseous and the juice of the tree is considered poisonous.

Sapindus Fruticosus.—Introduced from the Moluccas, flowers in racemes.

SAPINDUS EMARGINATUS. NAT. RITTAII.—Resembles the S. Indicus. The seeds are used medicinally, and also for washing the finer kinds of silk.

SARCOSTEMMA VIMINALE. *Apocynaceœ.* NAT. SOOM.—A valuable leafless plant, resembling the Euphorbia Tirucalli; flowers white in the rains, the Natives tie the stems up into a bundle and place them in the water-course of their wells for the purpose of preventing the attack of white ants.

SEMECARPUS ANACARDIUM. *Terebinthaceœ.* NAT. BHELA.—The juice of this fruit is particularly acrid, and is used for marking linen; the tree is very common in the Deccan.

SESAMUM ORIENTALE. *Pedalineœ.* NAT. GINGELIE.—A common plant springing up in waste places, and flowering towards the close of the rains; the flowers from the seed of which a bland oil is obtained.

SIDA ACUTA. *Malvaceœ.* NAT. KURETA.—A common plant, grows wild in many parts of the Deccan; flowers small, yellow, grows to the height of about three feet; and no doubt, like the S. Rhomboidea, a good fibre might be procured from it.

SINGHARA.—Vide *Trapa Bispinsa.*

SIPHONANTHUS INDICA. *Verbenaceœ.* NAT. BARUNGEE.—A tall, erect growing, suffruticose plant, with linear leaves; flowers white or cream coloured, with long tubes.

SIPHONANTHUS FRAGRANS. NAT. HATTI-KANA.—Double Variety. A native of China.

SLIPPER PLANT.—Vide *Euphorbia Tithymaloides.*

SNAKE FRUIT.—Vide *Eleagnus Conferta.*

SOAP NUT TREE. *Sapindaceœ.*—This tree is very common in the Deccan about villages. The leaves have a shining appearance, and the flower stalk a soft brown downy look, bearing a small whitish flower. The berries are used for washing by the Natives.

SOLANUM TUBEROSUM. *Solanaceœ.* NAT. ALOO.—Vide *Potato.*

SOLANUM MELONGENA. NAT. BINEGUM.—Vide *Egg Plant.*

SORREL.—This is grown by sowing the seed broad-cast and thinning the plants to the distance of eight or ten inches from one another. It may be sown at the commencement of the rains.

SORREL PLANT. *Hibiscus Sabdariffa.*—An annual, native of the West Indies, but now cultivated in most Indian gardens.

The part of the plant made use of is not the fruit, but the thick succulent sepals which envelope it. There are two kinds, white and red, the former is less acid. The seeds are sown in May at a distance of four feet apart. It grows to the height of three or four feet, and bears a yellow flower with crimson eye.

SOUR SOP.—Vide *Anona Muricata.*

SPATHODEA UNCINATA. *Bignoniaceæ.*—This genus of plants are showy and handsome, the colour of the flowers being yellow, purple, and red; they are easily propagated by seed or cuttings, and require a good garden soil.

SPONDIAS MANGIFERA. *Spondiaceæ.* NAT. AMBARA.—The hog plum; a large tree with pinnate leaves; deciduous in the cold weather; they have a peculiar smell when bruised: the fruit is acid, and only used in curries.

SPONDIAS ACUMINATA. NAT. AMBUT.—A middle-sized elegant tree, with shining leaves; fruit, the size of a small egg.

SPONDIAS DULCIS.—The Otaheite apple, much cultivated in the Society Islands. Introduced into Bombay.

STACHYTARPHETA MUTABILIS. *Verbenaceæ.*—A shrubby plant with variegated scarlet flowers in terminal spikes; propagated by cuttings.

STACHYTARPHETA JAMAICENSIS.—Species. An annual, with blue flowers in terminal spikes; common.

STAPELIA BUFFONIA.—*Asclepiadaceæ.* NAT. KAR-ALUM.—The Toad-like Stapelia.

STAPELIA GRANDIFLORA and S. VARIEGATA.—These species are stemless plants with fœtid flowers, star-shaped, colour resembling a toad's back: the plants should not have much water or be exposed to the sun; easily propagated by seed or cuttings.

STAR APPLE.—Vide *Chrysophyllum Acuminatum.*

STERCULIA FŒTIDA. *Sterculiaceæ.* JUNGLY BADAM.—Poon tree; grows to a very large size, with digitate leaves; deciduous in the cold weather. Flowers in March and April, of a dull crimson colour, and of an offensive odour: the seeds are roasted and eaten.

STERCULIA GUTTATA. NAT. GOLDAR.—A large erect tree; leaves long petioled, villous underneath; flowers in simple terminal racemes, pubescent on both sides, outer and inner of a pale yellow colour, marked with purple spots; deciduous. Carpels the size of a large apple, three or more growing together, of a reddish colour; seeds size of a chesnut, roasted and eaten by the Natives.

STERCULIA COLORATA. NAT. BHAEE OR KARAKA.—A large tree with palmated five-lobed leaves; deciduous in the cold season; flowers in March and April; carpels of a bright red, somewhat resembling the broad pod of a pea opened with the peas adhering; the tree when covered with them has a strange appearance.

STERCULIA URENS. NAT. KAVALI.—A large tree; leaves round, cordate and five-lobed; deciduous in the cold weather; flowers in February and March, very small; the carpel is covered with rigid bristly hairs, which puncture like the mucuna pruriens. The bark of the trunk is white, and gives the tree a dead appearance.

STERCULIA VILLOSA.—A large tree; leaves palmated, five or seven-lobed.

STRAWBERRY.—Vide *Fragaria.*

STRYCHNOS NUX VOMICA. *Strychnia.* NAT. KOOCHLA.—This tree grows in the hilly parts of the Concans; the nuts are used for poisoning fish.

STRYCHNOS POTATORUM. CLEARING NUT. NAT. NIRMULLEE.—This is a middle sized tree; grows in various parts of the Deccan,—flowers in March and April, of a greenish yellow colour. The ripe seeds are used by the Natives for clearing water, by merely rubbing the inside of a vessel with them, then allowing the water to settle, when all its impurities fall to the bottom. As this seed can often be obtained when alum cannot, I mention this circumstance.

STRYCHNOS COLUBRINA. NAT. KOOCHILA-LUTA.—A scandent shrub with tendrils; fruit, the size of an orange. The Telingees esteem the root as an infallible remedy in the bite of the cobra snake.

SUGAR-CANE.—Vide *Saccharum officinarum.*

SWIETENIA FEBRIFUGA. *Cedrelaceæ.* NAT. ROHUN.—A large tree with pinnate leaves; flowers in April and May, in terminal panicles; capsule size of a small apple, five-celled and five-valved, opening from the apex; the bark is a powerful febrifuge, and an excellent substitute for Peruvian bark; grows in the jungles of Goozerat and the Deccan.

SWIETENIA TUBULARIS.—A magnificent tree with pinnate leaves, leaflets tomentose, capsule four or five-valved; seeds arranged in a horizontal position, ripen in January.

SYMPHOREMA INVOLUCRATA. *Verbenaceæ.*—A species of St. Peter's Wort, cultivated by seed or cuttings.

TABERNÆMONTANA CORONARIA. *Apocynaceæ.* NAT. TUGGAI.—A common shrub in gardens with dark shining leaves, flowers generally double, colour pure white, resembling wax, having a faint pleasant smell; propagated readily by cuttings.

T. DICHOTOMA. DOODEE-KA-JHAR.—A small tree, with fragrant white flowers, grows wild, the leaves are used by the Natives in a decoction for curing sores on cattle.

TALLOW TREE.—Vide *Sapium Sebiferum.*

TAMARINDUS INDICA. *Cæsalpinieæ.* NAT. UMLEE.—This tree is too well known to need any description here. The red tamarind, which is scarce, is the most valuable, the seed yields a fine clear oil.

TAMARIX INDICA. *Tamariscineæ.* NAT. JHAU.—A small tree or shrub; grows abundantly in the beds of many rivers, and affords great shelter for all sorts of game.

Tamarix Dioica.—A very graceful shrub, with numerous small rose-coloured flowers in terminal drooping spikes; common in the beds of rivers.

Tapioca. Mandioc or Cassava Plant.—A shrub about eight feet high, cultivated for food all over the tropical parts of the world. The roots are rasped, the pulp well bruised and well washed, after which it is placed on iron plates to be heated. The season for removing the roots is January, at the same time cuttings two to three feet long in rows of four feet apart are put down. It will thrive in any soil, sandy loam is the best.

"*Preparation.*—Twelve months after planting the roots are fit to be dug up. They must then be well washed, and put into a trough with water, in which they are allowed to remain six hours, when the outer bark will be easily removed by a pressure of the hand. The next process is to grate the roots, and then press out the milky juice, which is poured into a flat tub. This is now suffered to rest for eight hours, when all the flour will subside to the bottom. The water is then poured off, and the meal laid upon wicker-frames to dry in the sun for two or three hours. The flour is then placed upon hot plates, and well-stirred to prevent it burning.

"The heat will cause the amylaceous substance to coagulate into small irregular lumps of a transparent and gelatiniform colour. The Tapioca is then ready for use.

"This is the best mode of preparing Tapioca, as customary at the Mauritius."

Tecoma Capensis. *Bignoniaceæ.*—An elegant creeping plant with orange-coloured flowers, well adapted for covering a wall or running up a trellis work, grown from seed in common garden soil.

Tecoma Jasminoides.—This plant is cultivated in the same way as the former. The colour of the flowers pink.

Terminalia Catappa. *Combretaceæ.* Nat. Budam.—This tree grows commonly in all parts of the Deccan. It is raised easily from seed, and in a good light soil, well watered, will in two years be ten or more feet in height, and give blossom. It is rather a handsome tree, and, from its large leaf (which turns red previous to its falling off,) has a very striking appearance. The fruit is of the size of a coarse plum, and the kernel, contained within the shell, resembles the English Filbert in flavour. It is produced at table with the dessert.

TERMINALIA BELLERICA. NAT. BUHIRA.—A very large tree; leaves deciduous about the beginning of the hot season, when the flowers appear; fruit round, covered with a grey silky down; common in the Deccan. The flowers have an offensive scent.

TERMINALIA CHEBULA. NAT. HAR-HARA.—A large tree; flowers in May. The moochies use the fruit to form a black dye.

TERMINALIA NITIDA. NAT. YELLA.—A large tree with oblong fruit, from which an intoxicating liquor is made.

THEOBROMA CACAO. *Byttneriaceæ.* CHOCOLATE TREE.—This tree has been introduced into Travancore where it thrives well, the fruit is round but smaller than that produced in South America.

THEVETIA NERIIFOLIA. *Vide* EXILE TREE. YELLOW OLEANDER.—This plant is common in the gardens of the Deccan; grows to the height of ten or twelve feet, with long tapering leaves; it is grown from seed, and blossoms throughout the year.

THYMUS VULGARIS. *Lamiaceæ.* THYME. NAT. IPAR.—A delicate plant to rear. Is best performed by seed, but it may be increased by slips, and dividing the root. It requires a rich soil, and the space of six inches between each plant. Best grown in pots.

TOBACCO.—Vide *Nicotiana.*

TRAPA BISPINOSA. *Onagraceæ.*—The Singhara is a water plant, and is cultivated in many of the tanks. There are two kinds,— one with a hard thick shell, and the other with only a soft skin. The former, when ripe, has the appearance of a bullock's head, from two sharp spear-like processes growing from it. The fruit when boiled resembles a chesnut, and is sold in the bazaar. The seed is also made into a coarse flour, and cakes are made from it; the thin-shelled kind both fish and tortoise feed upon.

In some parts of the country, great care is taken to preserve the seed for planting the following season, which is done by treading it into the beds of tanks and such places. The fruit is fit to be eaten at or about the close of the rains.

TRIBULUS LANUGINOSUS. *Zygophyllaceæ.*—A common annual with yellow flowers and angular thorny fruit.

TRICHOSANTHES ANGUINA. *Cucurbitaceæ.* NAT. CHICHONDA.—The Snake Gourd. This vegetable is cultivated by the Natives grown on trellis work, the fruit long and spindle-shaped is used chiefly in curries, &c.

URANIA SPECIOSA. *Musaceæ.*—An elegant tree, a native of Madagascar: spreads its leaves out like an open fan, forming a semi-circular head. It has a short solid trunk, with leaves like a plantain; and in a border, or at the end of a walk, when growing, forms a perfect screen: its peculiar appearance strikes a person immediately when seen for the first time. It bears a small fruit like the drupe of a plantain, which is of a bluish colour. Rox. says—"The plant has the property of rendering water or milk, either hot or cold, mucilaginous, without altering the taste, colour, or smell, of the liquid in its former state." Butter-milk and water is often thickened with the juice of this plant, and then sold as an unadulterated article of the richest and best description. Is propagated by seed and suckers. Fifteen feet space should be allowed between each tree.

URTICA INTERRUPTA. *Urticaceæ.*—The Nettle, a large annual plant, grows during the rains. The whole plant is covered with stinging hairs, like the common nettle. It grows wild: there are several indigenous species.

UVARIA ODORATA. *Anonaceæ.* Sweet Scented Uvaria.—A small tree, flowers white, delightfully fragrant, introduced from China.

UVARIA TOMENTOSA.—A tree, the fruit of which is about the size of a Nutmeg; flowers of purple colour, and hang in clusters.

VATERIA INDICA. *Dipterocarpaceæ.* CAN. PYNEE.—A large tree, with fragrant flowers in terminal panicles; said to yield the resin called Copal.

VERBENA OFFICINALIS. *Verbenaceæ.*—A shrub common in most gardens, it is well known for its strong aromatic lemon scent. It grows from cuttings or layers, and no doubt would also from seed, as it blossoms freely.

VERBENA TRIPHYLLA. NAT. PEELA-BHUNGARA.—The Lemon-scented Verbena.

VISCUM. *Loranthaceæ.*—The Mistletoe is a well-known parasite, readily propagated by sticking the berries on thorn or apple-trees, after a little of the outer bark has been cut off, and tying a shade or mat over them, to protect them from the birds. Its branches are much sought after at Christmas to hang up in houses along with other evergreens.

VITEX TRIFOLIA. *Verbenaceæ.* NAT. NERGOONDA.—A common shrub with pretty blue flowers, generally to be met with growing in patches, in moist places appearing in April and May, but more or less throughout the year.

VITIS INDICA. *Ampelideæ.* NAT. ANDHOUKA.—A wild shrubby climbing plant, common throughout the Deccan.

VITIS VINIFERA. NAT. ANGOOR.—The Common Grape. This fruit is cultivated in the greatest perfection in all parts of the Deccan, and the finest flavoured are found in the gardens in the neighbourhood of Dowlatabad, about seven miles North-West of Aurungabad. The mode of culture is as follows:—the trees are reared from slips taken at the time of first cutting after the rains, and when ready to be removed are put about seven or eight feet apart. They are for the first twelve months trained on dry sticks; after that, a large straight branch of the pangrah, with a fork left at the top to support the vine, is placed about twelve inches from it; if put at a greater distance it is apt to give a bend to the vine which is hurtful. The vine cannot be too straight, and the length of the prop should be about five feet.

VOLKAMERIA FRAGRANS. *Verbenaceæ.* NAT. IRUN.—A large common shrub with ovate, cordate, dentate leaves; white fragrant flowers (in the cold weather) in terminal panicles.

Volkameria Inerme. Nat. Sunghoopie.—A scandent ramous shrub, pure white flowers, in blossom nearly throughout the year, hedges are made with it.

Walnut.—Vide *Aleurites Triloba*.

Wood Apple.—Vide *Feronia Elephantum*.

Wrightia Coccinea. *Apocynaceæ.*—A large tree; flowers externally green, internally deep orange-red, having something of the perfume of the pine-apple.

Wrightia Tinctoria. Nat. Kala Kooda.—A small tree with pale green soft leaves; deciduous in the cold weather. On being bruised, a kind of Indigo exudes from them. Flowers in March and April; white follicles in pairs, from twelve to eighteen inches long, which as they ripen the ends of each pair curiously join. The wood is used by turners and cabinet makers.

Xylophylla Angustifolia. *Euphorbiaceæ.*—This is a small shrub growing to the height of three feet, the colour of the flowers is yellow and red.

Zanthoxylon Rhetsa. *Rutaceæ.*—A large tree armed with sharp prickles; capsules have a strong aromatic taste; the seeds are used instead of pepper.

Zizyphus Xylopyra. *Rhamnaceæ*. Nat. Gotti.—A small thorny tree, fruit round, used by the moochies for blackening leather.

Zizyphus Vulgaris. The Jujuba. Nat. Bier.—This is a common wild fruit tree, and grows in almost every jungle. The fruit is astringent, but sometimes of a pleasant sub-acid flavour—eaten chiefly by the poorer classes, and wild animals. It is more especially cultivated by Mussulmans round their tombs. The fruit is oblong, containing a stone, and bears twice in the year, the best crop about January: after this is over, the tree is pruned, by cutting off nearly all the smaller branches. A second crop succeeds on the new wood in the rains, but, from being full of maggots, is not eatable: even in the cold weather very few of the fruit are free from this insect. The Natives pretend that they have a remedy, which prevents the fruit from being attacked, but I have never known it succeed. The flavour is somewhat that of a fresh apple, and the fruit when large and fine is by no means to be despised. I have succeeded best by budding from a good tree on a common stock raised from seed. It will bear well in two or three years, but requires care and watering at first. A fine gum-lac is produced from this tree; the cocoon of the wild silk-worm is often found attached to it.

# GARDENER'S CALENDAR
### FOR
## BOMBAY.

### MAY.

But little can be done in the garden beyond breaking up the soil and collecting manure: on light and poor soils, the dry mud from the bottoms of tanks may be spread with advantage. Dry leaves and grass may be collected and spread on the beds, and burnt a week or two before the rains set in, for manure.

### JUNE.

But little more can be done than in the previous month. After the first rain has fallen, the growth of weeds is so rapid that constant attention is required to prevent the soil being impoverished by them. The best way to get rid of weeds, and roots of grass, is by trenching the soil two spades depth, and turning it over previous to burning; or after the first fall of rain, when the ground has become well softened. The Doob or Hureealee grass roots (Agrostis Linearis) are the most troublesome.

At the commencement of this month you may put down beans, white and black; cucumber, gourds of sorts, Jerusalem artichoke, and sweet potato. It is generally best to wait until the first heavy burst of the monsoon is over, in July, before transplanting all sorts of Europe vegetables, from turnips to lettuce and radish, for heavy continual rain is usually detrimental to the young plants. The climbers may be sown. Turnips, onions, tomato in baskets, and also nole-cole, cabbage of sorts, vegetable marrow, parsley, lettuce, and radish, for early sallads, and most Native vegetables.

### JULY.

This is generally the month in which the rain is heaviest. The use of the plough when practicable will be of great assistance in checking the weeds. It is of importance to ascertain beforehand whether your seeds be good, by putting them into water before sowing; such as are light, and float on the surface, are to be rejected. Vegetable seeds may be sown in boxes and baskets, but not too thickly; they must be sheltered from the weather, and require great care. The young leaves must be examined every morning, and cleared of all insects, particularly of a small slug or caterpillar: the transplanting must be frequent, and the young plants allowed room. Cauliflower, broccoli, cabbage, celery, and beet, may be thus brought forward, till at the season (*August*) for planting out they may have attained four to six inches high—a sufficient size to be put each in a small basket, from which the plant can be removed without disturbing the root, and an early crop secured.

Put down beet, lettuce, cabbage, turnips, nole-cole, asparagus, beans of sorts, spinage, country gooseberry, and tomato. It being sometimes difficult to get beans to germinate readily, they should be steeped in soft water for twenty-four hours previous to sowing, which will effectually remove this difficulty.

## AUGUST.

Plants of the cabbage tribe that have been grown in boxes or baskets will now require great attention, both in daily picking off insects and protecting them from heavy rains. A species of caterpillar, dark in colour—some smooth and some hairy—have been found most destructive in this month. A solution of tobacco, lime, and wood-ashes, effectually destroys them. Continue to sow lettuce, plant out celery, country gooseberry, tomato, brinjals, cucumber, vegetable marrow, and parsley.

In sheltered spots and light soils, lettuces may be brought to a very fair state of perfection.

## SEPTEMBER.

After Cocoanut Day, which usually falls in the end of August, the heavy rains generally cease, and you have passing showers with occasional sunshine. After transplanting, care should be taken to shade the young plants during the day with the shade-baskets, and to preserve them from the wet by earthing up.

The ground should now be well manured and prepared for

the young plants, which may be set as soon as the rains hold off. This may be expected early in the month, but as the heat is great, care must be taken that they do not grow too luxuriantly: to prevent this, frequent transplantation is the most effectual check. For cauliflowers the soil can hardly be too rich: when the plant attains strength, dried fish pounded and applied to the roots will be found beneficial, water must be liberally supplied, and the beds frequently flooded. Trenches, eighteen inches deep and twelve or fifteen wide, should be dug for celery, and the young plants put in about eight inches apart. The soil should be rich but light, and in positions where the black earth prevails, a mixture of sand will be found advantageous. Towards the end of this month and the next, transplanting must continue.

Sow peas if in a favourable situation, artichoke, beans, carrots, spinach, cabbage, cauliflower, lettuce of sorts, and early sallading: attend to strawberry plants, and prune all your fruit trees moderately.

Strawberry runners, which, during the heavy period of the monsoon have been placed in baskets, should also be now planted out in beds. These, as well as the vegetables, will require shelter from the sun as they attain strength: additional manure must be applied, and they should be flooded at least every other day. When they begin to produce blossom, straw or hay should be placed under them: it keeps the ground moist, and preserves the fruit from being injured by the water. Towards the middle of the month open the roots of your rose bushes, and do not water them for ten or fifteen days; cut the plants to within a foot of the ground, and at the expiration of the above period cover the roots well with rich manure and fish, and water abundantly. Lettuce plants should now be put out, and the first crop of potatoes planted. The best plan seems to be to place the cuttings, which should each have at least two eyes, on the sides of ridges; these should be about a foot apart, leaving a trench between them for watering, which should not be more frequent than every third day; the root requires three months to bring it to perfection, but in six weeks young potatoes may be dug for daily use. The best soil is the red earth or sand. They will grow to equal size in the black, but the produce is generally inferior in flavour. Where water is abundant, Lucerne may be sown in beds of convenient size. Parsley, turnips, spinach, radish, &c., may be sown in beds, and the first crop of peas; these may be either planted in rows or circles; in the latter way they occupy more space, but are more ornamental, and the produce is more easily gathered. They should be sheltered from the north-westerly winds as much as possible, and well watered. In planting the peas in circles, the best plan is to put the seeds in two concentric circles about three or four inches apart, the outer circle being from three to five feet in diameter, according to the height to which the plant is expected to grow,—strong supporting sticks being placed in the centre. As it requires full two months to bring them to perfection, no seed should be put in after December.

The system to be adopted from this period throughout the cold season, is so similar to that pointed out in the Deccan Calendar, that it is unnecessary to add anything further now.

The season for trimming vines is the latter end of September and beginning of October, and the system of treatment pointed out for the Deccan has been successfully followed in Bombay: great care must be taken in smoking the vines every evening about sunset while in blossom, and till the fruit is well set. After the smoking, the stem should be gently tapped with a stick, to shake off a small insect which is most destructive to the blossom. With respect to directions for the culture of the different vegetables and trees enumerated there can be little added; and the instructions regarding budding, grafting, and enarching elsewhere mentioned cannot be too closely attended to.

Now plant out strawberry runners, also your cabbage plants: sow celery, beet, spinach, onions, salsify, and sweet herbs, also turnips and carrots. Towards the end of the month, trim your roses and get ground ready for potatoes. Peas may be put down safely.

## NOVEMBER.

Plant out all the cabbage species, York, drum-head, Savoy, red pickling Savoy, also cauliflower. Sow crops of peas, turnips, carrots, salsify, beet, spinach, radishes of sorts, onions, leeks, shallots, celery, lettuce, and endive.

## DECEMBER.

Plant out cauliflowers, cabbages, peas, beans, knolkhol, lettuce, salsify, scorzonera, radishes, onions, leeks, tomato, carrots, and turnips.

## JANUARY.

The same as last month, after which your vegetables will continue in perfection until the different crops are over; but radishes, sallads, and other such esculents, may be continued to be put down until the end of February.

# GARDENER'S CALENDAR
### FOR
## THE DECCAN.

## MAY.

This month is so hot and dry that very little can be expected from your garden, though much may be done in clearing away weeds, dead leaves, and plants, that are about and under your trees. Plough up your ground well for ensuing crops, and as the clods of earth become dry, have them knocked to pieces, and the weeds removed. Collect now your manure for after use.

Fruits in season are—mangoes, peaches, pumplemose, pomegranates, plantains, grapes, melons, oranges, pine-apples, a few strawberries, and apples.

VEGETABLES, EUROPEAN—are nearly out. The following are to be had, but not by any means in perfection:—cabbages, asparagus, artichokes, beet-root, carrots, red cabbages, lettuce, potatoes, and celery.

VEGETABLES, COUNTRY.—Cucumbers, brinjals, dill pussund, bulam-keira, kuckrie, peeaz root, tur cuckrie, umbarie ka bajee, chillies, and various others. Strawberries are not abundant, and can only be preserved with great care. In the part of the Deccan about Poona, pine-apples and grapes are brought into the market in abundance,—the latter chiefly grown at Sattara.

Asparagus beds may be opened and trimmed: if well watered, they produce fine heads towards the end of the month.

*Obs.*—Onions, if not taken up before, should now be stored, and when sorted, dried for a few hours in the sun: after that, remove them into baskets, or lay them on the ground in a dry place, secure from rats and other vermin.

Towards the latter end of this month, if the appearance of the season indicates an early setting in of the rains, then get ready boxes, or baskets, with light rich earth for sowing the following seeds: cabbage, knolkhol, celery, parsley, beet, lettuce, and sea-kale. If the seed is fresh and good, the cabbage will be up in five or six days. Great care is requisite both for watering and protecting the plants from birds, which at this season eat every sort of young green vegetable they can get at: covering the boxes or baskets with dry thorns is the most efficient method of protecting them. The boxes or baskets should for the first fortnight be kept under a shed or verandah, and from heavy rain.

In the garden you may, towards the latter end of the month, put down French beans, cucumbers, vegetable marrow, lettuce, peas, radishes, and various sorts of Native vegetables, also Jerusalem artichokes.

Rain generally falls towards the latter end of the month, and the average at Aurungabad may be calculated at two inches. The thermometer ranges in the shade from 90 to 100 deg. The nights are mostly cool, as the hot winds cease soon after sunset.

## JUNE.

In the early part of this month the rains generally commence, and much depends on the mildness of the season for the thrift of the garden. If your young plants, sown last month in boxes or baskets, are looking well, remove them into beds that have been a little raised and edged with tiles or bricks, so that the rain does not lodge: put in the plants about four inches apart; protect them still with thorns, and examine them as often daily as you possibly can. A small fly settles on them during the evening and deposits its eggs, which are hatched in a few hours, when a small caterpillar is produced, hardly perceptible at first to the naked eye: in the course of a few days it has arrived at maturity, during which time it had been feeding, if left unmolested, upon the tenderest leaves of the cabbage plants. The centre of the sugar-loaf cabbage they seem most fond of; knolkhol next. This small caterpillar has the power of protecting itself from dust or water by spinning a thread from one edge of the minute leaf in which it is hatched to the other, thereby drawing them together; when it feeds in security. I think that I have observed that they cast a skin once during this stage, and, like the silk-worm, cease to feed for a time: when removed, they again feed voraciously and become quite green. If you shake the leaf and detach one, he immediately emits from his mouth a fine thread, by which he suspends himself, at the same time that he is connected with the spot to which he can and does draw himself up again for food. About the fifth day he ceases to feed, when he sets to work and spins a cocoon of silk over itself; in a few hours, about twenty-four, it has assumed a chrysalis state, and in three days after becomes a most beautiful little brownish golden-coloured fly, which I have since observed on the table-shades of an evening. It seems to hop more than fly, or rather makes strong bounds of at least a foot. As I have found the male and female together on the leaves, no doubt the female soon lays her eggs and then disappears. These observations were made by me, being desirous to trace the insect through all the stages. When I found that it had formed its cocoon, I placed it in a covered wine-glass, and the little golden-winged fly was the result.

Fruits procurable are, mangoes, pumplemose, pines, melons—going out; plantains, pomegranates, a few oranges, and late peaches, if the rain has not been very heavy.

EUROPE VEGETABLES.—Beet-root, celery, asparagus, artichokes, and small salad.

COUNTRY VEGETABLES.—The same as last month.

*Obs.*—Sow peas, French beans, and other runners; parsley in beds, where it is to remain; also spinage, turnips, turnip-radishes, and Native vegetables. You will find the small caterpillar very destructive to your young plants: look them over continually, and scatter wood-ashes from the kitchen over them; although this is not an effectual method of destroying them, it is useful. Carrots for an early crop may be sown on ridges, also onions. Beet, endive, and lettuce for early salading. If you find towards the end of the month any young shoots round the old celery, have them carefully taken up and planted in rows: they will in the course of eight weeks make an excellent addition to your vegetables. Towards the end of the month cucumber plants and French beans should be well forward. If much rain has not fallen, keep them well irrigated by any means you possess. Potatoes for a first crop may be sown, but, except in *particular* situations I have seldom seen them thrive; for if there is too much rain, they run to stalk; and if too little, from the very great heat, they wither and dry. The potatoes produced are so small and few that it is almost labour thrown away. Weeds are now also very troublesome, and require to be removed.

The average of rain this month may be calculated at about four inches; the Thermometer in the shade from eighty-six to ninety-two degrees.

## JULY.

This month is excessively warm, and your plants will require much water if the rain has not fallen regularly, and also protection from the sun, though the cabbage plants should not have too much, and are better watered by the hand: be careful to earth up your peas and beans, which are now sufficiently forward to climb the sticks, and should be towards the latter end of the month in flower.

EUROPE VEGETABLES in season are—radishes, turnips, cabbage-sprouts, and knolkhol from old plants; lettuce and French-beans.

COUNTRY VEGETABLES.—Turnips, radishes, pumpkins, mathie ka bajee, coolfie, maut ka bajee, chooka, &c.

*Obs.*—Peas when about six inches high may be brought into blossom earlier, by having their tops nipped off about half an inch.

Fruit is now very scarce: plantains, jamoon, and a few oranges, to be had. Mangoes by the latter end of the month gone out. In Bombay, pines and pumplemose in abundance, also custard-apples and guavas. Sow carrots, pumpkins, vegetable marrow, artichokes, onions, peas, beans, turnip-radishes, &c., and all the Native greens enumerated in another part of the work. Be careful to smoke well your orange plants morning and evening, by burning damp litter under, to windward of those that are bearing, to protect them from a fly or gnat very destructive to the young fruit. Rain this month about nine inches. Thermometer from seventy-six to ninety degrees.

## AUGUST.

The weather still very hot during the whole of this month, but as there is generally much rain, all vegetables grow fast. Those now coming, and in season, are—

EUROPE VEGETABLES.—French-beans, peas,* cabbage-sprouts, spinage, celery, lettuce, turnips, and cucumbers.

NATIVE VEGETABLES of all sorts, gourds, chillies, radishes, &c.

FRUITS.—Oranges, custard-apples, limes, figs, jamoon, plantains, pumplemose, pine-apples, &c.

*Obs.*—Sow vegetable seeds as last month; plant out your cabbages from the nursery beds, also beet and celery. Trim and cut blackberries; put down cuttings of every description required, shading them from the sun during the day by mats or otherwise, and take care that rain is never allowed to lodge in the beds. Weed all your plants carefully earthing up such as require it; and during the mornings and evenings burn all the rubbish you can collect, as directed last month for the orange trees. Apples begin now to blossom. Towards the end of the month, prepare your strawberry beds for putting down the first stock of runners.

The average rain this month is from nine to twelve inches. The Thermometer as last.

## SEPTEMBER.

The weather is still warm and close, the same as last month. Native vegetables are now brought into the market in great abundance; and about Poona, some grapes, but green and only fit for tarts—these are from their second crop.

EUROPE VEGETABLES procurable are—knolkhol, peas, French-beans, white beet tops, spinage, radishes, lettuce, turnips, small

---

* Peas sown the latter end of this month, and during the next, do not bear so abundantly; the stalks get mildewed in the latter end of the rains.

carrots, Jerusalem artichokes, onions, asparagus, celery, parsley, and a few potatoes.

NATIVE VEGETABLES are—pumpkins, turnips, Native greens of all descriptions, sweet potatoes, Indian corn, brinjals, kurrala, keira, and numerous other sorts.

FRUITS.—Oranges, pumplemose, guavas, plantains, papaw, mulberries, figs, rose-apples, sweet and sour limes, cocoanuts, loquats, pomegranates, roselle, white and red hibiscus, and custard-apples.

*Obs.*—Now plant out your strawberries from the nursery, selecting the first runners from the old plant. Sow the following seeds in boxes or baskets, for your cold season crop, as they can be better looked after than in beds, using the same precaution for their preservation as recommended in May :—cauliflower, broccoli, cabbage, knolkhol, &c.

In the garden you may put down potatoes, asparagus, artichoke, cucumbers, salad of every description, onions, beet—white and red, peas, beans, and all other kinds of runners; scorzonera, leeks, cress, turnips, and carrots. Also plant out any of the above from the nursery, if ready, in beds, where they are to remain. The latter end of this month is a good time for budding trees, such as apple, peach, orange, &c.; also to prune your vines. Mulberry cuttings thrive remarkably well if put down.

Average of rain, five or six inches. Thermometer as last month, from seventy-five to ninety degrees.

## OCTOBER.

The weather continues hot during the early part of this month, but about the 20th a change is very perceptible, and the first crop of vegetables, or rain crop as it may be called, are now going out.

EUROPEAN VEGETABLES in season are—peas, radishes, love-apples, beet—red and white, vegetable marrow, and Jerusalem artichokes.

COUNTRY VEGETABLES.—Pumpkins of every description, also Native greens, carrots, irvia, brinjals, sweet potatoes, &c.

Fruits.— The same as last month.

*Obs.*—Put down vegetables as directed for last month. Sow kidney-beans, parsnips, carrots, peas, potatoes, and all vegetable seed for the cold season. Attend particularly to your vines, open apple trees, &c. This is the best month for planting out strawberries.

The rain varies very much during this month; seldom any quantity falls—from two to three inches, when the monsoon may be considered over. Thermometer until the 20th or 25th from seventy-five to eighty-four degrees.

## NOVEMBER.

Now the cold season has set in, and your garden should be well stocked with young plants. The Europe vegetables which would not come to perfection before, if planted now will thrive well; such as broad-windsor and kidney-beans, and parsnips.

Europe Vegetables in season, the same as last month.

Country Vegetables.—Almost every description enumerated in the list.

*Obs.*—Plant out your cabbages, cauliflower, broccoli, celery and beet.

Sow turnips—white and red, Cape carrots, and onions for stock.—Look to your artichoke plants; have them well earthed up: remove weeds well from strawberry beds, and put out plants for the latest crop. Cape gooseberry and roselle are now in abundance, and fit for preserves. Open your peach trees. Blackberries coming in. Towards the end of the month your apples and peaches are in blossom. Put down potatoes; earth up the Jerusalem artichokes; cover the globular kind with ashes all over, to protect them from flies, which do great damage. Rain seldom falls this month, though the clouds are heavy and threatening, generally end in a blight. The grape-vines suffer most—those that have not been cut and opened until late, particularly.

## DECEMBER.

In this delightful cool month your garden should be in the best and most promising condition, and the European vegetables well forward: and those now in season are—

Europe.—Savoy, sugar-loaf, and drum-head cabbages, (broccoli and cauliflower coming on); knolkhol, potatoes, beet-root, French-beans, peas, love-apples, Jerusalem artichokes, radishes, leeks, scorzonera, lettuce, carrots, asparagus, cucumber, water cress, &c.

Country Vegetables.—Lussun, coolfie, chooka ka bajee, brinjals, umbarie, soe, pollok, &c. Fruits as last; oranges particularly fine.

*Obs.*—A fine crop of potatoes may be expected if sown as late as the 30th. Plant out onions for store, sow beet for a late stock, and put out the last of cabbage and broccoli plants. Bud any trees you require, and graft by approach: plant out cuttings that may have taken root in the nursery, and attend to your grapes. The common sort are, near the latter end of the month, brought in for sale, and sell when in full season from twelve to thirty seers, or more, for the rupee. Sugar-cane is now ripening.

## JANUARY.

The weather continues fine, as last month, and your garden is now in its best condition: all vegetables, enumerated as coming forward last month, will be in perfection—the broad windsor beans and kidney in blossom; cauliflower in head.

Europe Vegetables.—Boor-cole, savoys, celery, beet, carrots, broccoli, broad beans towards the end of the month.

Country Vegetables.—Are all the vegetable greens, brinjals, bendee, yams, sweet potatoes, &c.

Fruits.—Apples, oranges, pumplemose, guavas, grapes, citrons, plantains, figs, blackberry, Cape gooseberry, papaw, and strawberries: roselle going out.

*Obs.*—Peas are now going out. Attend well to the earthing up of artichokes* and potatoes; if the former are much infested with flies, sprinkle them with tobacco water. During this month occasional showers of rain fall. Thermometer about fifty-seven degrees.

* But in some parts of the Deccan, at Hyderabad particularly, the artichokes sown in the latter end of May gave fruit in October, and crops continued until June in succession.

## FEBRUARY.

The weather now is becoming warmer, the dust annoying, the nights variable, and the garden shows great symptoms of change; vegetables droop during the day, and regular irrigation is required.

EUROPE VEGETABLES.—The same as last month. Artichokes, of the globular kind, are now coming in; broad beans continue.

COUNTRY VEGETABLES.—Of almost every description, yams and sweet potatoes, in abundance.

FRUITS.—Towards the latter end of the month, a few early peaches. Strawberries in abundance; the other fruits the same as last month.

*Obs.*—Now take up all your yams and Jerusalem artichokes for seed. Attend to the watering of fruit trees: put out any cabbage plants you may have remaining, as they will, during the hot winds in May, serve to be cut as sprouts.

The nights still continue cool, and sometimes the thermometer will be found as low as sixty-four degrees in the early part of the morning; during the warmest part of the day eighty-four degrees.

## MARCH.

Now begins every appearance of hot weather, though the nights are cool. Much is not now to be expected from the garden. Peas are quite out, so are broad beans; parsnips just coming in.

EUROPE VEGETABLES.—Cauliflower still continues good; cabbages getting hard and coarse. Knolkhol may be had; artichokes in abundance. Scorzenora, potatoes, endive, French-beans, leeks, celery, and lettuce, good.

NATIVE VEGETABLES.—Irvia, sweet potatoes, carrots, brinjals, and almost every other Native produce for the bazaar.

FRUITS.—Grapes in perfections; oranges getting scarce; guavas, peaches, apples, figs, plantains.

*Obs.*—By the latter end of this month, if the hot season is advanced, it will be necessary to take up your potatoes sown in December; but the longer you can keep them in the ground the better. During this month, showers continually fall. Be careful to attend to, and water your fruit trees. Porcupines and other animals are very destructive in gardens at night time, owing to all the grain in the fields being now gathered in. Thermometer from eighty-four to ninety degrees.

## APRIL.

The hot weather has now decidedly set in. The vegetables in the garden, half an hour after sunrise, look in a drooping state, and regular irrigation is necessary.

EUROPE VEGETABLES now procurable, but by no means in perfection, are—cabbages, artichokes, asparagus, celery, beet-root, carrots, tomatoes, salads.

NATIVE VEGETABLES are—cucumbers, dill-pussund, kuddoo, mathie, soe, pollok, kumruk, brinjal, gajur, &c.

FRUITS.—Grapes, peaches, strawberries, rose-apples, apples, oranges, pines, plantains, melons (mangoes just making their appearance towards the latter end of the month); besides many sorts of Native fruits.

*Obs.*—Very little can be done in the garden now, as it is useless putting out plants. Constant irrigation is necessary for all vegetables, and the more they are sheltered from the hot winds the better. Ground may be ploughed and got ready for the ensuing rains. Now lay out your garden walks, as the Mallies have not much to do. Asparagus beds will be in full perfection if attended to and looked after. The small kinds of tomatoes continue, and salad, if well sheltered by the shade of plantains, or other trees, may be preserved.

Rain occasionally falls this month. The Thermometer in the shade ninety-two degrees and upwards. No doing without tatties from the middle of the month.

# EUROPE VEGETABLES.

Anise. *Hind.* Sonf.—Sown in a light soil after the rains, and allowed to remain where sown, thinning out the weaker plants.

Artichoke.—Of the four species—only two are cultivated for use. They have large pinnatifid leaves, erect, and of about two or three feet long. From the centre arises a long stalk, which gives off branches, on the top of which is a large round head composed of numerous oval scales enclosing the florets sitting on the receptacle, commonly called the artichoke bottom, and which, with the fleshy part on the base of the scales, is the only part eaten.

The two sorts grown are, the French conical spine-leafed, and round Dutch globular-headed. The seed may be sown in June, and continued during the rains; the soil should be light and of a good loamy description; the seed sown at least six inches apart. When they are in four or six leaves, they may be transplanted in rows, and in open situations and good soil, three or four feet asunder. The ground should be of a light consistence and well manured. Let the trenches be about six inches deep, and at least from one to two feet broad: they will require occasional irrigation if the weather is dry, after having been well watered by the hand. When first removed, at the latter end of the rains, and the plants have arrived at almost their full size, a small black fly collects upon them in the greatest abundance, and destroys the whole of the leaves. This also happens to plants raised from seed sown in October, or at the close of the rains. When the plants, in January, February and March, have arrived at their full perfection, they may be propagated from slips that grow on the side of the old plants, which wither and dry as soon as the fruit is ripe and gone to seed. Care must be taken in removing both plants and shoots, that a sufficient quantity of earth is taken up with the roots, so that the spongioles are uninjured. When they appear to have taken root well, let the ground occasionally be loosened round them, and the stalks well earthed up. The best means of preserving the plants from being destroyed by the fly, is to cover the leaves well over with ashes from the kitchen, or to sprinkle them with tobacco water. The seed from Europe, the Cape, Persia, and Hindoostan, all grow well, but those which have succeeded best with me were from the upper provinces of Bengal : they were of the large globular kind, and from being acclimatised, I thought they did not suffer so much from the fly as others. More than one head should not be allowed on each stalk: pick all the others off. If a piece of stick is run through the stalk, a cross under each head, I think that it tends to enlarge it. The seed may be collected whenever ripe, which is mostly in May or June. The largest and finest heads do not always give the most seed—often the reverse. Young artichoke shoots if blanched may be eaten as salad.

ASPARAGUS.—The species are many, but only one is cultivated for use. The roots of the wild species, "Asparagus Sarmentosa," are made into a preserve and also candied by the Chinese. The method of first raising the plants from seed, is either by sowing broad-cast, in beds of six feet square, or in long beds of about two feet broad, where they are to remain. If sown in square beds, when the grass is about six or ten inches high, and begins to bear small flowers, it may then be transplanted, and must be carefully taken up with a sufficiency of earth attached to the roots, and planted in trenches at least six inches deep and eighteen broad. Between each trench should be a space of one foot or more. The plants may then be laid down in double rows in the trench prepared at six or eight inches asunder—perhaps a greater distance may be better. The roots must be carefully covered, and well watered. The beds cannot be of too rich and light a soil, and must be kept clear of weeds, and watered as occasion requires. When the asparagus is sufficiently strong to commence working the beds after the stalks have gone to seed, the watering should be discontinued, and the stalks allowed to dry and wither; then uncover carefully the roots, being cautious not injure the crowns, cut or twist off the stalks, and cover up the crowns again with rich manure about two inches high; then turn over upon it the spare ground that has been left between the trenches. Thus you will have in the middle of the rows a water-course, which will serve to irrigate the plants below. The watering must now be continued daily if necessary, which will cause the plants to send shoots up through the loose soil above them, and, if well managed, the grass will be white and fine. Before putting down your plants in trenches, plenty of good manure should be well dug into them, so as to form a rich soil for the roots to strike in. After the grass has been cut, and the shoots are getting thin, cease working the beds and let them go to seed, when they may be again worked. You will seldom get more than two crops in the year from the same beds, therefore you should have them in succession. I do not know of any animal, except rats, destructive to the roots: flooding with water is the only remedy.

BASIL. SWEET BORAGE.—Grows as a shrub, and is only used for seasonings with other sweet herbs.

Grows in all parts of India from seed, or slips, in any light soil. Is used chiefly for flavouring sherbet, &c.

BEANS, BROAD AND WINDSOR.—Should be sown in the cold weather, in drills, the same as peas, each bean at six inches apart; the rows sufficiently separated to admit a person to pass between them for picking, weeding, &c.

The best time in the Deccan for sowing is in November, and if the ground is light and well manured, there is no chance of failure. I would also recommend the seed to be changed every season. Rats and porcupines are very destructive to them.

BEANS, FRENCH—WHITE, BLACK AND YELLOW.—These beans are runners and dwarfs; they should be sown in rows about two feet apart, and you may commence sowing them at the close of the hot winds. The dwarf white are preferable at the early part of the season, as they bear sooner than the other sort, which require sticks at least six feet high, and strong, so that they may stand the rain and wind; you can continue to plant them until March with success. All that is necessary is not to put them too close, and to remove caterpillars that are found upon them during the months of July and August. These beans are very hardy, and grow well in almost any soil.

The Portuguese beans, or Chevaux de Frize, is cultivated like all other beans. Its pod has four-fringed angles, the edges jagged: they are dressed like French beans.

All the other sorts are grown in the same manner.

BEET-ROOT, RED AND WHITE.—Is grown from seed, and thrives best in a light grey soil. The seed may be sown in the latter end of May, and transplanted either in rows or beds. This crop will not produce such large roots as those sown later, but with care some roots fit for salad may be forthcoming in September; and I would advise the plants being grown on ridges during the rainy season. The leaves, when not too large, of both species, are used and eaten as spinage. The plants should be at least a foot apart, and in transplanting them, care must be taken to draw the root up unbroken, and the whole in which they are put should, with a dibble be made quite even, and the plant put in straight. They may be transplanted at any period of their growth, except when going to seed, which all the early sown is apt to do. Fresh seed, if procurable, is to be preferred, though I have no doubt if seed grown in the Deccan were sent to another part of the country it would thrive well. Beet-root is always the finest for not being transplanted. The soil cannot be too light, and should be of a rich old vegetable manure.

BOOR-COLE.—Grows to great perfection; the leaves are curled. The tops should be cut off when two feet high; the sprouts being the only part fit for use. It is cultivated in the same way as cabbages, and may be had all the year round.

BROCCOLI.—For culture, see Cauliflower.

CABBAGE.—I shall confine myself to two or three sorts—the drum-head, sugar loaf, and savoy, as all the others require similar care and attention. You may sow the seed in the latter end of May in boxes, or baskets, shaded at first from the sun, and kept continually moist. The advantage of sowing them thus early, is that the plants are strong by the time the rains set in, and the leaves do not offer to the small fly which settles upon them to lay its eggs, the nourishment necessary for the young caterpillar when hatched. The plants, when about three inches high, should be pricked out about two inches apart, into other boxes, and lightly covered over with dry thorns to prevent sparrows and other small birds from eating them. When large enough to be transplanted into nursery beds, use the same precaution with regard to thorns; and lastly, place them where they are to remain, in rows about eighteen inches apart, either on the top of the ridge, or in the hollow—the former method in the rains is to be preferred. The soil should be light and rich. In the cold season, the precaution of sowing the seed in boxes is unnecessary, as they grow very well in small beds sown broadcast, and watered at first by the hand, after which, when removed, they thrive extremely well. If the seed is sown as late as January, you may raise a stock of plants, which come but to a small size, and if kept in the beds and sheltered from hot winds may be tranplanted in the rains. They produce good sprouts for eating when other vegetables are scarce; as also the stalks of the old cabbages, of which, if towards the end of the rains the shoots be carefully stripped off, they may be planted, and a succession of cabbages be procured by this means. I have known this plan adopted for years: in fact, in my own garden, particularly the red cabbage I have cultivated in this way for many seasons.

*Obs.*—You cannot be too careful in examining your young plants twice or thrice a day in the early part of the season, and having all the caterpillars picked off or destroyed. Sugar-loaf cabbage and knolkhol are particularly invested with them. I found that sprinkling the young plants, after watering, with a little black pepper, caused the small green caterpillar to leave the plant immediately. Slugs and caterpillars have a great aversion to pounded turmeric.

CAPSICUM.[*] *Hind.* MIRCHEE.—This plant is so well known all over India has the large red pepper, that it is hardly necessary

---

[*] The Chinese produce the finest Capsicums I have ever met with.

to describe the method of culture, which merely consists in sowing the seed broad-cast, and when the plants are about six inches high, putting them either in rows or beds eighteen inches apart. The soil should be rich. They require watering, and being kept clear of weeds.

CARROTS. *Hind.* GAJUR.—This vegetable is so well known as to need little description. The two kinds in general use all over the Deccan or the red and yellow—(orange and lemon colour); they may be sown at the commencement of the rains, broad-cast, in beds of about six feet square, and should be thinned, leaving a space of six or eight inches at least between each root: this distance is sufficient for your first crop, but those that are sown later should have at least six inches space allowed between each root. If you wish to preserve your carrots until the commencement of the rains, in the months of March and April cut off the green tops, and let the roots remain in the ground; this checks their growth, and I have by this means had good carrots until the middle of July. I found the yellow Cape to answer the best for preserving; the seed was not sown until January. They bear transplanting well, and may be sown with advantage in drills. The soil should be light and good: care must be taken, the same as in moving beet not to break the root.

CARDOON.—This resembles the artichoke, but grows much higher. The tender stalks and leaves when blanched are used for soups and salads, and are cultivated in the same manner as the artichoke.

CAULIFLOWER.—The seed should not be sown until the latter end of August, as it does not always head well: it requires the same care as the cabbage, and should be planted in a similar manner. Removing the plants occasionally prevents their quick growth, and I think if the roots, when taken up, were divided into halves, or quarters, before being put into the ground, that it would facilitate its going to head. The soil in which I have seen the finest heads grown was of a greyish description, and the plants had little water given to them. In England the market gardeners seldom water cauliflowers, and once in four days is amply sufficient in the Deccan: no injury will accrue even if watered less frequently. The white broccoli is, I am sure, often taken for the cauliflower in this country, and I have seen heads large enough to be divided into two dishes, and then form a sufficiency to cover a dish in general use for vegetables. Broccoli, both red and white, should be cultivated in the same manner as cauliflower.

CELERY.—The seed may be put down at the commencement of the rains, and, like other plants at that season, is better for being first sown in boxes or baskets, for the convenience of being removed under shelter, if the weather is bad. When the plants are about two inches high, they may be pricked out into other boxes or baskets, two inches apart, where they remain for the first four or five weeks, and then removed into beds or rows: to the latter I give the preference at the early part of the season; after that put them into square beds of six feet, and about twelve inches apart. They then grow so close in the leaves that they protect each other's roots from the sun, and keep the beds moist, besides being very readily blanched, merely requiring a couple of half circular tiles to be put around the stem, tied with string or matting; then earth up the sides, which completes the business. In four or five days you may commence cutting, and by transplanting the off-shoots, have a succession the whole year round. The plant is very hardy, and goes to seed without any difficulty.

CELERIAC.—Another variety of celery, and is to be managed precisely in the same manner. It seldom grows above eight inches, and mostly spreads upon the ground. The root only of this is eaten: it forms rather a large white bulb, nearly the size of a parsnip, and has an exceedingly fine flavour. The root of the celeriac is used for stews rather than eaten raw.

CHIVES.—A species of shallot. Propagated either by slips or dividing the roots: this may be done at any season, but best after the rains. Nine or ten inches of space must be allowed between each bulb.

CRESS.— It is to be sown thick in very narrow drills, about one inch deep and few inches apart. It requires to be well watered, and is in season all the year round. It is only used for salading. The seed is sold in the bazaars, and known by the name of Hallim: it should be cut for use when two inches high.

CORIANDER. *Hind.* DHUNNIA, KOTMEER.—Grown in Native gardens.

CUCUMBER, GREEN AND WHITE.—This vegetable is grown from seed at all seasons. The plants should never be too close. It thrives in all parts of India, and grows with much or little water; and being a creeper, if allowed to climb over sticks, or trellis work, is more out of the way of jackals and porcupines, who are fond of the fruit. The natives grow them in their fields, in the cold season, amongst grain of various sorts, and in the sandy beds of rivers during the hot weather.

EGG-PLANT, or BRINJAL. *Hind.* BINEGUN.—Grown commonly in Native gardens; of this plant there are many varieties.

ENDIVE, CURLED AND FLAT-LEAVED.—The seed may be sown in the earliest part of the rains in beds or boxes; the plants when about two inches high should be pricked out into beds, or sown in drills. They should not be nearer than one foot, and when grown to their full size, must be tied up to bleach. If in the rains, it is requisite that the plants should be every now and then opened, to let off the water that may have collected inside the plants, otherwise they soon decay. The method adopted in England of placing a board on the plants for the purpose of bleaching, will not succeed here, as the white ants attack them, and the board stopping the free circulation of air, prevents their growth and causes decay immediately.

FENNEL.—Grows in great abundance in all parts of India. It is often confounded with aniseed. It may be sown in beds, or rows, and does not require any particular care. It has a perennial root, the stem dies as soon as it has given seed.

GARLIC. *Hind.* LUSSUN.—This is common all over India, and may be grown from seed or roots—the latter method is most in practice. One of the bulbs is broken and the cloves taken out and planted in beds about four inches apart: no particular care is required save watering and keeping clear of weeds. When the leaves dry and wither, then take up the roots and preserve in a safe place.

GINGER. *Hind.* ADRUCK.—Is a Native of India, and is sown at the commencement of the rains in beds of about six feet square, and in a rich cultivated soil. The planting consists in dividing part of the green root, which the Natives first soak in a mixture of cow-dung and water; it is then planted about two inches deep and about one foot apart; it requires a great deal of water, and to be kept clear of weeds. When the stalks dry, the ginger may be taken up, although it is sometimes left in the ground for a couple of years. It is better for remaining twelve months, and must be watered during the dry season.

HORSE RADISH.—I have never seen the plant in India: * a substitute is the scraped root of the moringa, which grows wild; and the pods, when young, are used as a vegetable, both boiled and in curries. The tree is easily propagated by seed, and only requires watering for a few months when first sown.

JERUSALEM ARTICHOKE.—This is a species of sunflower, and is, I believe, a Native of South America. It goes to seed generally in October and November, and may be raised from it, or by dividing the root, planting them the same as potatoes. They should be put down in January or February, and will require occasional watering until the rains, when they make their appearance. As the plants grow they must be well earthed up, and if very tall, may probably require to be supported with sticks. This vegetable is ripe as soon as the stalk withers, and the best method of preserving them is to let the roots remain in the ground,—that is, if the white ants and other insects do not attack them. If you are obliged to take them up, keep them in a safe place, in earth, watering them occasionally. To sow them, put either a half or a whole one, at a foot distance, in rows, the same as potatoes, and attend to them in like manner.

* I have since heard it is, and has been, grown in Candeish.

Leeks.—The seed may be sown at the commencement of the rains, or after, in beds, broad-cast. When about six inches high they require transplanting into large beds, or rows, at least one foot apart: they go to seed in the course of six months, and grow very well in all parts of the Deccan.

Lemon Grass, or Sweet Rush.—This is a fine aromatic grass, and flourishes well in any good soil. It is propagated by slips from the root, and only requires watering. It is used as an infusion.

Lettuce.—There are various sorts: the most esteemed are the cabbage, red and brown cos-lettuce. For early salading the seed may be sown at the commencement of the rains, although neither are in perfection until the cold season. They are mostly raised in small beds, and then transplanted into others at about one foot apart, or on ridges around other vegetables; they do not require any particular care. The ground should be light and rich, and when the plants are of a sufficient size they should be tied up; and this may be done with shreds of plantain-leaf or twine.

Love Apple, or Tomato.—The produce of South America—a genus of the same family as potatoes. There are two sorts, single and double: they may be sown immediately the rains commence, in beds; afterwards transplanted in rows, two feet apart, and trailed upon sticks of a strong description. If the soil is good, they will grow to seven or eight feet in height. The double, which are the finest, if sown in June, ripen in October. The lower branches should be pruned, and a succession of crops may be kept up until April. The small single tomato, with a slight protection from the dry winds, will continue until the rains.

Marjoram.—A native of India, and is very easily reared, in beds or pots, either by slips from the roots, or seed. It is used for flavouring ragouts, sauces, &c.

Melon.—The rock, green, and musk, (*Hind.* Khubbooza) are all sown in the Deccan at the same time,—generally in beds of rivers where the soil is light and sandy. They are very seldom sown in gardens. The seed is put down in November, three or four together, with as rich manure as can be procured. The plants must not be close together—a distance of from six to eight feet is generally allowed. They come in about March, and continue until the rains. In Bombay they are in season the same time, and a second crop is grown during the rains: this is not the case in the Deccan. The water melon (*Hind.* TURBOOZA) is also to be had at the same time, and grown in a similar manner. The seed should always be preserved from the finest and richest-flavoured fruit, and is better for being three or four years old. The green melon I think the finest flavoured, although many of the others are very good. I attribute the melons growing finer in the sandy beds of rivers to the temperature being more equal about the roots than it is in beds in the gardens—especially during the night.

MINT. *Hind.* PODEENA.—There are three sorts, Spear-mint, Pepper-mint and Penny Royal. The first is generally used for culinary purposes: it may be propagated by layers, or cuttings, or parting of the roots; it requires a moderate proportion of water. In the rains a small black caterpillar attacks the leaves, and will destroy the whole bed if not removed by hand, or flooding the beds, when the insect becomes detached from the leaves, and is easily destroyed.

MOREL.—This species of Fungus is found at the latter end of the rains, and generally dug of white ants' nests.

*Obs.*—The wholesome sorts of mushroom are readily distinguished by being of a pink or flesh colour in the gills, changing to a darker colour as they get older; they have also a peculiar sweet smell: and another criterion of their being edible is the outer skin pealing off easily.

MUSHROOM. *Hind.* KOODRUTTEE.—Commonly found all over the country during and after the rains.

MUSTARD. *Hind.* RAIE, EAST INDIA.—This is of two sorts, white and black: the former is generally cultivated for salad, and is grown in a similar manner to cress; the black mustard seed is used for sauces, pickles, and oil.

NASTURTIUM.—This is either grown from cuttings or seed, and merely requires to be protected from the hot winds to be in flower all the year round; it grows much better in beds than pots. The flower and leaf are eaten mixed with other salads, and the seeds when green are pickled.

KNOLKHOL—Is a plant of the cabbage species, and must be sown exactly in the same manner as that recommended for cabbage, broccoli, &c. It comes in early, and remains in season until April. If watered during the hot weather and taken care of, it will, when the rains commence, throw out sprouts, and form other knolkhol on the old stalk, which may either be used, or slipped off and planted: they will not be so fine as those raised from seed, yet are fit for use.

ONIONS. *Hind.* PEEAZ.—This vegetable is common all over India, and is sown broad-cast. When about six inches high it is pricked out into beds six fingers' breadth apart; they are sown at almost all seasons of the year, and go to seed without difficulty.

ORACHE, OR MOUNTAIN SPINAGE.—Of these there are several varieties, commonly known as red and green sag—the leaves are slightly acid; both sorts are boiled as spinage, but the red is most esteemed.

Propagated by seed—no particular soil required.

PARSLEY—Is cultivated from seed: may be sown in beds or rows, where it is to remain. The plants, when about two or three inches high, should be thinned, and a space of at least a foot left between each. It will, if watered and taken care of, continue all the year round. A good plan is occasionally to cut down the leaves to within four inches of the root, as it makes the parsley throw out young and fresh leaves. It bears transplanting well. Always give the preference to Europe seed. The common parsley of the country is very insipid. The roots of parsley are much used in French cookery.

PARSNIPS.—This vegetable is very difficult to rear, as it does not often happen that the seeds come up; they should be sown broad-cast in beds of a rich soil, and the plants, when of a sufficient size, carefully thinned, leaving a space of one foot between each plant, and removing all weeds. They may be transplanted, but it must be done with the same care as recommended for beet-root. The proper time for sowing the seed is the latter end of July, and they will come in during March and April. It goes to seed freely, but the roots grown from it were by no means fine the second year.

PEAS. *Hind.* BUTTANA.—The large white, green, and brown, are now the common pea in the Deccan; the latter sort are boiled and eaten often in the shell. Peas may be sown in the beginning of June, and continued at pleasure until February, when the weather becomes warm and the stalks dry up, although I have known peas to be had much later in the sheltered gardens in the city of Aurungabad. The method of sowing is very simple: they should not be too thin, or placed deeper in drills than two inches, and a space of three feet between the rows. I generally sow my first crop in double rows, with a space of a foot between: when they are ready to climb, I earth up both sides well, leaving room for the water to run in the middle. I then place good strong sticks in the centre of the rows, and on the outer side of each lay good old manure, after which little trouble is required. Keeping them free from weeds is of course essential, and if you wish to preserve the seed, take care and remove any of the plants that appear of a different kind when in blossom; also draw out all the thin and bad looking plants, to prevent the pollen impregnating the good, and if this seed be the produce of the rain crop, you will find that if sown again in the cold weather they will be much finer and last longer than the seeds of the former season. I was led to observe this from seeds that had fallen and grown up of themselves. If you sow for late crops, I recommend their being put down in single rows, and the lines from east to west: this enables the sun to act upon the whole, and tends to prevent mildew from damp on the stalks. In growing crops that you do not intend to stick, it is advisable to put brushwood on one side for them to creep over, and prevent much loss in seed from damp and otherwise.

POTATOES. *Hind.* ALOO.—This vegetable, now so generally cultivated all over the Deccan, was a few years ago confined to Surat and Seroor. The former was generally the finer, and could only be had during the cold season; but now the potatoes are grown all the year round: on the Neilgherry and Mahabuleshwar hills they are in abundance. They should be planted in rows about one foot apart, and five or six inches deep; the space between each row, if ground can be spared, eighteen inches, otherwise a foot. The ground should be light and loamy, and as little infested with white ants as possible. They can be sown at the commencement of the rains, but the spot should be selected where the water cannot lodge, but be easily let off; which may be done by keeping the end of the channel between the ridges open. At this season plant your potatoes on the top of the ridges, and do not water them unless necessary, as too much water makes them run to stalk. If your ground has not been well ploughed previous to the rains setting in, and all the weeds destroyed, the chance is your crop will fail; but should you have your ground ready, take your potatoes, intended for seed, and cut them into pieces, taking care that each slice has at least two eyes in it; and as you cut the slices, whilst fresh, dip the cut side of each into wood-ashes, and let them dry well, which takes place in a few hours: this I think prevents the white ants' attack. Sow each slice from nine to twelve inches apart, and place by the side of each a small clove of garlic, which in some measure tends to prevent the attack of a large grub very destructive to the plant.

*Obs.*—Here I think I am in error with respect to the grub, as the insects' eggs must be in the manure when added to the soil, and I have little doubt but that if the manure was previously worked up with the soil two or three times during the hot season, and exposed to the heat of the sun, the eggs would be destroyed: or the same purpose might be effected with a little fresh lime. I am sure the caterpillar does not travel to the plant.

The finest crops in the Deccan are sown from the beginning of October to the latter end of December, and this last crop will be found the most productive. Fine crops of potatoes have been grown where hemp has been first sown, and when about two feet high ploughed up into the ground. If, when your potatoes are about flowering, you perceive any of the stalks wither, carefully open the earth and look for a grub, which you may be certain is feeding upon it—of course destroy it. When these grubs are very numerous, it is necessary to search all the drooping plants daily : my idea is, that the larvæ is brought with the manure, and is the deposit of a beetle—however, nothing can be done but destroying them. I have heard recommended a bag with a small quantity of asafœtida to be placed in the water-course, as a remedy, when the plants were being irrigated. Here again is another insect which deposits its egg on the stalk of the plant. In the rains a small caterpillar eats its way into the stalk above the ground, when the plant immediately droops : the remedy is to remove the whole. Be careful at all seasons to keep the stalks well earthed up, and let the potatoes have a moderate supply of water—of course the season must be your guide. I, one year, at Kunhur, raised a very fine crop of potatoes during the rains, by sowing them on ridges, and only watered them at first in consequence of want of rain : they were sown in the beginning of July, and a few taken up in September (the latter end). Some of the potatoes weighed from five to seven ounces, and were equal to any I have seen grown on the hills.

In the latter end of August, by way of experiment, I tore off shoots from the lower end of the stalks, when they were abundant, and planted them in rows, the same distance as for seed ; and in November, on taking them up, was gratified by finding four or five large potatoes produced by each stalk, the size of a duck egg. This plan I strongly recommend to those persons who may not be able to get fresh seed after the rains. I did not find that the rows of potatoes from which the slips were taken produced fewer potatoes in consequence, as I weighed the whole and kept a memorandum in my journal.

PUMPKIN. *Hind.* KUDDOO—RED AND WHITE.—This vegetable grows in great abundance in all parts of the Deccan. It is much esteemed both by Europeans and Natives. It is generally sown at the commencement of the rains, and requires no particular care; the soil should be light and good. When young, about the size of a goose egg, if cut and boiled, it will be found to resemble the artichoke-bottom dressed in the same way.

PURSLANE. PORTULACA SATIVA AND OLERACEA. *Hind.* CHOOLEE.— Round stem, fleshy leaves, and slightly acid. It is used as an ingredient in salads. It is reared by seeds sown at the commencement of the rains, and will thrive in any soil.

RADISH. *Hind.* MOOLEE.—This vegetable may be sown at the commencement of the rains, either in beds broad-cast, or on ridges of beds where other vegetables have been planted. I prefer the ridges in the rainy season, as I think they grow better. You may continue to sow them until February. The turnip-radishes are of various colours—white, red, spanish black, and purple: also long, white, red and purple. The seed should be trodden in, or beaten down, and then a good watering given to them. When about three inches high, they must be carefully thinned, leaving at least a space of five fingers' breadth between each plant. They take from three to five weeks to come to perfection, and require a good share of watering. The seed pods are often used for pickles when green.

ROSEMARY.—This plant is an evergreen, and highly aromatic, and grown precisely the same as lavender, or oyster plant.

SAGE.—A perennial, native of South of Europe; it grows in all the gardens, and is propagated by seeds, layers, and slips, without any difficulty. It is used for seasoning.

SCORZONERA AND SALSAFY.*—This is a long milky-juiced root. Grows without any difficulty after the rains. It is an annual from the South of Europe. It should be sown either in beds, broad-cast, or planted out in rows at a distance of a foot apart. The root when boiled and dressed is rather a delicate vegetable. It comes to perfection in three or four months.

SHALLOT. *Hind.* GUNDHUND.—Propagated in the same way as the chive.

* SALSAFY.—This is the black scorzonera, and requires the same treatment.

SORREL.—This is grown by sowing the seed broad-cast and thinning the plants to the distance of eight or ten inches from one another. It may be sown at the commencement of the rains.

SPINAGE.—The produce of what country unknown. It may be sown in the rains, but it succeeds best in the cold season: it should be sown in lines a foot apart, or in beds, broad-cast, lightly covered over. It requires a moderate share of irrigation. The Native vegetable, called seo pollok, when boiled and dressed, very much resembles it.

SPINAGE, NEW ZEALAND.—Is a hardy annual, with fleshy leaves and numerous branches. As a spinage it is as valuable as the Orache. If watered, grows freely, and produces leaves in the hottest weather.

THYME. THYMUS VULGARIS. *Hind.* EEPAR.—Very delicate plant to rear. Is best performed by seed, but it may be increased by slips, and dividing the root. It requires a rich soil, and the space of six inches between each plant. Best grown in pots.

TURNIPS, ANNUAL.—The produce of Britain. They are cultivated in all parts of the Deccan at the commencement of the rains and the cold weather. They continue until the latter end of February, and go to seed easily. The soil should be rich and light, and they may be sown broad-cast, and then transplanted, either in rows or ridges, and a space of at least six fingers' breadth allowed between each. In the rains a small caterpillar is bred on the leaves, which, if not removed, will destroy the whole. The sorts are white, and red; one species grows above the ground.

VEGETABLE MARROW, OR SQUASH. *Hind.* SUPPARA ROOMRO.—This is a very delicate vegetable of the Gourd species. The crooked-necked, when about six inches long, is well flavoured, but soon gets hard and stringy. The pear-shaped is the best of any, but must be dressed when young.

Propagation only by seed, and the plants should never be removed, but remain where sown, only thinning the weakly ones.

The soil should be a rich loam, the same as for cucumbers. Train the plant on sticks. It is often necessary to fertilize the female blossoms, by approaching the anthers of the male flower when charged with pollen.

WATER CRESS.—A native of Great Britain. Is generally raised from slips. It thrives best in running streams, and is to be had all the year round. It is grown from seed in beds near a water-course, and the supply may be kept up for any length of time. A small black caterpillar is very destructive to it: the only remedy is flooding the plants for a short time.

# GARDENER'S CALENDAR
### FOR
## MADRAS AND BANGALORE.

## JANUARY.
### MADRAS.
*Mean temperature, 75·6.—Average fall of rain, 1·29 inches.*

The season is too far advanced to sow the generality of vegetables with much prospect of success; but turnips, carrots, love-apples, vegetable-marrow, lettuce, endive, radish, mustard and cress, spinage, and Nepaul spinage, may be sown during all this month; also successive crops of cabbage and knolkhol every fortnight. Turnips are said to succeed best when placed in rows; they should be thinned to a distance of six inches from each other. Carrots rarely succeed well when planted at this season: they should be thinned, but not transplanted, except when required for seed. Love-apples, when two or three inches high, should be planted out in beds at five inches apart: afterwards transplanted in rows two feet from each other with a frame-work to run upon. Vegetable-marrow should be sown in rich light soil: earth up the stems as they increase, and peg down the leading branches at a joint. Lettuce and endive should be planted in boxes, and transplanted at one foot apart from each other; they may also be sown in beds, and thinned to the proper distance: a few days before use they should be blanched. Radish, mustard, and cress, may be sown every week or ten days; the two last throughout the year. Spinage, to be sown in beds, and thinned until the plants are one foot apart. Nepaul spinage should be planted in rows, with trellis work to run over. This vegetable continues to flower and bring forth fresh leaves throughout the year, and requires no care. Cabbage and knolkhol should be planted in boxes, and transplanted into beds about three or four inches apart in three weeks or a month. They may be transplanted a second or third time, especially the latter. When transplanted for the last time, they should be put in well manured trenches, at two feet from each other. Horse manure and ground bones are strongly recommended for all the cabbage tribe. With care, cabbage and knolkhol may be procured during every month in the year.

Cape, or English seed potatoes may be planted during the first week of this month; and, if the season prove cool, they may be expected to arrive at considerable perfection. The early part of December is a more favourable time for planting potatoes; but it is hardly possible to procure fresh seed-potatoes from England before the beginning of January.

In this month the following vegetables and fruits are sometimes procurable in the market, in small quantities and at high prices,—carrots, turnips, cabbage, knolkhol, beet-root, salad, negro-salad, Bombay and country onions, Surat onions, beans, country beans, double beans, Vellore beans, French beans, white beans, Goa beans, and peas, (the last always dear, and seldom good,) pumplemose, Manilla and camala orange, chota orange, country orange, pomegranate, guavas, apples, limes, jack fruit, figs, red plantain, yellow plantain, thurmerten fruit, bilimbi, and occasionally mangoes.

### BANGALORE.
*Mean of the thermometer, 70.—Quantity of rain measured, none.*

In this month, most of the culinary vegetables are in great perfection. Grapes, apples, pine-apples, and also a few strawberries and peaches, are in season. Such apple trees as have finished bearing may be pruned, although it would be better to delay it until the ensuing month. Sow seeds of such vegetables as peas, radish, spinage, &c., that do not require more than three months to come to perfection.

## FEBRUARY.
### MADRAS.
*Mean temperature, 77·7.—Average fall of rain, 0·04 inches.*

The remarks on last month apply generally to this; but there is less chance of success in rearing vegetables, as they seldom acquire much strength before the hot winds set in. Turnips and carrots rarely succeed; but radish, mustard and cress, lettuce, endive spinage, and the cabbage tribe, should all be planted in this month, and throughout the year.

All the fruits, vegetables, and flowers, mentioned as procurable in the market in January, may be had in greater perfection, and cheaper, during this month.

In the beginning of the month peas are plentiful; and with care the following may be obtained of good quality :—Jerusalem artichokes, asparagus, duffin beans, French beans, scarlet runners, beet-root, broccoli, cabbage, carrots, cauliflowers, celery (in great perfection,) endive, lettuce, knolkhol, onions, parsnips, spinage, turnips, and yams; also the following fruits,—custard apples, Brazil gooseberries, guavas, lemons, mangoes, mulberries, pumplemose, raspberries, sapadilloes, tomatos, and occasionally apples.

### BANGALORE.
*Mean temperature, 74½.—No rain.*

In this month, peaches, grapes, and apples are in great abundance, strawberries are getting plentiful. Sow Portulaca and Gold Feather, graft peaches and apples, and prune the latter. Beet and celery are in perfection.

## MARCH.
### MADRAS.
*Mean temperature, 80·8.—Average fall of rain, 0·70 inches.*

Few vegetables come to any perfection that are sown in this month, but it is desirable to sow successive crops of cabbage and knolkhol, which may be planted in beds that are partly protected from the sun, and transplanted into rows as required. With care, salad may be grown in this month, and generally throughout the year.

In the market, brinjals, carrots, and turnips, may be procured in considerable quantities, and pretty good. Turnips are generally very stringy towards the end of March. Country radish, and all kinds of country greens, may be had in large quantities; but no fruits can be obtained in the market except the red and white plantain, which are always in season.

## BANGALORE.

*Mean temperature, 80.—Quantity of rain measured, 2¼ inches.*

During this month, the roots of apple trees should be opened by those who approve of that system and very strong manure should be applied. Strawberries, grapes and peaches, are still in season. Vine trees should be dug about and manured, the high winds and hot air of this month begin to tell on gardens, though still many very gay flowers are out. Stocks, lark spur Lobelia, Gazania, Verbena and Phlox are in full blaze of flower.

## APRIL.
### MADRAS.

*Mean temperature, 80·37.—Average fall of rain, 0·40 inches.*

The remarks on March apply equally to this month; but as the hot season advances, the chances of success in rearing most kinds of vegetables diminish. Melons and cucumbers should be sown during this month. Sow melons in rich light soil, giving the plants plenty of room to run. When they have made four leaves stop them by pinching off the leading bud; they will then produce two lateral shoots, which stop in a similar manner: and so continue to treat each new formed shoot, stopping it at the second or third joint. When the plants begin to show fruit, stop the fruiting branches two joints before the fruit. Cover the ground with leaves or straw, to keep the roots cool, and to prevent the fruit from becoming spotted.

In this month yellow and red plantains, pine-apples, grapes, pumplemoses, chota and camala oranges, are procurable in the market, carrots, turnips, beans, and cabbages, are reduced in quantity, and their prices are considerable. Brinjals, radishes, water pumkins, pavekah, peerkengah, and greens, are to be had in abundance.

### BANGALORE.

*Mean temperature 80¼.—Quantity of rain measured, 3¼ inches.*

Pot off Gladioli bulbs, Achimenes, Gloxinia, Gesnera, Caladium, remove to sheltered places, Gold Feather and Stackys edgings, dig up all beds, sow Zinnias and Canna.

## MAY.
### MADRAS.
*Mean temperature, 86·8.—Average fall of rain, 0·77 inches.*

Melons, cucumbers, love-apples, and Nepaul spinage, may be sown during this month; also successive crops of the cabbage tribe, and mustard and cress. Mangoes, oranges, pine-apples, pumplemoses, red and yellow plantains, and grapes, are supplied abundantly. Brinjals, greens, peerkengah, drumstick or moorungakaw; and in flowers, all sorts of mallgay flowers are to be had plentifully in the market.

### BANGALORE.
*Mean temperature, 81.—Quantity of rain measured, 3 inches.*

Sow vegetable marrows, pot off more Gladioli and Achimenes, plant Dahlia roots, after the 20th sow a first supply of Asters, Balsams, Amaranthus, Convolvoli, Verbena, Petunias, prepare and manure grass land.

## JUNE.
### MADRAS.
*Mean temperature, 88.—Average fall of rain, 1·46 inches.*

If the season is at all favourable, this is a very desirable time to sow the first crop of celery, beet-root, and asparagus, in boxes, for transplanting towards the latter end of August or beginning of September.

Cabbage seed may be sown in boxes in all this month. If the weather be favourable for transplanting, they should be put out in beds in the following month, and finally transplanted in August. In ordinary seasons good cabbage may be procured in this manner during the whole of October, November and December, by which time peas and other vegetables become abundant. If the weather should continue very hot during September, without showers, the plant should be kept in the boxes until the end of September or beginning of October.

As it is desirable to get strong celery plants before the monsoon, fresh seed should be sown every fortnight from the middle of June until the end of October. Beet also should be sown in successive crops, and transplanted once or twice. This vegetable is not likely to be injured by the heavy rains of the monsoon. Asparagus seed should be sown in boxes towards the latter end of the month, and transplanted in November, in rows two feet apart, and the plants one foot from each other. The soil should be mixed with a large portion of rotten horse manure: it is scarcely possible to make the ground too rich for asparagus. Fresh asparagus seed should be sown whenever procurable, and especially between the end of June and the beginning of December.

In this month mangoes, oranges, pine-apples, pumplemoses, plantains, pomegranates, cucumbers, melons, green melons, and limes, are abundantly supplied, at low prices, in the market. Carrots, turnips, cabbage, and other European vegetables, are scarce and dear; but pavekah, podalongah, greens, and brinjals, are procurable in small quantities.

The following fruits and vegetables are also to be had in this month:—custard apples, sapadilloes, lemons, mangosteens, parsnips, salad, and vegetable-marrow.

### BANGALORE.

*Mean temperature, 76.—Quantity of rain measured, 4 inches.*

Sow Nasturtiums, more Asters, Geraniums, Lobelia, Ramosa. Mignonette, Salvia, Balsams, Cocks-combs, Phlox, Datura—manure and prune rose trees, plant out Altenanthera, Gold Feather, Stackys, sow peas, beans, celery, knolkhol, carrots, lettuce, plant a small crop of potatoes.

## JULY.
### MADRAS.

*Mean temperature, 85·7.—Average fall of rain, 3·73 inches.*

In this month, it is desirable to sow celery, beet, knolkhol, cabbage, cauliflower, broccoli, asparagus, endive, lettuce, carrots, and turnips.

CELERY.—Sow in boxes in this and the two following months. Remove to beds when about three inches high, and into trenches, as required, after being a month in the beds. The trenches should be two and a half feet deep, filled up with a foot of light soil and stable manure, and afterwards gradually, as the plant grows, with light soil, till within about six inches of the top. Water for the first two months with hand, after which they may be occasionally flooded.

*Another way.*—Having sown and transplanted as above, remove into trenches four feet apart, and about eighteen inches deep, nearly filled with horse manure and rich earth. As the plant grows, bank up into ridges, with light soil. By this method the root of the plant, and not the stem, is watered when flooded.

KNOLKHOL, CABBAGE, CAULIFLOWER, AND BROCCOLI.—Sow in boxes during this and five following months. Remove in beds when two inches high, and transplant the cabbage and knolkhol twice, and cauliflower and broccoli at least three times, allowing the growth of a couple of new leaves between each planting.

ASPARAGUS.—Sow in beds in July, and remove the plants in November into raised beds of one or two rows. When the berries become red, cut the plants two inches above the ground and dress the tops, when they will be ready to cut in ten days. By dressing the beds in succession, asparagus may be produced for the table all the year. Stable manure is the best, and the plant should invariably be watered by the hand, and never flooded except in the hot wind season. Plants if taken care of will produce for eight or ten years; they should however be wintered (roots cleared of the earth and exposed for some days,) and the ground dressed, every second year.

LETTUCE AND ENDIVE.—Sow in boxes and pots surrounded with water till the plants appear, otherwise the small red ant will destroy them: plant out as required, and tie up a few days before you cut for use. Black Town, or St. Thomé manure is the best.

CARROTS.—Sow in a light deep sandy soil.

TURNIPS.—Sow in a rich soil well manured.

PEAS.—Should the fall of rain be considerable throughout

June, and in the early part of this month, a few peas may be sown once a fortnight until the monsoon, but the plants die so soon after they begin to pod, even in the most favourable seasons, that the produce is generally less in quantity than the seed sown.

In the market, all European vegetables are scarce and dear this month. Brinjals, greens, vendakaw, and other Native vegetables, are supplied in small quantities. Mangoes and pine-apples are getting out of season. Plantains, cucumbers, and melons, are plentiful.

### BANGALORE.

*Mean temperature, 75.—Quantity of rain measured, 4 inches.*

Sow second supply of flower seeds as in June, layer Heliotrope and roses, bud roses, strike cuttings of foliage plants, sow Dahlia seed. Balsams are in full flower.

## AUGUST.
### MADRAS.

*Mean temperature 84·6.—Average fall of rain, 4·76 inches.*

Successive crops of all the vegetables sown in July should be planted this month, more especially celery and beet, which should be fit to transplant a second time before the monsoon. These two vegetables are less likely to suffer by excessive rain than most others. Artichokes should be sown in beds during this month, three inches between each seed, so as to allow the removal of the plants in November without disturbing the roots. To propagate by suckers, take off the suckers, and prick them out six inches apart; and when they become well rooted, transplant into deep rich soil, setting them two feet apart. If large, suckers may be planted at once where they are intended to remain.

To prevent artichokes running to leaf, and producing small heads, when the plants are from ten to fifteen inches high cut them off close to the ground, and cover them over with light dry old manure; when they have advanced a few inches repeat the operation. If the young plants are tied up for a few days before being cut off, they will become blanched, and may be eaten as salad.

French beans and scarlet runners may be sown during this month, and until February. They should be planted in rows two feet apart, north and south, and be well supported with sticks, or with an arched bamboo trellis, which is very ornamental.

European vegetables continue scarce and dear. Brinjals, greens and other Native vegetables, are to be had. Mangoes, pineapples, and oranges, are very scarce. Plantains continue in abundance.

## BANGALORE.

*Mean temperature, 74.—Quantity of rain measured, 5⅜ inches.*

Asters will be ready to plant out early in the month. Sow cauliflower. Oranges, loquats and alligator pears, in season. Insects are excessively numerous and destructive. The orange tribe should be budded and inarched, and propagated by gooties. Plant beds with early strawberries. Still sow a few vegetable and flower seeds. Continue grafting mangoes. Transplant cotton. Propagate carnations and pinks by layers. Begin collecting seeds of early flowering annuals. Dahlias are in perfection.

# SEPTEMBER.

## MADRAS.

*Mean temperature, 83·7.—Average fall of rain, 5·30 inches.*

Continue to sow all the vegetables mentioned for August. Transplant cabbage, cauliflower, broccoli, beet, celery, endive, and lettuce. Two or three crops of peas may be sown during this month, if the weather is favourable, but not with much prospect of success. The seed peas that answer best in Madras are those grown at Bangalore.

Peas should be planted in well raised beds, in double rows, about two feet apart. They should be watered by hand for the first fortnight, and afterwards flooded. Peas require no manure, but should be planted in good soil.

### BANGALORE.

*Mean temperature, 75.—Quantity of rain measured, 8½ inches.*

Asters, Phlox, Nasturtiums, Cocks-combs, Mignonette are in full bloom. Zinnias and Balsams over, the gardens generally suffer from the heavy rains prevalent at night. All delicate seedlings should be under cover at night during this and the following month. Sow beet, cabbage, knolkhol, brinjals, transplant cauliflowers and early cabbages and knolkhol.

## OCTOBER.
### MADRAS.

*Mean temperature, 82·0.—Average fall of rain, 11·12 inches.*

The remarks on last month apply equally to this. Continue to sow all kinds of vegetable seeds in boxes; transplant from the boxes into beds, and immediately after the first heavy fall of rain remove into rows and trenches,—more particularly celery, beet, cabbage, knolkhol, cauliflower, and broccoli. Care should be taken in finally transplanting all the cabbage tribe, to provide against heavy falls of rain, by making trenches to carry off the water. Crops of peas should be sown every week or ten days from the beginning of this month until the 10th of December; peas sown after that time seldom pod.

Onions and leeks should be sown during this month in light rich earth, carefully covering the seed. When leeks are a few inches high, plant them in drills, eighteen inches apart, and nine inches plant from plant. As they increase in size, draw up the earth to their stems, in order to blanch them: leeks are much improved by blanching.

Sow parsnips in rich deep soil. Trench the ground two feet deep; sow the seeds in drills one foot apart, and thin the plants so as to leaf eight inches from each other.

But few fruits, vegetables, or flowers, are procurable in the market this month; but cabbages, carrots, and spinage, may be produced from your own garden with ordinary attention.

### BANGALORE.

*Mean temperature, 74.—Quantity of rain measured, 4 inches.*

Plant out cauliflowers, cabbages, brinjals, sow more lettuce and beet-root and dwarf cabbage, Mignonette, Phlox, Japan Pinks, Nasturtiums, Lark-spur, Pansies, Stocks. Winter Gladioli, Achimenes, Caladiums, Gloxinia, Dahlia, layer Verbenas for beds, plant Potatoes.

## NOVEMBER.
### MADRAS.
*Mean temperature, 78·9.—Average fall of rain, 14·13 inches.*

This is the month for activity in the vegetable gardens, as but few things arrive at much perfection which are not planted before the end of this month. The principal crops of peas should be sown during the first week, and continued every three days during the month; also French beans, scarlet runners, broad beans, and Windsor beans: the two last have rarely succeeded in Madras. Sow beet, knolkhol, cabbage, broccoli, and cauliflower, in boxes: transplant from boxes into beds, and remove from beds into rows. Transplant celery and remove into trenches. Plant out artichokes and asparagus. Broccoli and cauliflower seed planted on the 25th of this month, and transplanted on the 20th December, in a sandy soil, with a small quantity of horse dung soil with common manure, produced fine heads on the 18th of February. They were watered by hand for the first fortnight, and afterwards flooded in the usual way.

Potatoes should be sown towards the end of this month. They should be planted in light red soil in which no horse dung is mixed. The potatoes should be cut according to the number of eyes, taking care that each piece is of sufficient size. When planted, not more than one inch or one and a half inches of soil should be placed over it; and it should not be watered oftener than once in four days, even during the hottest weather. As it grows up, the soil should be banked up to the stalk. Great care should be taken not to give too much water, and not to put too much soil upon the potato when first planted.

It has lately been recommended to plant potatoes whole instead of cutting them as formerly: it is also said that the produce is much increased by taking off the flowers as they form; but potatoes flower so seldom in Madras, that it is hardly possible to offer a practical opinion on the subject.

### BANGALORE.

*Mean temperature 72.—Quantity of rain measured, 2¼ inches.*

All English annuals may be put out in the beds. Geraniums will do in the borders also, the white grub being no longer to be feared, cauliflowers and cabbages will be near heading.

## DECEMBER.

### MADRAS.

*Mean temperature, 76·4.—Average fall of rain, 4·61 inches.*

In the beginning of the month sow French beans, scarlet runners, broad and Windsor beans. Peas sown in this month rarely pod, although they grow luxuriantly. Plant out celery from boxes to beds, and remove from beds to trenches. Sow cabbages and knolkhols, and transplant as above. Vegetable-marrow may be sown in the early part of this month in light rich soil. Earth up the stems of the plants as they increase in growth, and peg the leading branches down at a joint, and they will strike root.

Potatoes may be planted until the end of this month; but those sown during the first fortnight are most likely to succeed. Seed potatoes produced from England or the Cape, are greatly to be preferred to those grown in this country. When potatoes are planted whole, the produce is finer than when they are divided into two or three pieces; but the same number of potatoes yield a larger crop by the latter than by the former method. Cape potatoes planted on the 18th of December made their appearance on the 30th of that month, and were ripe on the 16th of March. Potatoes should be planted in beds fully exposed to the sun. In rather shady places the crop is small, and when altogether excluded from the direct rays of the sun, they produce nothing.

European vegetables are scarce during the early part of the month; but all sorts of pavekah, pumpkin, water pumpkin, brinjals, podalangaw, sweet potato, or velly kelingoo, saury kelingoo, yams, aivully kelingoo, and leno vulty kelingoo, are plentifully supplied in the markets. Fruits are scarce, except plantains, guavas, and oranges. The saminthee flower and rose are to be had in great abundance.

## BANGALORE.

*Mean temperature, 69.—¾ inches of rain measured.*

Cauliflowers and all the cabbage tribe, beet, celery and lettuce are full grown.

# GENERAL REMARKS.

## MADRAS.

Winter and dress figs, mulberries, and custard apples. Dress pines in September, and remove the suckers, and dress again with stable manure, red earth, and sand, in January. Sprouts of cabbage, cauliflower, broccoli, and knolkhol, taken in February, March and April, and even in May, afford a good vegetable during the hot season.

Plantains, pine-apples, and figs, may be watered in the morning; but everything else in the evening only. The seed peas that answer best for Madras are those from Bangalore—the common white pea of Mysore. The best carrot, turnip, and onion seed is from Hyderabad; knolkhol from the Cape; and cabbage, cauliflower, beet, and celery, from England: other seeds from Bangalore and the Neilgherries.

Good manure for all sorts of flowers, is red earth and sheep's dung, in nearly equal quantities.

## BANGALORE.

The meteorological observations of three years—1834-5-6—were one very hot, and one very rainy season: this may therefore be regarded as a very fair average when taken together.

# NATIVE VEGETABLES, GREENS, ROOTS, LEGUMES, ETC.

ADRUK. *Zingiber Officinale.*—Ginger. It is a native of India, and is sown at the commencement of the rains in beds of about six feet square, and in a rich cultivated soil. The planting consists in dividing part of the green root, which the Natives first soak in a mixture of cow-dung and water; it is then planted about two inches deep and about one foot apart. It requires a great deal of water, and to be kept clear of weeds. When the stalks dry, the ginger may be taken up, although it is sometimes left in the ground for a couple of years. It is better for remaining twelve months, and must be watered during the dry season.

AJMOOD. *Apium Petroselinum.*—Parsley. See *Parsley.*

AJOWAN. *Ligusticum Ajowan.*—Lovage. This plant is grown by the Native gardeners for the seed only, which, from its highly aromatic property, is used for culinary and medicinal purposes. Propagated by seed and grown in square beds; the seed is sown in September and October and sold at five pice the seer.

ALOO. *Solanum Tuberosum.*—See *Potatoes.*

ANASPHUL. *Illicium Anisatum.*—Star Anise. Is brought chiefly to India from China, and is used for flavouring Native dishes.

AMBAREE KEE BHAJEE. *Hibiscus Cannabinus.*—Hemp-leaved Hibiscus. This is an erect growing plant, of the height of about four feet. It is slightly prickled over the stem. The leaves have an acid taste, and are used as a pot herb.

There is a dark purplish coloured species, the leaves of which are used for a similar purpose; they are both grown all the year round, and sold at five seers for one pice.

Propagated by seed, and grown in any common garden soil.

BAUJERA. *Holcus Spicatus.*—This is a very common grain, not so heating as Jawarie, and may be made into cakes or porridge. Sown in fields at the commencement of the rains.

BAKLA ZUN. *Phaseolus Vulgaris.*—Kidney Bean, dwarf. See *Beans.*

BAKLA. *Vicia Faba.*—Garden Bean. This is cultivated at the same season and manner as the kidney.

BHANG-U-GUNDUNA. *Allium Tuberosum.*—Indian Chive. This very much resembles the English chive; it is grown in square beds or rows and should be planted at the close of the rains; it is easy of culture either by slips or dividing the roots; it should be set about twelve inches apart, and when the bunches have increased to a large size, must be again divided.

It is used in various ways for the table.

BHENDEE. *Hibiscus Esculentus.*—Bandaykaye. This plant is very common; the long capsules, when green, are used for various purposes, either boiled whole and eaten or sliced and put into soup or curries; the inside is of a slimy consistency, but, when dressed, not unpleasant. The seed is sometimes laid upon toast with butter, pepper and salt. Another species, the Okro, has a smaller capsule which grows upright, the seeds when rubbed between the fingers have a strong scent of musk; the Arabs flavour their coffee with it.

BOODUNK. *Mentha Pulegium.*—Penny Royal. Cultivated the same as thyme.

BOORUNK KALA. *Ocymum Basilicum.*—Sweet Basil. Grows common in Native gardens; the seeds are used medicinally an infusion being considered very cooling.

BOOTA. *Zea Mays.*—Maize Grown at the commencement of the rains and sown in beds or in the common fields; it requires little care; the heads are either boiled or roasted before eaten. The ground should be well manured before the seed is sown.

BRINJALS or BAYENGUN. *Solanum Melongena.*—Egg plant. There are several varieties of this plant—a large round-shaped fruit, both purple and white; another, white, thin and long; a smaller species again, pear-shaped, red and purple striped; and one seldom exceeding the size of an egg. They are all dressed alike and used both in curries and other Native dishes.

Propagation—by seed, at the commencement of the rains. The young plants are placed at about eighteen inches apart and require watering every third or fourth day; they are sold from one to three pice a seer.

BUKUM. *Cæsalpinia Sappan.*—Narrow-leafed Brasiletto. This is a common shrub in most parts of India; the seed is used for colouring milk, and the wood as a red dye.

BULLUR. *Var: of the Dolichos Lablab.*—Small Bean. This is a shrubby plant, bearing a small bean, sown in June and ripe in October; it is boiled plain and eaten, or put into curries; the Natives also give it to cattle.

BUNBURBUTTEE. *Phaseolus Lunatus.*—Duffin Bean. Sown in rows the same as other beans, but with a much greater space between; they require very strong sticks for support, and are ready in about six months. No very particular care is necessary.

BURRIE TOOVAR. *Cytisus Cajan.*—Large Dhal. This is sown in fields at the commencement of the rains in June and sometimes much later; it is ripe in December. The seeds are sometimes ground into flour or split like dry peas: for the latter they are an excellent substitute. There are several varieties, which sell from 30 to 40 seers for the rupee.

BUTANEE. *Pisum Sativum*—Common Pea. The native country pea is sown after the rains in drills, and varies in price according to the quality; when green they are tolerable as a vegetable, but are best in soup. Procurable in December and January.

CHEENA. *Cicer Arietinum.*—Chick Pea or Gram. Grown in fields and sown after the rains. Price various.

CHOOLAEE. *Amaranthus Polygamus.*—Common Bajee. Much cultivated by the Natives. It is sown broad-cast in beds from

June to March. The leaves are sold in the bazaar at one pice the seer. Used as greens and also in curries.

CHUCHOONDA. *Tricosanthes Anguina.*—The Snake Gourd. This is sown in rains, and grown generally over a high paudal, that the fruit may have space to hang down from; a small stone or weight is then tied to the end to increase its length, which varies from a foot and a half to three feet or more. Raw, it resembles a cucumber in flavour, but is better dressed in a stew or curry.

CH'HOTA KULPA. *Borago Indica.*—Indian Borage. This is a common plant, and grows wild in many parts.

CHOTIE SAYME KE PULLIE. *Dolichos Lablab.*—Native Bean. This is a smaller species of the *Dolichos Lablab;* the legume and seeds are both eaten; it is sown in the rains and sells from one pice to two a seer.

CHOOLAEE. *Spinacia Tetrandra.*—Spinach Tetrandous. This is a common sort of Native greens, and, when boiled, resembles spinach; it is procurable nearly all the year round.

CHOOKEH. *Rumex Vesicarius.*—Sorrel. This is also of common Native growth, and where water is abundant may be had for eight months in the year; it is sown in drills or on the edges around other beds; the leaves are sold in bundles from one to two pice a seer. There is also another species called the Indian Red Sorrel.

CHUCKOONDA. *Beta Vulgaris.*—Common Beet. This is the common beet.

CHOOPREE ALOO.—Tubers roundish, very large, white inside and much esteemed; the skin thin and smooth like a potato. The stems require strong sticks to creep over; it bears a large roundish fruit, like an oak apple in appearance, which is also edible.

DARCHEENEE. *Laurus Cinnamomum.*—Cinnamon. This is brought from Ceylon and the Spice Islands.

DHAN OR CHOUL. *Oryza Sativa.*—Rice. Is so common as not to need any description here.

DHUNNIA. *Coriandrum Sativum.*—Coriander seed. This is also imported.

DILL PUSSUND. *Cucurbita Lagenaria.*—Small Pumpkin. This is a small species of round squash or gourd, and is grown in the bed of rivers with the melons; it much resembles, when dressed, the vegetable-marrow, and is thought by some to be even superior.

ERVIE. *Caladium Esculentum.*—Urvie. This is a small bulbous root sown from March to July, in rows or beds, mostly along a water course where ginger is planted. It requires much water, and takes from six to seven months to ripen. When boiled and then roasted it is very wholesome and somewhat resembles a yam in taste; the Natives also put it into curries.

GAJUR. *Daucus Carota.*—Carrot.

GUNDUNA. *Allium Porrum.*—Leek.

GURANYO ALOO. *Dioscorea Rubella.*—Red Sweet Yam. This is oblong and red skinned root tuberous, deeply tinged with red under the skin, but the colour does not penetrate deep; they are sometimes as much as three feet long in a rich light soil.

GURANYO ALOO LAL. *Dioscorea Purpurea.*—Purple Yam. Root oblong; throughout of a lighter or dark purple, but always considerably deep in tinge. This colour is permanent.

ZEMMY KUND. *D. Atro Purpurea.*—Another species. Tubers sub-rotund purple throughout, very large, of an irregular, smooth, roundish shape, and growing near the surface, so as to appear in dry weather through the cracks they make by raising the soil over them.

HULDEE. *Curcuma Longa.*—Turmeric. There are four species of this plant, one a small and very fine sort; the other longer and coarse; the third the Ambie used chiefly as medicine, the fourth a wild species. That which is cultivated for domestic culinary purposes is sown in beds like ginger, and when ripe in twelve months, taken up and dried. It is extensively cultivated in most parts of India, and sells, green, from eight to eighteen seers the rupee.

HULEEM. *Arabis Chinensis.*—Cress. Described elsewhere.

ILLACHEE. *Elettaria Cardamomum.*—Cardamum. This specie is also imported.

IPAR. *Thymus Vulgaris.*—Thyme. Elsewhere described.

JAWORIE. *Holcus Saccharatus.*—Grown in fields and sown during the rains; it is the common food of the poorer classes, made when ground into cakes.

KALA KUSTOORIE. *Abelmoschus Moschatus.*—Musk Okro. See *Bhendee.*

KALEE SEEM. *Stizolobium Altissimum.*—Assam Bean. This bean is grown like most others, and may be first sown at the commencement of the rains and continued during the cold season.

KALEE TULSEE. *Ocymum Sanctum.*—Basil. This is grown in almost every Native garden, and is used for various purposes by Europeans, for flavouring sauces, wine or vinegar.

KALEE MIRCHEE. *Piper Nigrum.*—Black Pepper. Although principally the produce of the Eastern Islands, it is grown of a superior quality in the Malabar Coast. The root is a tonic and cordial.

KAM ALOO. *Dioscorea Alata.*—Winged Yam. Tubers oblong, brown on the surface, internally white of a great size. Besides the tubers the proper roots of all those plants are fibrous, springing chiefly from and about the union of the stems with the tubers, and spreading in every direction.

KHEERA. *Cucumis Sativus.*—Cucumber, common. See *Cucumber.*

KHUSH KHUSH. *Papaver Somniferum.*—Poppy Seed. This is simply the seed of the poppy and used in confectionary, as well as to make oil.

KOOLEE BAYNEGUN. *Solanum Longum.*—Egg Plant, cylindrical. See *Brinjals.*

KUDDOO. *Cucurbita Lagenaria.*—Bottle gourd. This is grown at the commencement of the rains; a good soil is all that is necessary, requiring no further care.

KUKREE. *Cucumis Utilissimus.*—Green Cucumber. A large, coarse kind of cucumber, sown with the melons and other fruit, in the beds of rivers.

KULAEE. *Phaseolus Trilobus.*—Three-lobed Bean. Sown like other Native beans.

KULMEE SAG. *Convolvulus Repens.*—Creeping Bind Weed. This grows wild; the leaves are eaten by the Natives.

KULT'HEE. *Dolichos Biflorus.*—Two-flowered Bean. This is grown in fields after the rains, and chiefly used for cattle; when given to horses it must first be boiled; they soon become very fond of it, and keep in as good condition as upon any other grain.

KURBOOZAH. *Cucumis Melo.*—Melon. See *Melon.*

KUREELA. *Momordica Charantia.*—Bitter Hairy Gourd. This is a creeper, sown at the commencement of the rains, and may be continued during the cold season; it is a bitter fruit, very rough skinned, and from four to five inches long; the edges have a very wrinkled appearance; when ripe it is of a beautiful deep red and yellow. The Natives fry and eat them, but they are principally used in curries; they require to be soaked in salt and water before dressing. They sell from one to two pice a seer.

KURSUMBUL KE PULLIE. *Dolichos Lunatus.*—Duffin Bean. This is a very fine sort of large bean, and when dressed resembles the Windsor; it is grown like all other beans that require sticks for support.

LAL SAG. *Amarantus Giganticus.*—Spinach. The leaves of this plant is eaten as a spinach; it is generally sown broad-cast, and procurable all the year round.

LOOBEA. *Dolichos Sinensis.*—Asparagus Bean. This bean is sown at the commencement of the rains; it has a very long and slender pod, and is boiled and eaten as French beans; the bean itself is small.

LUSSUN. *Allium Sativum.*—Garlic. See *Garlic.*

MATKEE BHAJEE. *Amarantus Oleraceus.*—Greens. There are

two sorts of these common greens, cultivated in all Native gardens; the leaves are eaten as spinach or put into curries.

Meet'hee. *Trigonella Fœnum, Fœnum Grocum.*—Fœnugreek. This is a small annual, commonly cultivated during the cold season. The greens are used by the Natives and the seed in curries. It is sown like all other common greens.

Meet'hee Kuthoo. *Cucurbita Pepo.*—Sweet Pumpkin. This is grown at the same time as all the other species, and if hung up in a dry place is an excellent store vegetable, keeping for several months.

Moong Arood. *Phaseolus Mongo.*—Green Gram. This is chiefly grown in the upper parts of Hindoostan; it is eaten by the Natives dressed in various ways.

Moong P'hulee. *Arachis Hypogœa.*—Earth-nut. This is grown under ground, the legumes of which contain the nuts; they are small and white, and require to be roasted before eaten; they are not in much esteem.

Mukhum Seem. *Dolichos Gladiatus.*—Sabre Bean. This is a large kind of bean, sown at the same time as others; it requires strong support to run over. The beans are dressed as French beans but are not so tender.

Mirchee. *Capsicum Frutescens. Capsicum.*—See *Capsicum.*

Mutke ke Pullie. *Dolichos Fabœformis.*—Small Sabre Bean. This is grown the same as the larger sort.

Nubcha. *Corchrus Olitorius.*—Sag Greens. These greens are common amongst the Natives; it is an erect growing plant, and flowers at the close of the rains.

Paluk Sag. *Beeta Bengalinensis.*—Bengal Beet. The leaves only of this vegetable are eaten; when boiled it resembles spanish in flavour. The roots are tough and stringy. It may be sown in beds or rows. The leaves shoot out again after being cut down.

Pan. *Piper Betel.*—Betel Pepper. This is cultivated in pots by itself; it requires much water and care, and is too well known to need any further description here. The leaves are eaten raw.

PEEAJ. *Allium Cepa.*—Onion. See *Onions*.

PEEAZ. *Allium Ascalonicum.*—Shallot. This is cultivated in a light rich soil, and propagated by dividing the clustered roots; it should be sown in beds at the commencement of the rains, and will give a crop during the cold weather.

PENDALOO. *Dioscorea Aculeata.*—The Small Yam. This is a very valuable and delicate root, somewhat resembling the sweet potato in appearance; tubers of an oval form and very white, generally weighing about two pounds.

PHOOT. *Cucumis Momordica.*—Field Cucumber. A wild species of cucumber sown generally in the fields amongst Jaworie, and is something between the melon and cucumber; it keeps for a long time if not too ripe and would be valuable as a store vegetable for sea.

PIPILIE. *Piper Longum.*—Long Pepper. This is a creeper of easy culture and should be trained on poles, or have strong sticks to grow upon. It is common in all parts of India.

PODEENA. *Menthœ Verticulata.*—Mint. See *Mint*.

POEE. *Basella Alba et Rubra.*—Malabar Nightshade. This is a twining, succulent plant, with smooth fleshy leaves; it grows very rapidly and is generally cultivated as a spinach. There are two sorts.

PULWUL. *Trichosanthes Dioica*—Dioceous Snake Gourd. This is one of the snake gourd species, of a small description, the size of an egg; the seed is sown in the cold season and yields fruit from March to September.

PULPUL. *Myrtus Pimenta.*—Allspice. This is imported.

RAE. *Sinapis Trilucularis.*—Mustard. See *Mustard*.

SALBEA. *Salvia Officinalis.*—Sage. See *Sage*.

SHULGUM. *Brasica Rapa.*—Turnip. See *Turnip*.

SONF. *Anethum Panmori.*—Sweet Fennel. See *Fennel*.

SAYME KE PULLIE. *Dolichos Lablab.*—Native Bean. This bean is sown in the fields like all others in rows, and are eaten both boiled or put into curries.

Sayme ke Pullie Lal. *Dolichos Lablab Rub.*—Native Bean, red. This bean when young, is eaten pod and all; when full grown, the seeds only are used. It is about five inches long and has got its name from the reddish colour of its edges.

Soot'hnee. *Dioscorea Fasiculata.*—Yam. Consists of many tubers, about the size and shape of an egg. They are covered with a light coloured thin skin; internally they are white. They are not only eaten, but starch is made from the roots.

Sukur Kund. *Convolvulus Batata.*—Sweet Potato. A sweet-tasted nutritious root, of which there are two sorts, red and white. The tubers are long, and, when boiled or roasted, very wholesome. They are sown precisely in the same manner as a potato, after the hot season, and are fit to be taken up in six months. They sell from two to four pice a seer.

Sufed Tulsee. *Ocymum Alba.*—White Basil. Chiefly grown in Native gardens.

Sufura Roomro. *Cucurbitis Ovifera.*—Vegetable Marrow. See *Vegetable Marrow.*

Thurbooj. *Cucurbita Citrullus.*—Water Melon. This is grown in the bed of rivers in the hot season, but may be cultivated in gardens during the rains.

Zeera. *Cuminum Cyminum.*—Cummin Seed; black and white. This is grown in beds the same as the coriander; the seeds are used for seasoning curries. Much is brought from China and the Persian Gulf.

Zurumbad. *Curcuma Zerumbet.*—Zeodary; four sorts. See *Huldee.*

# NATIVE VEGETABLES, GREENS, ETC.
## WHEN PROCURABLE IN THE DECCAN.

Ambaree, procurable all the year round.

Bhendee, September to March.
Brinjals, ditto ditto.
Bullur, sown in June, ripe in October.
Bhoe, September to January.

Chooka, from June to March.
Chowlie, sown in June, and ripe from September to January.
Choukundar, from May to January.
Chundoric, to be had all the year round.
Chankoorah, or Pothee, from March to July.
Chundan Butwar, to be had all the year round.
Chul, ditto ditto.
Chackoondrah, April to July.

Dill Pussund, ditto ditto.

Gajur, from October to June.
Gownwhar ka phull, from October to June.
Good Alloe, January to June.
Gurrieg phull, October to June.

Huldee sown in June, remains twelve months.
Hudgar, from September to February.

Kurralah, August to March.
Kumruck ka pullie, September to March.
Kura, September to November.
Kuckrie, March to July.
Kutchna, during the cold season.
Kuldie, or Kuddar, September to March.
Karmonie, September to January.
Kotemeer, sown in September, and ripe in three months.

Lussun, September to January.

Mooringa, the pods are procurable almost all the year.
Maut ka bajee, all the year round.
Mathee and Mathar, all the year round.
Mirchie, from July to April, but procurable all the year.
Peeaz, all the year round.
Pend Allo, sown at almost all seasons of the year, chiefly in the rains.
Poot, from July to January.
Pookelah, from July to April.
Poce or Butchlar, during the rains and cold season.

Ruthree ka bajee,      ditto        ditto.
Raje Gurah,            ditto        ditto.
Rut Alloe, ripe from December to April.

Shulgum, August and September, and from January to March.
Seo Pollok, September to July.
Sonf do., procurable during the rains and cold season.
Sayme ke pullie, September to March.
Saymee, or Sayndah, from September to January.
Sursoh, all the year.
Sooriakhund, in the cold season, two sorts, bitter and sweet.
Soorie, common in pawn gardens,—See medicinal qualities.
Soorun, after the rains.

Turrie, at all seasons.
Thur Kukrie, April to July.
Thurbooj, April to September.
Thuzzotals, during the rains and cold season.

Urvie, September to January.
Udruck, sown from March to July, and ripe in nine months.

Wachvee, during the rains and cold season.

# INDEX

OF

## ANNUAL, BIENNIAL, AND PERENNIAL, FLOWER-PLANTS.

The following are best known by the English names, but as the Scientific names are requisite to show the genus to which they belong, they are also given. Such popular names as Convolvulus Minor, Flos Adonis, &c., have no affinity with the Latin, and are not to be considered as translations.

1st Column.—Hardiness and Duration of each plant.
2nd Ditto.—Colour of Flower.
3rd Ditto.—Height.
4th Ditto.—Price.—Packets may also be had of those marked 3d., of James Carter, Seedsman and Florist, 238 High Holborn, London; also of Minier, Adams and Nash, 63 Strand: and should instruments such as saws, pruning-knives, &c., &c., be required, I would recommend Mr. Weiss of the Strand.

| A—is employed to indicate varieties. | | H. & Dur. | Col. of Fl. | Height. | Price. | |
|---|---|---|---|---|---|---|
| | | | | feet. | s. | d. |
| Aster Chinese, m | Aster Sinensis, pl. var. | hha. | div. | 2 | | 3 |
| — Quilled (German) | — Fistulòsus, 20 v | — | — | — | | 6 |
| — Dark blue | — Atro-cærùleus | — | d. b. | — | | 3 |
| — Light blue | — Læte-cærùleus | — | l. b. | — | | 3 |
| — Dark red | — Atrorùbens | — | d. r. | — | | 3 |
| Aster Rose | Aster Ròseus | hha. | rose | — | | 3 |
| — Turkey | — Turcicus | — | c. r. | — | | 3 |
| — White | — Albus | — | wh. | — | | 3 |
| — New Globe | — Globòsus Nòvus | — | div. | — | | 6 |
| — New Pyramidal | — Pyramidális | — | — | — | | 6 |
| — Variegated | — Variegátus | — | — | — | | 6 |
| — New Dwarf | — Nánus Nóvus | — | — | 1 | | 6 |
| Auricula, Alpine | Prímula Aurícula | hp. | — | ½ | | 6 |
| Finest Prize | ...... | — | — | — | 2 | 6 |
| Balsam, Finest m | Balsámina Hortensis | ta. | — | 2 | | 6 |
| Double Purple | — Purpúrea Pléna | — | pur. | — | | 3 |

| A—IS EMPLOYED TO INDICATE VARIETIES. | | H. & Dur. | Col. of Fl. | Height. | Price. | |
|---|---|---|---|---|---|---|
| | | | | feet. | s. | d. |
| Balsam, Dark Rose | ... Balsámina Atro-rósea... | ta. | rose | 2 | | 3 |
| —— Scarlet | ... —— Coccínea ... | — | sc. | — | | 3 |
| —— White | ... —— Candida ... | — | wh. | — | | 3 |
| —— Striped | ... —— Striáta ... | — | div. | — | | 6 |
| —— Camelia | ... —— Camellieflóra ... | — | — | — | | 6 |
| —— Dwarf Scarlet | ... —— Coccínea Nòva ... | — | sc. | 1 | | 3 |
| —— Mixed Dwarf | ... —— Nàna Nóva ... | — | div. | — | | 6 |
| Broom, Ornamental | ... Cytisus et Spartium ... | hp. | y. & w. | 5 | | 6 |
| Candytuft, White | ... Ibéris Amára, (bitter).. | ha. | wh. | 1 | | 3 |
| Purple | ... Unbelláta ... | — | pur. | — | | 3 |
| New Crimson | ... —— Phœnicea ... | — | cr. | — | | 3 |
| New Blush | ... —— Carnea Nóva ... | — | blsh. | — | | 3 |
| New Rocket | ... Coronária ... | — | wh. | — | | 3 |
| Fragrant | ... Odoráta ... | — | — | — | | 3 |
| Mixed | ... ...... | — | div. | — | | 3 |
| Canterbury Bells | ... Campánula Médium ... | hp. | bl. | 2 | | 3 |
| White | ... —— Alba ... | — | wh. | — | | 3 |
| Double | ... —— Flóre-pléno ... | — | w. & b. | — | | 6 |
| Capsicum, 10 var. | ... Capsicum Annuum, &c. | ta. | y. & r. | — | | 6 |
| Catchfly, Lobel's | ... Siléne Arméria ... | ha. | red | 1 | | 3 |
| White | ... —— Alba ... | — | wh. | — | | 3 |
| Chrysanthemum, m | ... Chrysan., 2 var. ... | — | y. & w. | 3 | | 3 |
| Tricolor | ... Carinátum ... | — | 3 col. | 1 | | 3 |
| New Golden | ... —— Flávum ... | — | yel. | — | | 3 |
| Showy | ... —— Speciòsum ... | — | — | — | | 3 |
| Clary, Red-topped | ... Salvia Hormìnum ... | — | red | 1½ | | 3 |
| Purple-topped | ... —— Purpúrea ... | — | pur. | — | | 3 |
| Cockscomb, Dwarf | ... Celósia Christáta, Nána. | ta. | — | 1 | | 6 |
| Columbine, Double | ... Aquilègia Vulgáris ... | hp. | div. | 2 | | 3 |
| Convolvulus Minor | ... Convolvulus Trícolor ... | ha. | b. v. | tr. | | 3 |
| New Dark | ... —— Atropùreus ... | — | pur. | — | | 3 |
| Large Flowered | ... —— Grandiflòrus ... | — | — | — | | 6 |
| New Variegated | ... —— Variegátus Novus | — | var. | — | | 6 |
| White | ... —— Bícolor ... | — | w. & y. | — | | 3 |
| Mixed | ... ...... | — | div. | — | | 3 |
| ...... | Nos. 867 to 872 ... | — | — | — | 1 | 6 |
| Convolv. Major, m | ... Ipomæa Purpúrea ... | hha. | — | cl. | | 3 |
| Extra Fine, 20 v | ... | — | — | — | 1 | 0 |
| New Crimson | ... —— Kermesínus ... | — | cr. | — | 1 | 0 |
| Rose-coloured | ... —— Roseus ... | — | rose | — | | 3 |
| Spotted | ... —— Punctátus ... | — | sp. | — | | 3 |
| Striped | ... —— Striàtus ... | — | st. | — | | 3 |
| Violet | ... —— Violáceus ... | — | vi. | — | | 3 |
| Very dark | ... —— Atroviolúceus ... | — | d. v. | — | | 3 |
| ...... | Nos. 875 to 881 ... | — | div. | — | 3 | 0 |
| Cowslip, Mixed | ... Prímula Véris ... | hp. | — | ½ | | 3 |
| Cyanus, Sky-blue | ... Centaurea Cyánus ... | ha. | bl. | 2 | | 3 |
| Brown | ... —— Brunnea ... | — | br. | — | | 3 |
| Fine Mixed | ... ...... | — | div. | — | | 3 |
| Egg Plant, Purple | ... Solánum Ovìgera ... | ta. | pur. | — | | 3 |
| White Fruited | ... —— Leucocarpon ... | — | wh. | — | | 3 |

| A—IS EMPLOYED TO INDICATE VARIETIES. | | H. & Dur. | Col. of Fl. | Height. | Price. | |
|---|---|---|---|---|---|---|
| | | | | feet. | s. | d. |
| Flos Adonis | Adónis Æstivális | ha. | sc. | 1 | | 3 |
| Flame-coloured | Flammea | — | fl. | — | | 3 |
| Fraxinella, Red | Dictamnus Fraxinella | hp. | red | 3 | | 3 |
| White | Albus | — | wh. | — | | 3 |
| French Honeysuckle | Hedysarum Coronárium | hha. | sc. | 2 | | 3 |
| White | Album | — | wh. | — | | 3 |
| Globe Amaranthus | Gomphròna Globósa | fgh. | pur. | — | | 3 |
| White | Alba | — | wh. | — | | 3 |
| Mixed | ...... | — | div. | — | | 6 |
| Gourd, Bottle | Lagenariá Vulgáris | fa. | yel. | tr. | | 6 |
| Hercules' Club | Claváta | — | — | — | | 6 |
| Mammoth | Cucurbita Pèpo | — | — | — | | 3 |
| Orange | Aurantia | — | — | — | | 3 |
| Striped Pear | Ovífera | — | — | — | | 3 |
| Mixed | ...... | — | — | — | | 3 |
| Hawkweed, Purple | Crépis Rúbra | ha. | pur. | 1 | | 3 |
| Snowwhite | Nivàlis | — | wh. | — | | 3 |
| Yellow | Tolpis Barbáta | — | yel. | — | | 3 |
| Silvery | Argentea | — | sil. | — | | 3 |
| Heartsease (Pansy) | Viola Tricolor | hp. | div. | — | | 6 |
| Hollyhock, Antwerp | Althæa Ficifòlia | — | buff. | 7 | | 3 |
| Double Rose | Rósea | — | rose | — | | 3 |
| —— Black | —— Nìgra | — | bla. | — | | 3 |
| —— Purple | —— Purpúrea | — | pur. | — | | 3 |
| —— Red | —— Rúbra | — | red | — | | 3 |
| —— Yellow | —— Lútea | — | yel. | — | | 3 |
| —— White | —— Alba | — | wh. | — | | 3 |
| 30 Var. Mixed | ...... | — | div. | — | 1 | 0 |
| Chinese | Althæa Chinensis | — | vio. | 3 | | 3 |
| —— Purple | —— Purpúrea | — | pur. | — | | 3 |
| —— Mixed | ...... | — | p. & v. | — | | 3 |
| ...... | Nos. 909 to 919 | — | div. | 3-7 | 3 | 0 |
| Horn Poppy, Mixed | Glaucium, pl. var. | ha. | — | 2 | | 3 |
| Scarlet | Phœnìceum | — | sc. | — | | 3 |
| Violet | Rœmeria Hybrida | — | vio. | — | | 3 |
| Ice Plant | Mesemb. Crystallinum | ta. | wh. | tr. | | 3 |
| Jacobœa, dou. m | Senècio élegans, fl. pl. | hha. | div. | 1½ | | 6 |
| Double Crimson | Kermesina | — | cr. | — | | 3 |
| —— Mulberry | —— Rùbro-Purpùrea | — | ml. | — | | 3 |
| —— Purple | —— Purpùrea | — | pur. | — | | 3 |
| —— Rose | —— Ròsea | — | rose | — | | 6 |
| —— Violet | —— Violàcea | — | vio. | — | | 3 |
| —— White | —— Alba | — | wh. | — | | 3 |
| ...... | Nos. 925 to 931 | — | div. | — | 2 | 0 |
| Larkspur, Dwarf m | Delphínium Ajàcis | ha. | — | 1 | | 3 |
| Dwarf, German | Hùmile pl. var. | — | — | — | | 6 |
| —— Blue | —— Cæleste | — | bl. | — | | 3 |
| —— Rose | —— Ròseum | — | rose | — | | 3 |
| —— White | —— Album | — | wh. | — | | 3 |
| —— Unique | —— Bícolor | — | r. & w. | — | | 3 |
| Tall m. | Elàtior, pl. var. | — | div. | 1½ | | 3 |

| A—IS EMPLOYED TO INDICATE VARIETIES. | | H. & Dur. | Col. of Fl. | Height. | Price. | |
|---|---|---|---|---|---|---|
| | | | | feet. | s. | d. |
| Larkspur, Tall German | Delphinum Elàtior, var. | ha. | div. | 1½ | | 6 |
| —— Blue | —— Cærùleum | — | bl. | — | | 3 |
| —— Rose | —— Ròseum | — | rose | —. | | 3 |
| —— White | —— Album | — | wh. | — | | 3 |
| Branching Ger. | Consòlida, pl. var. | — | div. | 2 | | 6 |
| —— Blue | —— Cœleste | — | bl. | — | | 3 |
| —— Rose | —— Ròseum | — | rose | — | | 3 |
| 10 fine var. sep. | …… | — | div. | — | 2 | 0 |
| Lavatera, Red | Lavatèrà Trimestris | — | rose | 3 | | 3 |
| —— White | —— Alba | — | wh. | — | | 3 |
| Love-lies-bleeding | Amaranthus Caudàtus. | — | red | tr. | | 3 |
| Lupins, White | Lupìnus Albus | — | wh. | 2 | | 3 |
| Dutch Blue | Canaliculàtus | — | bl. | — | | 3 |
| Large Blue | Hirsùtus | — | — | — | | 3 |
| Large Rose | Piòsus | — | rose | — | | 3 |
| Yellow | Lùteus | — | yel. | 1½ | | 3 |
| Straw-coloured | —— Stramíneus | — | str. | — | | 3 |
| Mixed | …… | — | div. | 2 | | 3 |
| Mallow, 5 var. sep. | Malva, pl. sp. et var. | — | — | — | 1 | 0 |
| Marigold, French, m. | Tagètes pátula, 10 var. | hha. | — | 1½ | | 6 |
| French, Dwarf | —— Hùmilis | — | — | 1 | | 3 |
| —— Superb Striped | —— Striàta Superba | — | str. | 1½ | | 6 |
| —— Quilled | —— Fistulósa | — | div. | — | | 3 |
| —— African, m. | Erecta, pl. var. | — | y. & o. | 2 | | 3 |
| —— Lemon | —— Citrina | — | lem. | — | | 3 |
| —— Orange | —— Aurantìaca | — | or. | — | | 3 |
| —— Quilled | —— Fistulósa | — | y. & o. | — | | 3 |
| Cape | Calendula Pluviàlis | ha. | wh. | 1 | | 3 |
| Hybrid | Hybrida | — | — | — | | 3 |
| Double, Pot | Officinális, fl. pl. | — | yel. | — | | 3 |
| Marvel of Peru | Miràbilis Jalpa | hhp. | div. | 3 | | 3 |
| Purple | —— Purpúrea | — | pur. | — | | 3 |
| Red | —— Rúbra | — | red | — | | 3 |
| Striped, 3 var. | —— Striàta | — | stri. | — | | 3 |
| Yellow | —— Flàva | — | yel. | — | | 3 |
| White | —— Alba | — | wh. | — | | 3 |
| Long-flowered | —— Longiflòra | — | — | — | | 3 |
| 12 fine var. mix. | …… | — | div. | — | 1 | 0 |
| Mignonette, lb. 8s. | Resèda Odoràta, oz. 6d. | ha. | buff | 1½ | | 3 |
| Monkshood, mixed | Aconìtum, pl. sp. | hp. | b. & w. | 2 | | 3 |
| Nasturtions, Tall | Tropæolum Màjus | ha. | o. & y. | cl. | | 3 |
| New Carmine | —— Miniàum | — | car. | — | | 3 |
| Dark Red | —— Atrosanguineum | — | d. r. | — | | 3 |
| Shillings | —— Shillingii | — | spot. | — | | 3 |
| Three-spotted | —— Trimaculàtum | — | — | — | | 3 |
| New Dwarf | —— Mìnus | — | s. & o. | — | | 3 |
| Common Dwarf | …… | — | or. | — | | 3 |
| Palma Christi | Rícinus Májor | hha. | gr. | 6 | | 3 |
| Pea, Tangier | Làthyrus Tingitànus | ha. | sc. | 4 | | 3 |
| New Striped | —— Striàtus Nòvus | — | str. | — | | 3 |
| Sweet, m. lb. 4s | Odoràtus, pl. var. | — | div. | — | | 3 |

| A—IS EMPLOYED TO INDICATE VARIETIES. | | H. & Dur. | Col. of Fl. | Height. | Price. | |
|---|---|---|---|---|---|---|
| | | | | feet. | s. | d. |
| Pea, Black | Odorátus Níger | ha. | bla. | 4 | | 3 |
| Painted Lady | —— Pictus | — | var. | — | | 3 |
| Purple | —— Purpùreus | — | pur. | — | | 3 |
| Scarlet | —— Coccíneus | — | sc. | — | | 3 |
| Striped | —— Striàtus | — | str. | — | | 3 |
| White | —— Albus | — | wh. | — | | 3 |
| Persicaria, Red | Polygonum Orientàle | — | red | 6 | | 3 |
| White | —— Album | — | wh. | — | | 3 |
| Mixed | ...... | — | r. & w. | — | | 3 |
| Polyanthus, ex fine | Primùla Elàtior, var. | hp. | div. | ½ | | 6 |
| Poppy, Double, m. | Papàver Somníferum | ha. | — | 2 | | 3 |
| Double Black | —— Nìgrum | — | bla. | — | | 3 |
| —— Carnation | —— Caryophylloìdes | — | var. | — | | 3 |
| —— Fringed | —— Fimbriàtum | — | div. | — | | 3 |
| —— Himelayan | —— Himelayanum | — | — | — | | 3 |
| —— Scarlet | —— Coccíneum | — | sc. | — | | 3 |
| —— Striped Rose. | Róseum Striàtum. | — | rose | — | | 3 |
| —— Striped Red. | —— Rùbrum Striàtum. | — | red | — | | 3 |
| —— White | —— Album | — | wh. | — | | 3 |
| French Double | Rhæas, fl. plèno | — | div. | 1 | | 3 |
| —— Bordered | —— Limbàtum | — | red | — | | 3 |
| —— Striped | —— Striàtum | — | str. | — | | 3 |
| Nos. 1,001 to 1,012 | ...... | — | div. | — | 3 | 0 |
| Primrose, mixed | Primùla Vulgàris | hp. | — | ¼ | | 3 |
| Prince's Feather | Amaranthus Hypocon. | ha. | pur. | 2½ | | 3 |
| Quaking Grass | Briza Maxima | — | gr. | 1½ | | 3 |
| —— Grass, Slender | —— Gràcilis | — | gr. | 1 | | 3 |
| Rocket, Purple | Hesperis Matronàlis | hp. | pur. | — | | 3 |
| Sweet | Tristis | — | wh. | — | | 3 |
| Scabious, Dwarf | Scabiósa Nàna | ha. | div. | — | | 3 |
| Very Dark | Atropurpùrea | hp. | pur. | 2 | | 3 |
| Splendid Ger. | —— Superba | — | div. | — | | 6 |
| Scotch Thistle | Carduus, sp. | — | pur. | 8 | | 6 |
| Sensitive Plant | Mimósa Sensitíva | fgh. | pink | 2 | | 6 |
| Spanish Broom | Spartium Junceum | hp. | yel. | 3 | | 3 |
| Snapdragon, m. | Antirrhínum Majus | — | div. | 2 | | 3 |
| Splendid m. 40 var. | ...... | — | str. | — | | 6 |
| Carnation | —— Caryophylloìdes | — | — | — | | 3 |
| —— Yellow | —— —— Lùteum | — | — | — | | 6 |
| Four-coloured | —— Quadrícolor | — | 4 col. | — | | 6 |
| Orange | —— Aurantíacum | — | or. | — | | 6 |
| Pale-yellow | —— Ochroleucum | — | p. y. | — | | 3 |
| Painted | —— Pictum | — | var. | — | | 3 |
| Scarlet | —— Coccíneum | — | sc. | — | | 3 |
| White | —— Album | — | wh. | — | | 3 |
| Yellow | —— Flávum | — | yel. | — | | 3 |
| Nos. 1,027 to 1,036 | ...... | — | div. | — | 3 | 0 |
| Stock, 10 week, m. | Mathìola Annua | hha. | — | 1¼ | | 3 |
| Scarlet | —— Coccínea | — | cr. | — | | 3 |
| Intermediate | —— Intermédia | — | — | — | | 3 |
| Large Scarlet | —— Major | — | — | 2 | | 3 |

| A—IS EMPLOYED TO INDICATE VARIETIES. | | H. & Dur. | Col. of Fl. | Height | Price. | |
|---|---|---|---|---|---|---|
| | | | | feet. | s. | d. |
| Stock, Purple | Mathìola Purpúrea | hha. | pur. | 1¼ | | 3 |
| White | —— Alba | — | wh. | — | | 3 |
| Grem, 20 v. | —— Annua, var. | — | div. | 1 | | 6 |
| Large Packet | ...... | — | — | — | 1 | 0 |
| Dwarf Carmine | Densiflórà, min. | — | ver. | — | | 6 |
| —— Dark Carmine. | —— Atro-Miniàta | — | d. v. | — | | 6 |
| —— Crimson | —— Kermesìna | — | cr. | — | | 6 |
| —— Dark Crimson. | —— Atrorùbens | — | d. c. | — | | 6 |
| —— Dark Blue | —— Atro-cærùlea | — | d. b. | — | | 6 |
| —— Lilac | —— Lilacìna | — | li. | — | | 6 |
| —— Light Blue | —— Læte-Cærùlea | — | l. b. | — | | 6 |
| —— Peach-bloss | —— Persiciflóra | — | p. bl. | — | | 6 |
| —— Rose-coloured. | —— Ròsea | — | rose | — | | 6 |
| —— Yellow | —— Lútea | — | yel. | — | | 6 |
| —— Violet | —— Violácea | — | vio. | — | | 6 |
| —— White | —— Alba | — | wh. | — | | 6 |
| Nos. 1,046 to 1,057. | ...... | — | div. | — | 5 | 0 |
| Prussian, m. | Græca (Cheirifòlia).. | — | — | — | | 3 |
| Purple | —— Purpùrea | — | pur. | — | | 3 |
| Scarlet | —— Coccìnea | — | cr. | — | | 3 |
| Rose | —— Ròsea | — | rose | — | | 3 |
| White | —— Alba | — | wh. | 1¼ | | 3 |
| Autumnal | Autumnális | — | div. | 2½ | | 6 |
| Brompt, m. | Mathìo, Simplicicaulis. | hb. | — | — | | 3 |
| Purple | —— Purpúrea | — | pur. | 2¼ | | 3 |
| Brompt, s. | —— Simplicicaulis | hb. | cr. | — | | 3 |
| White | —— Alba | — | wh. | 1½ | | 3 |
| Queen, m. | Mathìola Incana | — | div. | — | | 3 |
| Purple | —— Purpúrea | — | pur. | — | | 3 |
| Scarlet | —— Coccìnea | — | cr. | — | | 3 |
| White | —— Alba | — | wh. | — | | 3 |
| Imperial | Imperàlis | hp. | d. bl. | — | | 6 |
| —— Light Blue | —— Læte-cærùlea | — | l. bl. | — | | 6 |
| —— Red | —— Rùbra | — | red | — | | 6 |
| —— Rose | —— Ròsea | — | rose | — | | 6 |
| Nos. 1,073 to 1,076... | ...... | — | div. | — | 1 | 6 |
| Sunflower, d. tall | Helianthus Annuus | ha. | yel. | 6 | | 3 |
| Dwarf | Indicus | — | — | 3 | | 3 |
| Sweet Alyssum | Alyssum Marìtimum | hp. | wh. | 1 | | 3 |
| Sultan, p. | Centaurea Moschàta | hba. | pur. | 2 | | 3 |
| White | —— Alba | — | wh. | — | | 3 |
| Yellow | —— Suavèolens | — | yel. | — | | 3 |
| Venus's Looking-glass. | Campánula Spéculum.. | ha. | bl. | ¾ | | 3 |
| Rose | —— Ròsea | — | rose | — | | 3 |
| White | —— Alba | — | wh. | — | | 3 |
| 5 var. separate | ...... | — | div. | — | 1 | 0 |
| Navelwort | Cynoglossum Linifolium | — | wh. | 1 | | 3 |
| Virg. Stock | Malcòmia Marìtima | — | li. | ½ | | 3 |
| White | —— Alba | — | wh. | — | | 3 |
| Wallflower, Dark | Cheiranthus Cheiri | hp. | br. | 2 | | 3 |

## 230

| A—IS EMPLOYED TO INDICATE VARIETIES. | | H. & Dur. | Col. of Fl. | Height. | Price. | |
|---|---|---|---|---|---|---|
| | | | | feet. | s. | d. |
| Wallflower,Chameleon | Cheiranthus Variábilis . | hp. | var. | 2 | | 3 |
| Purple | —— Purpúrea | — | pur. | — | | 3 |
| Yellow | —— Flàva | — | yel. | — | | 3 |
| Double German | Flòre, Plèno | — | div. | — | | 6 |
| —— Black Brown | —— Nigrescens | — | d. br. | — | | 6 |
| —— Blue | —— Cœrùlea | — | bl. | — | | 6 |
| —— Large-flower | —— Grandiflora | — | br. | — | | 6 |
| —— Pyramidal | —— Pyramidàlis | — | — | — | | 6 |
| 20 var. mixed | …… | — | div. | — | | 6 |
| Winter Cherry | Physalis Alkakengi | ha. | wh. | 2½ | | 3 |
| Xeranthemum, p. | Xeronthemum Annuum | — | pur. | 1½ | | 3 |
| White | —— Album | — | wh. | — | | 3 |
| Yellow | Elichrysum Bracteàtum | hba. | yel. | 2 | | 3 |
| New White | —— Album Nóvum | — | wh. | — | | 3 |
| Splendid | —— Splendens | — | var. | — | | 3 |
| Zinnia, Golden yel. | Zínnia Aurea | — | yel. | — | | 6 |
| Large-flowered | Grandiflóra | — | red | — | | 3 |
| Mixed | …… | — | r. & y. | — | | 3 |

# CATALOGUE OF SEEDS.

### ASSORTMENTS OF FLOWER SEEDS.

h, *hardy*; hh, *half hardy*.

| | s. d. |
|---|---|
| 6 Fine var. Calliopsis, hha. | 1 6 |
| 7 ,, Clarkia, ha. | 1 6 |
| 6 Everlasting Flowers, hha. | 1 6 |
| 6 Fine Linária, ha. | 1 0 |
| 6 ,, Nemóphila, ha. | 1 6 |
| 8 ,, Œnothéra & Godétia, ha. | 1 6 |
| 6 ,, Lobélia, hh. | 2 0 |
| 6 ,, Marigold, hha. | 1 6 |
| 8 ,, Schizanthus, ha. | 2 0 |
| 4 ,, Sweet William, hp. | 1 6 |
| 6 ,, Wallflower, hp. | 2 0 |
| 50 Finest hp. Annuals, 10s.; 25. | 5 0 |
| 50 ,, h. do. 20s.; 25. | 10 0 |
| 50 Fine h. perennials, 10s.; 25. | 6 0 |

*The selection of the above must be left entirely to J. C.*

### FRUIT SEEDS—*Per Packet*.

| | s. d. |
|---|---|
| Currants, red, white, and black.. | 6 |
| Gooseberry, finest mixed | 6 |
| Melon, Beechwood, extra fine | 1 0 |
| — Carter's green flesh | 1 0 |
| — Early Cantalupe | 6 |
| — Evans' scarlet flesh | 1 0 |
| — Green flesh, fine | 6 |
| — Hardiest early Cantalupe | 6 |
| — Netted Persian | 6 |
| — Pekin, new and extra fine | 1 6 |
| — Scarlet flesh | 6 |
| — Snow's Prolific | 1 0 |
| — Sweet, of Ispahan | 1 0 |
| — Terry's green flesh, extra | 1 0 |
| — Windsor Prize, fine | 1 0 |
| — Fine mixed Melon | 6 |
| — 12 fine other var., separate | 5 0 |
| Mulberry, 3 fine species | 1 0 |
| Quince | 6 |
| Raspberry, red and mixed | 1 0 |

| | s. d. |
|---|---|
| Strawberry, red and white alpine | 1 0 |
| — British Queen | 1 0 |
| — Various fine sorts, mixed | 1 0 |
| — Finest mix., for preserving | 6 |
| Water Melon, fine mixed | 6 |

### FLOWERING BULBS.

| | s. d. |
|---|---|
| Achímenes, 12 in 4 fine sorts | 2 6 |
| Amaryllis Bella-Donna, each | 1 0 |
| — Formosissima | 6 |
| — 3 Greenhouse sp., each 3s. 6d. for | 10 0 |
| — 2 Species, South America, each | 3 0 |
| Ammocháris coránica | 4 0 |
| — Falcáta, 4s.; glauca | 4 0 |
| Anemones, finest new dou., per lb. | 7 0 |
| — 100 finest new var., separate. | 25 0 |
| — 50 do. 12s. 6d.; 25 do. | 7 0 |
| — Fine mixed new single, per lb. | 4 0 |
| Arum, fine new sp. Bolivia, each | 5 0 |
| Dahlia, extra, fine double, per doz. | 15 0 |
| Gladíolus oppositiflórus, new v., doz. | 2 0 |
| — Psittacinus (natalensis) | 1 6 |
| — Superbus (gandivensis), each | 2 0 |
| Lílium lancifólium, rubrum, ,, | 10 6 |
| — Album | 5 0 |
| Pancrátium illyricum | 1 6 |
| Ranunculus, finest mixed, per 100 | 7 6 |
| — 100 in 100 ext., fine var. named | 20 0 |
| — 50 do. do. 10s.; 25 do. do. | 5 0 |
| — Mixed Turban Ranunc., per 100 | 5 0 |
| Tigrídia Pavónia, 1s. 6d. v. large, doz. | 2 6 |
| — Conchiflóra, yellow ... doz. | 6 0 |
| — Superba, scarlet ... ,, | 18 0 |
| Tuberoses, double Italian ... ,, | 4 0 |

# KITCHEN GARDEN SEEDS.

## WARRANTED GENUINE.

| oz. ounce; lb. pound; qt. quart. | Price | pa. packet; bush. bushel. | Price |
|---|---|---|---|
| | s. d. | | s. d. |
| Artichoke, green ... per oz. | 9 | Broccoli, Chappel's cream | |
| Purple ... „ | 9 | ... per oz. | 1 0 |
| Asparagus, giant, oz. 2d. per lb. | 2 6 | Dwarf Siberian ... „ | 1 0 |
| Beans, early Mazagan ... per qt. | 6 | Ellison's new April... „ | 2 6 |
| Early dwarf Fan ... „ | 6 | Field's new white ... „ | 1 6 |
| — Long-pod ... „ | 6 | Grange's early ... „ | 1 6 |
| — Lisbon's do. ... „ | 6 | Hampsh. gr. ... „ | 1 6 |
| Johnson's Wonderful... „ | 6 | Hampton Court ... „ | 1 0 |
| Sword long-pod ... „ | 6 | Howden's superb ... „ | 1 6 |
| Green long-pod ... „ | 6 | Impregnated white... „ | 1 0 |
| Large Windsor ... „ | 8 | Invisible ... „ | 1 0 |
| — New thick do. ... „ | 8 | Knight's protecting... „ | 1 0 |
| — Taylor's do. ... „ | 8 | Lake's white ... „ | 1 0 |
| — Green do. ... „ | 8 | Large spring purple. „ | 1 0 |
| Beet, fine large red ... per oz. | 3 | —— White ... „ | 1 0 |
| New German ... „ | 6 | Late close-headed p.. „ | 1 0 |
| New black ... „ | 6 | — Purple ... „ | 1 0 |
| New dark crimson ... „ | 6 | — White ... „ | 1 0 |
| Green ... „ | 3 | London, particular... „ | 2 6 |
| Silver-stalked ... „ | 3 | Miller's late ... „ | 1 0 |
| White ... „ | 3 | New Victoria ... „ | 1 6 |
| Silesian sugar ... per lb. | 2 0 | Portsmouth ... „ | 1 0 |
| Borecole, or Kail, brown.. per oz. | 3 | Potter's new pink ... „ | 2 6 |
| Green curled dwarf ... „ | 3 | Snow's superb ... „ | 1 0 |
| Curled tall ... „ | 3 | Sulphur ... „ | 1 0 |
| New Asparagus ... „ | 6 | Very late Danish ... „ | 1 0 |
| Buda ... „ | 6 | White Southampton.. „ | 1 0 |
| Variegated, &c., &c. ... „ | 6 | Wilcox's large wh. ... „ | 1 0 |
| Broccoli, ear. pur. Cape.. „ | 1 6 | 8 best for succession. „ | 8 0 |
| White Cape ... „ | 1 6 | 4 do. do. ... „ | 5 0 |
| Green Cape ... „ | 1 6 | Brussel's sprouts, fine... „ | 6 |
| Early Cauliflower ... „ | 1 0 | Imported Belgian ... „ | 1 0 |
| — Close-headed ... „ | 1 0 | Cabbage, Atkins' Match „ | 6 |
| — Malta ... „ | 1 0 | Carter's Matchless ... „ | 1 0 |
| — October ... „ | 1 6 | Early dwarf ... „ | 6 |
| — Purple ... „ | 1 0 | — Battersea ... „ | 6 |
| — Sprouting ... „ | 1 0 | — London Market ... „ | 1 0 |
| — Walcheren ... „ | 2 0 | — Nonpareil ... „ | 6 |
| — White ... „ | 1 0 | — Sugar-loaf ... „ | 6 |
| Adams' new dwarf ... „ | 1 6 | — Wonder ... „ | 1 0 |
| American ... „ | 1 6 | — York ... „ | 6 |
| Brimstone ... „ | 1 0 | — Enfield, new early, „ | 1 0 |

## 233

oz. ounce; lb. pound; qt. quart.  pa. packet; bush. bushel.

| | Price s. d. | | Price s. d. |
|---|---|---|---|
| Cabbage, Large Battersea. per oz. | 6 | Cress, Water ... per pa. | 6 |
| — Imperial ... „ | 6 | Cucumber, fine frame ... „ | 6 |
| — Pomeranian ... „ | 1 0 | Fine long prickly ... „ | 3 |
| — York ... „ | 6 | Fine ridge ... „ | 3 |
| — Drumh., lb. 3s. ... „ | 3 | Short prickly ... „ | 3 |
| — Scotch, lb. 3s. ... „ | 3 | Turkey, wh. or gr. ... „ | 3 |
| Paignton ... „ | 6 | Carter's Champion ... „ | 1 0 |
| Shilling's Queen ... „ | 6 | Colney Hatch, ex. ... „ | 1 0 |
| Spotboro' new ... „ | 1 0 | Cuthill's blackspine ... „ | 6 |
| Vanack ... „ | 6 | Manchester Prize ... „ | 6 |
| 6 finest for succession... „ | 3 6 | Man of Kent ... „ | 6 |
| Red Dutch ... „ | 6 | Roman Emperor ... „ | 6 |
| Dwarf red ... „ | 6 | Sion House ... „ | 6 |
| Savoy, dwarf green ... „ | 6 | Snow's white spine.. „ | 6 |
| — Drumhead ... „ | 6 | Stewart's Ringleader „ | 1 0 |
| — Globe ... „ | 6 | Superb white spine.. „ | 1 0 |
| — Yellow ... „ | 6 | Victory of England.. „ | 1 0 |
| Couve Tronchuda ... „ | 1 0 | Walker's superb ... „ | 1 0 |
| — New curled ... „ | 1 0 | Weedon's frame ... „ | 6 |
| Chou de Milan, imp. ... „ | 1 0 | Young's Champion, &c. „ | 1 0 |
| Carrot, early Morn ... „ | 3 | Cucumbers, 6 finest varieties. | 5 0 |
| Early scarlet frame ... „ | 3 | Endive green curled ... per oz. | 6 |
| Long Surrey ... „ | 3 | White curled ... „ | 6 |
| — Orange ... „ | 3 | Batavian, green ... „ | 6 |
| — New Brunswick ... „ | 3 | — white ... „ | 9 |
| Altringham ... „ | 3 | New German ... „ | 9 |
| White Belgium ... „ | 3 | French beans, Chinadw., per qt. | 1 3 |
| Cauliflower, early Engl.... „ | 1 6 | Dwarf dun ... „ | 1 3 |
| Late English ... „ | 1 6 | Dark dun ... „ | 1 3 |
| — Asiatic ... „ | 1 6 | — Fulmer's ... „ | 1 3 |
| — Cyprus ... „ | 1 6 | — Negro ... „ | 1 3 |
| Fitch's new late ... „ | 2 6 | — Negro Major ... „ | 2 0 |
| Popart's early Engl. ... „ | 2 6 | — Speckled ... „ | 1 3 |
| Late Dutch ... „ | 1 6 | — Turkey ... „ | 2 0 |
| Walcheren ... „ | 1 6 | Runners, scarlet ... „ | 1 3 |
| Cardoon, Spanish ... „ | 6 | — French Haricot ... „ | 1 6 |
| New large purple ... „ | 1 0 | Painted Lady ... „ | 1 6 |
| Celery, soild white ... „ | 3 | Turkey ... „ | 2 0 |
| Soild red ... „ | 3 | Ice plant, garnishing ... per pa. | 3 |
| Giant red ... „ | 4 | Indian Corn ... „ | 3 |
| Giant white ... „ | 4 | Leek, London, Flag ... per oz. | 6 |
| Jones' new Matchl. ... „ | 6 | New Giant ... „ | 1 0 |
| New curled Paw ... „ | 4 | Lettuce, Cos, Ady's . ... „ | 1 0 |
| Seymour's white ... „ | 4 | Cos, Artichoke-leav.... „ | 1 0 |
| Wheeler's pink ... „ | 6 | — Bath ... „ | 1 0 |
| Large-rooted ... „ | 4 | — — Bl. seeded do. ... „ | 1 0 |
| Chervil, curled ... „ | 4 | — — Broad leav. do... „ | 1 0 |
| Corn Salad ... „ | 3 | — Brighton ... „ | 1 0 |
| Cress common ... per qt. | 1 0 | — Brown ... „ | 1 0 |
| Triple curled ... „ | 1 6 | — Egyptian ... „ | 1 0 |
| Golden ... „ | 1 6 | — Florence ... „ | 1 0 |
| Perennial Amer. ... per oz. | 3 | — Green ... „ | 1 0 |

oz. ounce; lb. pound; qt. quart.   pa. packet; bush. bushel.

| Item | Unit | s. d. | Item | Unit | s. d. |
|---|---|---|---|---|---|
| Lettuce, Cos, Kensington. | per oz. | 1 0 | Peas, Early Race-horse | per qt. | 9 |
| — Nonpareil, w. | ,, | 1 6 | — Warwick | ,, | 9 |
| — Nonpareil, gr. | ,, | 1 6 | — Charlton, 2nd early. | ,, | 8 |
| — Paris | ,, | 1 0 | — Bishop's dwarf | ,, | 1 0 |
| — Snow's matchl. | ,, | 1 6 | — Champion of Eng. | ,, | 5 0 |
| — White | ,, | 1 0 | Later sorts | | |
| — — winter | ,, | 1 0 | Carter's Lilliputian | ,, | 2 6 |
| Cabbage, wh. | ,, | 6 | — New Colossus | ,, | 1 6 |
| — Asiatic | ,, | 1 0 | — Victoria | ,, | 3 0 |
| — Brown Dutch | ,, | 6 | Glory of England | ,, | 1 0 |
| — Drumhead | ,, | 1 0 | Marrow, dwarf wh. | ,, | 9 |
| — Hardy Hammers | ,, | 6 | — Dwarf green | ,, | 9 |
| — Malta | ,, | 1 0 | — Tall white | ,, | 9 |
| — Marseilles | ,, | 1 0 | — Tall green | ,, | 9 |
| — Mogul | ,, | 1 0 | Woodford's green | ,, | 1 6 |
| — New Winter | ,, | 1 0 | Victoria | ,, | 1 0 |
| — New pink-edged | ,, | 1 0 | Knigh's Marrow, d. | ,, | 2 0 |
| — Tennis ball | ,, | 1 0 | Matchless Marrow | ,, | 1 0 |
| Silesian, brown | ,, | 1 0 | Bedman's Imperial | ,, | 1 0 |
| — White | ,, | 1 0 | Groom's superb | ,, | 9 |
| 8 Finest sorts | ,, | 7 0 | Prussian blue | ,, | 8 |
| Love Apple or Tomato | ,, | 1 0 | Queen of the dwarfs | ,, | 2 6 |
| Yellow | ,, | 1 0 | Scimitar | ,, | 1 0 |
| Mallow, garnishing | per pa. | 3 | 10 best for succession.. | ,, | 15 0 |
| Mustard, white | per qt. | 1 0 | Potato early | per pa. | 1 0 |
| Onion, blood-red | per oz. | 6 | Late | ,, | 1 0 |
| Deptford | ,, | 6 | Silver-skin Dutch | ,, | 1 0 |
| Globe | ,, | 6 | Purslain, gr. or gold | per oz. | 6 |
| — New white | ,, | 9 | Radish, long frame | per qt. | 2 0 |
| James' keeping | ,, | 9 | Wood's new frame | ,, | 2 6 |
| Lisbon | ,, | 6 | Early scarlet | ,, | 2 0 |
| New Giant | ,, | 9 | Early short-topped | ,, | 2 0 |
| Pickling | ,, | 9 | Rong Salmon | ,, | 2 0 |
| Portugal, white | ,, | 6 | White Naples | ,, | 2 6 |
| Reading | ,, | 6 | Red Turnip | ,, | 2 6 |
| Silver-skinned | ,, | 9 | White Turnip | ,, | 2 6 |
| Spanish, white | ,, | 6 | Mixed Turnip | ,, | 2 6 |
| — Brown | ,, | 6 | New Olive | per oz. | 2 |
| Strasburg | ,, | 6 | Spanish, Black | ,, | 2 |
| Tripoli, large | ,, | 9 | Rampion, pa. 3d. | | |
| Two-bladed early | ,, | 6 | Rhubarb, Victoria | ,, | 1 0 |
| Welch | ,, | 6 | Tobolsk, &c., &c. | ,, | 1 0 |
| 6 Finest sorts, 2 ounces | ea. | 7 0 | Salsafy | ,, | 6 |
| Parsley, extra curled | ,, | 3 | Scandix bulbosa, root | ,, | 6 |
| Myatt's garnishing | ,, | 4 | Scorzonera | ,, | 6 |
| Large-rooted | ,, | 4 | Sea Kail | per qt. | 2 0 |
| Parsnip, best large | ,, | 3 | Skirret | per oz. | 8 |
| Peas, early Kent | per qt. | 8 | Sorrel | ,, | 6 |
| Early Frame | ,, | 8 | Spinach, Round | per qt. | 1 0 |
| — May | ,, | 8 | Prickly | ,, | 1 0 |
| — Prince Albert | ,, | 1 0 | Broad Flanders | ,, | 1 0 |
| — Shilling's Grotto | ,, | 1 0 | New Zealand | per oz. | 6 |

| oz. ounce ; qt. quart. | Price | pa. packet ; bush. bushel. | Price |
|---|---|---|---|
| | s. d. | | s. d. |
| *Carter's Victoria Pea warranted superior in size and flavour to any other. | | Hyssop, per oz. 6d., per pa. | 3 |
| | | Lavender ,, 1s. ,, | 3 |
| | | Marjoram, pot ,, 1s. ,, | 3 |
| | | —Sweet ,, 1s. ,, | 3 |
| Squash, fine mixed ...per pa. | 6 | Marigold, pot ,, 6d. ,, | 3 |
| Turnip, early Dutch ...per oz. | 3 | Rosemary ,, 1s. ,, | 3 |
| Early, Mousetail ... ,, | 3 | Rue ,, 1s. ,, | 3 |
| —Snowball ... ,, | 3 | Wormwood ,, 6d. ,, | 3 |
| —Nonsuch ... ,, | 3 | Sage ,, 6d. ,, | 3 |
| —Stone or stubble ... ,, | 3 | Savory, Sum ,, 1s. ,, | 3 |
| —Large white ... ,, | 3 | —Winter ,, 1s. ,, | 3 |
| Yellow Altringham ... ,, | 3 | Thyme ,, 1s. ,, | 3 |
| —Maltese ... ,, | 3 | Tobacco (fumigating) ,, | 3 |
| —Stone ... ,, | 3 | | |
| Swedish ... ,, | 2 | ROOTS, PLANTS, &c. | |
| Teltau, German ... ,, | 6 | | |
| Vegetable Marrow ...per pa. | 6 | *The prices variable.* | |
| SWEET HERBS, &c. | | Artichokes ... per bush. | |
| | | Asparagus, all sorts... ,, 100 .. | |
| Balm, per oz. 1s., per pa. | 3 | Garlic ... ,, lb. ... | |
| Basil, sweet ,, 1s. ,, | 3 | Horse Radish ... ,, doz.. | |
| Basil, Bush ,, 1s. ,, | 3 | Mushroom, Spawn ... ,, bush... | |
| Borage ,, 6d. ,, | 3 | Potato, early forcing ... | |
| Buglos ,, 6d. ,, | 3 | Late varieties ... ... | |
| Burnet ,, 6d. ,, | 3 | New ,, ... ... | |
| Capsicum ,, 1s. ,, | 3 | Rhubarb Roots, all sorts, each... | |
| Chilis ,, 1s. ,, | 3 | Shallots ... per lb ... | |
| Clary ,, 6d. ,, | 3 | Sea Kale ... per 100... | |
| Fennel ,, 6d. ,, | 3 | Strawberry Plants ... ,, | |
| Florence Fennel,, 6d. ,, | 3 | Raspberry Plants ... ,, | |

# ORNAMENTAL FOLIAGE PLANTS.

## CONTRIBUTED BY Mr. J. M. GLEESON,
### SUPERINTENDENT OF THE AGRI-HORTICULTURAL GARDENS.

## CROTONS.

THIS interesting genus of plants, which are chiefly natives of New Guinea, the Moluccas, and South Sea Islands, has deservedly gained a place in popular favour of late years. When this useful little hand-book of gardening made its appearance in 1859, these plants were almost unknown, the old Croton *Pictum* and *Variegatum* being the only two kinds in general cultivation. Owing to their liability to variation, both under artificial fertilization, and by the agency of insects in their native country, an enormous number of strange-formed and brilliant-coloured foliaged plants have resulted. Artificial crossing still presents a wide field for the introduction of new varieties, which may probably transcend in beauty all those now or heretofore in cultivation.

To increase our stock of any desirable kind which we may have from seedlings or from older varieties, propagation from cuttings is the most certain to produce nice plants in a short time. The cuttings should be three to five inches long, from the young growth, taking care that the base is tolerably firm, but not woody, as these latter take longer to form roots. The lower two or three leaves may be cut away, but the upper leaves should be left intact. They may be put down to strike in any ordinary garden soil, but pure white sand, not sea sand, is the most convenient medium in which to insert the cuttings, taking care to slightly water the sand before insertion and a good watering after to settle the cuttings firm. Large seed pans, with some broken pots or bricks for drainage with a layer of old cocoanut fibre over the latter to prevent the layer of sand in which they are to be inserted from washing away through the drainage, are to be used. The plants should be shaded by means of palm leaves or mats or any other suitable materials at hand. The shading should only be used in bright sunshine, the covering being taken off at night and whenever the sky is cloudy. Making beds under trees for cuttings should be avoided if possible. With ordinary care cuttings may be made at any season, but the commencement of the rains is the most suitable time, as little or no care is then required for watering. They generally take root in fifteen or twenty days in favourable weather.

When transplanting, the plant should be taken up singly, care being taken to leave untouched whatever sand adheres to the roots. Drainage should be liberal, and the pots should be no larger than suffices to conveniently contain the individual plant. Good virgin loam, with leaf mould and about one-sixth silver sand, should be used. If good leaf mould is not procurable, good loam and sand will suffice. The mistake of putting a small plant in a large pot should be avoided. The use of large pots certainly saves future pottings, but in this case the plants never maintain so healthy a root action as when successively potted into larger pots as required. The central shoot should be stopped at about twelve inches. This causes the plant to throw out branches from the lower part, so that when full grown it is well foliaged down to the pot. Though in growing a few of the narrow-leaved varieties, for table decoration, the principal shoot may remain intact until the plants get too large for that purpose. They may then be cut back to about a foot and allowed to grow on for large specimens. Their quick growth, comparatively easy propagation with their gorgeous colouration and adaptability to either pot-culture or permanent planting out in the garden, to contrast with dark masses of foliage, places them in the first rank of decorative plants. Though certainly making a more vigorous growth under the influence of shade, they lose much in the splendid variations of colour which are never so vivid as when fully exposed to the sun. In places further more inland than Madras, &c., pot-cultivation is perhaps to be recommended, as the plants could thus be arranged outside in the cold season and a slight amount of shade might be found beneficial in the hot season. In the latter case they could be removed to a Plant-house of light materials, the semi-shade being obtained by having the roof formed only of light bamboo screens.

The number of varieties of Crotons, advertised in the most recent catalogues, amounts to over two hundred; but the following list of the principal kinds of Crotons arranged to shew their principal characteristics, may be found useful to amateurs. Those with only pale yellow and green colouration are marked with an*; those suitable for table decoration with a †.

**A.** *Large leaves, broader at the upper portion.*
*Gladstonii,*—blotched green and cream colour, very large, bold striking foliage.
*Williamsii,*—dark green, crimson veining, very rich in colour.
*Hendersonii,*—rich green, lemon-coloured veins and margin, very bright.
*New Guinea,*—as *Hendersonii*, tinted with crimson.
*Baptistii,*—bright green, orange crimson marks.

**B.** *With large broad leaves of about equal width.*
*Maximum,*—green with bold yellow veins: requires semi-shade.
*Macfeanus,*—blotched piebald-looking leaves, green and cream, very effective.
*Grande,*—bright green, veins pink: requires semi-shade.
*Aureum,*—bright green, flushed here and there with yellow.
*Rotundifolium,*—similar to last, but smaller leaf.

**C.** *Medium-sized leaves.*
*Pictum,*—generally rich, olive green, sometimes beautifully blotched with pink.
*Metallicum,*—very dark olive colour, very rich and sombre: useful contrast plant.
*Oblongifolium,*—bright green and gamboge yellow, marbled.
*Variegatum,*—rich green, veins all bright yellow.

**D.** *Medium size with undulated margins.*
*Undulatum,†*—black green with rich crimson, marbling, margins undulated: a superb and rich variety.

**E.** *With medium oval-shaped leaves.*

*Rosea-Picta,*—green, orange crimson veining, rich.
*Royal Prince,*—green, and lemon veins tinged with pink.
*Andrieanus,*—green, with orange pink veining.
*MacArthurii,* No. 37,—somewhat similar, but more effective than *Rosea-Picta.*

**F.** *Leaves long and of moderate breadth.*

*Veitchianus,*—green, centre of the leaf yellow, with crimson midrib.
*Hookeri,*\*—rich green, yellow veining : bold foliaged plant.
*Weismanii,*\* †—green and yellow : one of the best for specimen purposes.
*Superbiens,*—yellow and crimson, with green blotches.
*Concinnus,*—green, with orange crimson veins.
*Splendidus,*—like *Veitchianus,* but smaller.
*Goldiana,*\*—lemon yellow, with irregular green blotches.

**G.** *Long lance-shaped leaves.*

*Lancifolium,*—green with crimson midrib.
*Wilsonii,*\* †—rich green, yellow midrib and mottled all over with yellow : very effective.
*Macfarlainii,*—similar to *Wilsonii,* perhaps the best tinged rose.
*Queen Victoria,*—similar to *Sunset* : markings carmine.
*Lord Ripon,*\*—rich green, bright gamboge yellow, veins rich and bright.
*Sunset,*—dark green, blotched irregularly with orange crimson, some leaves totally crimson.

**H.** *Leaves long and irregular in breadth, not twisted.*

*Youngi,*†—bright green markings on a yellow ground, blotched with crimson.
*Lowii,*†—similar to last.
*Truffantianus,*†—green, broad crimson centre, curious variegation.
*Nobilis,*†—(also called *Jacksonii*) rich green yellow centre, crimson midrib.

**I.** *Leaves long and slightly twisted.*

*Toughii,*—(also called *Irregulare*) green, with pale yellow centre.

*Angustifolium giganteum,*—yellow with green blotches.

**J.** *Leaves large, very long and twisted.*

*Schomburgkiana,*—dark green and crimson, curiously twisted, one of the best.

*Challenger,*—green, spotted pink, margin and midrib crimson.

*Rex,*—green, slightly twisted, central line orange crimson.

*Australian Longifolium,*—dark green, twisted.

*Washingtonii,*—as the last, but narrower leaf.

**K.** *Leaves narrow, twisted and interrupted.*

*Interruptum,*—yellow, crimson and green.

*Duke of Edinburgh,*†—cream colour, blotched green, one of the best.

*Duchess of Edinburgh,*—green, spotted pink.

*Mutabilis,*—some very dark, others almost orange crimson.

*Majesticus,*—broad crimson central space, with green margins.

*Picturatus,*—green and pink, mottled and blotched.

*Torquatus,*—dark green and scarlet lake, one of the best.

**L.** *Leaves thin and narrow, slightly twisted and undulated.*

*Johannis,*†—green and pale yellow, most effective.

*Longifolium,*—yellow and green, one of the most graceful in cultivation.

*Microphyllum,*—a most desirable variety: one of the most effective.

**M.** *Leaves twisted more or less.*

*Spirale,*—twisted, some leaves dark green, others yellow and crimson.

*Crispum,*—twisted, green-margined, yellow and crimson centre.

*Camptophyllum,*†—twisted, pale yellow with green blotches.

*Amabilis,*†—green and yellow, delicate narrow foliage: pretty.

**N.** *Leaves horned; curious shaped.*

*Cornutum,*—green margin with yellow and crimson centre.

*Imperialis,*—dark green with pink midrib and margins: both broad and narrow-shaped leaves.

O. *Leaves long, breadth variable, form grotesque.*

*Multicolour,*—strange-formed leaf, broad top, tricolored, very brilliant.

*Variabilis,*—blotched irregularly with green, white, grey, yellow and crimson : a beautiful variety.

*MacArthurii,*\*† No. 11,—ragged-looking leaf, irregularly formed of yellow and green : one of the best.

P. *Extremely long leaf, not twisted.*

*Mooreanus,*\*—a most effective variety, yellow with green blotches, sometimes with short lobes at base.

Q. *Trilobed varieties.*

*Alberti,*\*—yellow centre, green at lower part of leaves.

*Disraeli,*\*†—narrow, yellow with green markings: sometimes five-lobed.

*Lord Cairns,*—green, yellow and crimson.

*Evansiana,*†—green with yellow feather-like mark in centre, tinted with crimson.

*MacArthurii,* No. 85,—green, with yellow midrib and lobes.

*New Guinea,*—green and yellow lobes, a peculiar narrow trilobe.

*Dormanianus,*—a voluted trilobe, dark green, yellow and crimson-spotted.

R. *Voluted leaves.*

*Volutum,*†—curious form, very effective, green with yellow veins and crimson midrib.

S. *Various-shaped leaves, all spotted.*

*Acubæfolium,*—one of the best old varieties, the spots yellow with crimson centres.

*Maculata,*\* †—green, spotted cream colour.

„ *Katoni,*\* †—green, with cream spots, a trilobe.

*Cromatum,*†—green, irregularly and thickly spotted with orange crimson.

# CROTONS.

### CONTRIBUTED BY AN AMATEUR.

No one who has attended the Annual Flower-Shows of the Agri-Horticultural Society for the past few years can have omitted noticing the immense piles of Crotons and other foliage plants exhibited year after year, the grand effect produced by the huge piles of Crotons alone testifying (if any proof were wanted) the increased interest taken by Amateurs in the cultivation of ornamental foliage plants; therefore, in issuing this new edition, a few hints on their cultivation have been added.

Crotons deservedly occupy the leading position among ornamental foliage plants not only because the Indian climate, especially that of Southern India, is peculiarly adapted for their successful propagation, growth, and development, but also because in this group of plants is to be found not only the grandest, but also the most fantastic and grotesque foliage, which, in the generality of cases, is extravagantly variegated, and thus rendered unexceptionably beautiful.

There are, at the present time, in the trade, upwards of two hundred distinct varieties, from which the most fastidious taste may be easily satisfied, besides these, are the endless variety of nameless seedlings raised by Amateurs and Horticultural Societies, and to these additions are being continually made by new introductions from Australia, New Guinea, the South Sea Islands, and the New Hebrides besides Hybrids raised by Horticulturists. (Hybrids are plants raised by the mixture, or crossing of two different species, with the object of producing a new species; or a new plant with the qualities of two plants combined in one). With such attractions as these, there is no doubt that for many years to come, Crotons will continue to be regarded as the most desirable foliage plants suitable for decorative, and exhibition purposes.

## PROPAGATION.

All the known varieties of the Croton family can be very easily propagated, namely, by cuttings; for this purpose, sometime before the rains come down, matured branches must be selected from the most vigorous and healthy of the Croton trees of the collection at disposal (tender branches are next to useless, as they seldom take root, and when they do, a sickly miserable specimen is the result). The selection having been made, cut off the branches with a sharp knife; if any of the branches are too long, divide them in two or three pieces, taking care that none of the pieces are less than three inches in length; the pieces thus cut should, without loss of time, be planted in seed pans into which Compost No. 1* has been previously put; the pan or pans must then be put in a place where they will have plenty of shade and light, and will not be shut out from rain and dew when they fall; the cuttings, if regularly watered from a can, will, in a short time, take root. If the operations detailed above are carefully conducted in the cool of the evening, or on a rainy day, there will be very few casualties among the cuttings; the coarser natures very seldom fail, but should some of the rare kinds fail, fresh cuttings of those particular kinds must be taken, and put into a separate pan, and grown under a glass cover. Should the quantity of cuttings required to be put down at one time be so large that they cannot be dealt with in pans, then the cuttings of the common varieties may be put into a bed in the ground conveniently situated, as to shade, and open to rain and dew.

Within three weeks or a month, the cuttings will have rooted, and as soon as they have put forth three or four leaves, they are ready for transplantation into nursery pots, say seven inches deep, seven inches wide at the top, and six inches at the bottom,

---

* COMPOST No. 1.—Stable manure, containing a large quantity of the refuse of grass on which horses have been fed, and which generally consists of roots, should be laid up to rot for some time until the roots are dead—then mixed with an equal quantity of red earth and laid by in a shady place for a month, the heap should be watered if the weather is dry. This will make an excellent soil suitable for the majority of Exotics and Indigenous shrubs cultivated in pots, especially Roses, or for renewing flower-beds.—*Hints to Amateur Gardeners, by A. T. Jaffrey.*

filled with new soil similar to that in which they were propagated; in these pots they may safely remain for a season, when they must be transferred into larger pots, say twelve inches deep, twelve inches wide at the top, and eight inches at the bottom, (inside measurement).

## PROPAGATION BY SEEDLINGS.

*Croton Seedlings.*—For the benefit of those who care to raise seedlings, a few hints are included for their guidance. Most of the common varieties of the Croton flower and perfect their seed, the quantity of seed produced is very variable; the female flowers are borne on a spike six to eight inches long, resembling the tendril of a climbing plant; the flowers mature and are succeeded by globular fruit; these must be enclosed by a very light coarse muslin bag, so that, when they become ripe and burst, the seed contained in the berry may not be lost as they are scattered to a great distance: by the use of the muslin bag, not only are the fruit and seed secured, but light and air are admitted into the bag; when all the fruit from the spike or tendril have dropped into the bag, remove it and place it in the sun for a few hours, then sow the seed immediately (as they invariably deteriorate very rapidly by keeping); if fortune is propitious, some very fine plants may reward the patience and perseverance bestowed in raising the seedlings. If the raising of seedlings is made one of the customary gardening operations, it will soon, by habit, become an amusement.

## GROWTH AND DEVELOPMENT.

Crotons, like all other plants, absorb the nutriment they require by their roots; this is passed through the stem into the leaves where the greater portion of the liquid of which it is composed is discharged, and the residue is submitted to the action of the atmosphere; Carbonic acid is thus generated, which is decomposed by the action of the light; Carbon is then fixed under the form of a nutritive material which is re-conveyed into the system of the plant, and thus its growth and development are secured in proportion to the supply of the nutriment. But it has been ascertained that a proportion of this secreted matter is subsequently discharged by the roots into the soil, thus rendering the soil unfit for the cultivation of the same species, although plants of other species may be raised in the contaminated soil without much apparent injury.

It is very remarkable in plants which ripen their seed and throw out suckers or shoots, that these suckers strike out to a considerable distance from the parent plant, as if endeavouring to avoid the soil contaminated by the excrementitious discharge from the roots of the parent tree.

It is, therefore, evident that periodically a change of soil is essential, and that plants in pots must be transplanted annually, and where this change cannot be effected, the soil around the plant must be very carefully removed without injuring the roots, and new soil substituted for that which has been already removed; this operation of transplanting or changing of the soil must invariably be performed shortly before the rains commence.

It must be borne in mind that the operation of transplantation will, more or less, effect the foliage or flowers put forth immediately after, or which were in course of being perfected when the transplantation took place, the result depending very much on the care bestowed in the carrying out of the operation; when carelessly done, not only is there the risk of the subsequent foliage or flowers being diminished in size, or distorted, but it may result in the loss of the whole of the foliage, or flowers, or in the total loss of the plant itself, therefore plants intended for exhibition or show-purposes should not be interfered with; even if by accident the earthen pots containing them are fractured, they should be retained as they are, and the change into the new pot effected on the evening preceding the morning of the show, so that the foliage or bloom of the plant may be in perfection for the occasion.

## ALPHABETICAL LIST OF CROTONS,
### WITH A SHORT DESCRIPTION OF A FEW OF THEM.

*C. Alexandra* is a tender but rare broad-leafed variety; leaves being twelve to sixteen inches in length by five inches in breadth, of a dark green colour, irregularly spotted and streaked with orange yellow and carmine; as the leaves mature, these colours change into bronze and rich crimson; should be grown in the shade, and cuttings will only succeed under glass.

Croton Albicans.

*C. Amabilis.*—A hardy narrow leafed variety produces green leaves, four inches long by half an inch wide with midrib and margins marked creamy white; wants shade only in the very hot months, cuttings root easily. This plant can be grown for a long time in a small pot or vase for table decoration.

*C. Andreanus.*—Richly-coloured large-leafed variety; must be grown in the shade; the leaves are twelve to fourteen inches long by five inches at the broadest part; the ground colour is green, on which the midrib and veins are marked out in light creamy white; as the leaves mature, these markings become a rich crimson; cuttings succeed well. This plant must be "stopped," that is, the top must be pinched off to make it branch.

Croton Aneitumensis.  Croton Argus.

*C. Appendiculatus.*—Hardy variety with small green, unmarked, interrupted leaves, that is, two leaves are grown which are connected by a costa or thread-like rib, about one and a half or two inches long; wants protection during the very hot months only; cuttings root easily.

| Croton Augustifolia. | Croton Aureo—lineata. |
| " " gigantea. | " " —maculata. |
| " Aucubæfolius. | " " —phinecia. |
| " Attunata (Vivicans.) | " Baptisti. |

*Baron Frank Selliere.*—This hybrid has leaves twelve inches long by four wide, of a pleasing green, with irregular markings of a creamy yellow; wants shade, cuttings, if not treated with care, will not root.

*Baron James De Rothschild.*—Also an hybrid of rare beauty; grows very slowly, but the leaves are richly marked with bright crimson at a very early stage; they are obovate in shape, nine inches long by four wide; must be grown in the shade, and cuttings raised under glass. This plant must be "stopped" to branch, and its slow growth and brilliant colours make it very suitable for table decoration.

*Barton Westii.*—This is a plant introduced by Mr. West of Calcutta from the South Sea Islands; has very long leaves from twenty-four to thirty-six inches in length, and about two inches in breadth, but as the leaves are rolled backwards, they appear much narrower than they really are. The ground colour is a pleasing green with a narrow golden central band with occasional patches of the same colour; must be grown in the shade; cuttings root easily.

        Croton Bicolor.        Croton Bismarkii.
        Croton Braegæanus.

*C. Bergmanni.*—This variety is of continental origin with bright green leaves, a foot in length and six inches in breadth, with the veins and central band marked out in ivory white; wants shade; cuttings must be treated with care.

*C. Broomfieldii.*—A narrow leaf variety, with very dark green leaves, nine inches long by two and a half wide, with the midrib and margins marked in bright crimson and golden variegations, in the shape of spots and bars freely distributed all over the leaf; must be grown in the shade; cuttings require care.

        Croton Braithevaitei.        Croton Burtoni.
        „      Camptophyllus.        „      Carrieri.
        „      Cascarilla.        „      Chrysophyllus.

*C. Challenger (Imperator).*—This is an old favourite, and deservedly so, having graceful drooping leaves from a foot to a foot and a half in length by two or three inches in breadth; the young leaves are of a very light green with creamy white markings which leave very little of the green to be seen; as the leaves mature, much of the latter colour gives place to magenta which gives the leaves a very grand appearance; easily propagated, but must be grown in a very shady place.

*C. Chelsoni* comes to us from New Guinea; has small narrow leaves, very variable, some twisted, others plain, but all of them richly coloured with a peculiar tint of orange and bright crimson; wants shade; is propagated easily and very suitable for table decoration.

        Croton Comte de Germiny.        Croton Concinnus.
        „      Contortus.        „      Cornigerus.

*C. Cooperii.*—A very handsome long drooping-leafed variety, very finely marked; the foot-stalk, which is six inches long, is magenta, and this colour is carried through the length of the midrib of the leaf which is from twelve to eighteen inches long and three inches wide; the ground colour is dark-green with all the veins marked out in creamy white; the well-grown matured leaves have tints of crimson intermixed, and appear, when seen from a distance, as if they were covered with white lace with crimson threads run in here and there. This plant is very tender; wants shade, but will propagate easily; must be "stopped" to branch.

| | |
|---|---|
| Croton Cornutum. | Croton Countess. |
| ,, Cronstandti. | ,, Crown Prince. |
| ,, Cunninghami. | ,, Darciana. |

*C. Dayspring.*—This is a very pretty variety with glowing colours like "Sunset"; has semi-transparent leaves twelve to eighteen inches long and three inches wide; not only is the upper part of the leaf marked with orange-yellow and crimson, but the under part has a shade of red which is reflected through the leaf, giving it a fiery appearance; wants shade, and cuttings must be raised under glass.

| | |
|---|---|
| Croton Diadem. | Croton Diana. |
| ,, Diversifolia. | ,, Dodgsonii. |
| ,, Dormanianus. | ,, Droueti. |
| ,, Duke of Connaught. | ,, Duke of Buccleuch. |
| ,, ,, Edinburgh. | ,, Duchess of Edinburgh. |

*C. Eburneus* has lanceolate leaves, eight inches in length by an inch in breadth; the ground colour is green with an ivory white band half the breadth of the leaf running along the centre; propagates easily, but must be grown in the shade.

Croton Eclipse.

*C. Elegantissimus sp. W. Bull* has very long narrow leaves, the foot-stalks of which are of a bright red colour; the variegation of the leaf consists in blotches and patches of bright golden yellow and chrome yellow; is of hybrid origin; very tender; wanting shade, and difficult to propagate except under glass.

Croton Elegans.    Croton Evansiana.
„ Ensifolia.      „ Fenzii.
Croton Elegantissimum.

*C. Excelsior* has richly-coloured narrow leaves, about sixteen inches long by an inch and a half wide, of a deep green colour with yellow markings, which become a very bright crimson when the leaves mature; must be grown in the shade, and propagates easily.

*C. Formosus* has lance-shaped leaves, fifteen inches long and an inch broad; the stalks are crimson, which colour extends itself all along the midrib; the bright green leaves are marked with pale yellow bands, blotches and spots, which subsequently change into crimson; wants shade, and propagates easily.

Croton Fordii.    Croton Foxii.
„ Freckle.       „ Fucatus (lacteum).

*C. Gladstonii* has large bold leaves, sixteen inches long and four inches broad at the top, but tapers towards the stalk; the large green leaves are covered with pale yellow markings, sometimes in bands, sometimes in patches; must be grown in a shady place; propagates easily; must be "stopped" early if a widespread plant is desired.

*C. Gloriosus.*—A new introduction from the New Hebrides also known as the "Princess of Wales"; the leaves are narrow, being a little more than an inch in breadth, but about twenty-four inches in length; some of the leaves are very much undulated; the habit is arching, and the variegation is uncertain; in some leaves the ground colour is creamy yellow with clouded green blotches and spots, the smaller spots being confluent; in other leaves these conditions are reversed; this plant must be protected from the sun throughout the year, and cuttings will only root under glass.

Croton Goldie.    Croton Goldieana.
„ Goodeneoughti.  „ Gracilis.
„ Grande.         „ Grotesque.

Croton Hastiferus.   Croton Harlequin.
  „   Hawkerii.         „   Hendersonii.
Croton Henryanus (Macarthuri), No. 46.

*C. Heroicus.*—This plant has leaves resembling the tri-lobed variety; the leaves are obovate and having the front portion of the leaf narrower than the back; the bright green leaves are copiously marked with yellow; in some cases the whole of the leaf is covered with this colour, on others it is mixed with a rosy crimson tint; wants shade, and cuttings must be treated with care; is very suitable for table decoration.

Croton Hillianus.   Croton Hybridum.
Croton Hookerii.

*C. Illustris* is a fantastically grotesque-looking plant with a very good sprinkling of three-lobed green leaves attached to purplish foot-stalks, and spotted and blotched with golden yellow; must be grown in the shade; this is a new plant not yet propagated in Southern India; cuttings should be raised under glass to prevent disappointment.

Croton Imperialis.   Croton Imperialis—aurea.
  „   Interruptum.    „   Interruptum—aurea.
  „   Insignis.       „   Irregular.

*C. Jamesii*, a very distinct variety with leaves from three to four inches in length by two inches in breadth; the ground colour is ivory white with scanty irregular markings in green of two or three shades; a very delicate plant; wants plenty of shade, this plant must be "stopped" and compelled to branch early; cuttings succeed well; very suitable for table decoration.

*C. Johannis.*—This is a long narrow-leafed variety (resembling the old "longifolium"); the leaves are from ten to fourteen inches in length and less than half an inch in breadth; the ground colour is green, which in the young leaf is suffused with yellow markings, but when the leaf matures, scarcely any of the green ground colour remains to be seen, the leaves being almost entirely yellow; will stand a moderate amount of sun; cuttings grow easily.

Croton Jubilee.   Croton Jacksoni (Noblis).

*C. Kingianus*, as its name denotes, is the grandest and noblest of the Crotons, with rich bright green leaves, some of which are twenty inches in length and nearly eight inches in breadth, brilliantly variegated with golden yellow markings; the plant must be grown in the shade where plenty of light is available, or the golden markings will not come out to advantage; cuttings easily root.

*C. Lady Zetland* is a densely-leaved variety of drooping habit; the leaves are a foot long, but only an inch wide, of a shining green splashed with yellow; the midrib being dark orange margined with crimson; wants shade, and cuttings must be raised under glass.

Croton Laingi.
  „ Latifolius.
Croton Lancifolius.
  „ Longifolium (Salicifolium).

*C. Longifolium* (Australian).—This is a fine long-leafed variety with spiral and undulated dropping leaves eighteen to twenty inches long, of a dark bronze, (nearly black,) the young light green leaves being a striking contrast next to the black matured leaves; will stand a moderate amount of sun; propagates easily.

*C. Lord Ripon.*—This plant is very much like the well-known "C. Hookerii," only the leaves are very much larger, and the golden markings are much richer and less of the green is seen; will grow in the sun except in the very hot months; cuttings succeed easily.

*C. Lowii* (*Handburyanus*) is a very handsome Croton, with long pendulous leaves about eighteen inches in length and three in breadth, of a bright green colour with patches of light yellow, which become suffused with crimson markings as the leaves mature; the underside of the leaves have a shade of crimson which makes them very rich in appearance; must be grown in the shade; cuttings want care.

Croton Linearis.    Croton Lord Belhaven.

*C. Macfeeanus* is a plant with foliage like Croton "Maxima," with a large patch of creamy yellow, sometimes covering nearly two-thirds of the leaf and at others only one side of the leaf, leaving the opposite side perfectly green; must have shade; cuttings grow easily.

| Croton Macfarlanei. | Croton Macarthuri. |
| --- | --- |
| ,, Macarthur Species. | ,, Macarthuri, Nos. 11, |
| ,, Maculata-Kattonii. | 37, 47, 56, 85. |
| | ,, Maculata—var. |

*C. Magnolifolius* is one of the few large-leafed Crotons that has the primary veins of the leaf distinctly marked in crimson on a bright green ground; the leaves are twelve to fourteen inches long and five inches broad; will grow to advantage next to "Kingianus;" is very delicate, and if placed where there is too much sun or shade, will deteriorate very rapidly; cuttings raised under glass.

*C. Majesticum*, a bright-looking plant, with narrow leaves about fourteen inches in length; the ground colour is light green with the central rib marked out in creamy yellow, but as the leaves mature, the green and yellow are replaced with a dark shade of red, and the middle of the leaf has a bright crimson band; the leaves being long and drooping, makes the plant very handsome; must be grown in the shade; cuttings succeed well.

*C. Mirabilis* is a richly marked plant, with leaves ten inches in length by three inches in breadth; the bronze green leaves are marbled, blotched and veined with rosy crimson which gives it a rich appearance; wants shade; cuttings require care.

*C. Morti* has leaves eight inches in length by about four inches in breadth in the broadest part, that is, near the apex; the leaf tapers towards the foot-stalk; the ground colour is a bright green on which the midrib and primary veins are very broadly marked in creamy yellow; wants plenty of shade; cuttings rather delicate.

| Croton Maxima. | Croton Microphyllum. |
| --- | --- |
| Croton Medium. | |

*C. Mooreanus* has long drooping leaves sixteen to eighteen inches in length by one and a half inches in breadth; the ground colour is a bright green with bright yellow markings consisting of a yellow midrib and primary veins with numerous yellow bars across the leaf; in some cases the yellow is very profuse, but this condition is only obtained by exposure to the sun; a moderate exposure, during the cooler months only, will produce a very handsome plant; cuttings grow very easily.

   Croton Mrs. Dorman.  Croton Multicolour.

*C. Multiformis* grows a variety of leaves, that is, of different shapes, the most interesting of them being the spiral and interrupted ones which are about a foot long and an inch in breadth; the ground colour is bright green spotted with pale yellow and tinted with crimson; requires shade; cuttings must be treated with care.

      Croton Murillo.

*C. Mutabilis* (*Princep's*), as its name denotes, grows leaves of a variety of shapes; the most remarkable are those that are interrupted and which are enlarged towards the apex into a cuplike termination, from which a rib or thread grows for two or three inches in length, and a second leaflet also very variably in shape is formed; the colours are dark-green, marked with shades of yellow and pink, which, when matured, become bright orange and magenta; must have shade; cuttings easily root, but in selecting branches, one with the largest number of interrupted leaves on it should be chosen.

   Croton Neptune.  Croton Nevilliæ.
    „ Newtonii.  „ Negro-rubra.
      Croton Nigrum.

*C. Ornatus* has oblong deep green leaves, with partially undulated margins, a central band, and long parallel veins of creamy yellow, also irregular blotches of the same colour which becomes tinged with crimson; some of the leaves are bronzy green with lines and blotches of rosy pink and a midrib of rosy crimson; propagated easily.

   Croton Orestes.  Croton Ovalifolium.

*C. Prince Albert Victor.*—An Australian variety of dense drooping habit; some of the long pendulous leaves are completely spiral, others have a twist only, but they are invariably undulated; the leaf is dark-green, handsomely spotted and margined with yellow; requires plenty of shade, and cuttings are propagated easily; must be " stopped " to branch.

*C. Prince of Wales.*—This plant has been cultivated under the name of "Schomburgkiana"; it is too well known to require description; it is, however, very difficult to obtain a position for this plant in the garden so that the leaves may be well coloured; a well coloured plant should have its leaves almost entirely pale yellow, margined and blotched with rich carmine, with irregular patches of light green, the midrib and leaf stalk being bright magenta; cuttings root easily.

Croton Parkerii.  Croton Pictum.
" Picturatus.  " Pilgrimii.
" President.  " President Cherreau.
" Paradoxus.  " Prima Donna.

*C. Recurvifolius.*—This plant is a great improvement on Croton "Volutus," the leaves growing more densely, being twice the breadth, and the midrib and veins being marked in rich crimson, makes it a grander plant; the leaves have also a rugged and waved appearance as the veins are much sunk below the surface; must be "stopped" to branch; propagated easily.

*C. Roseo-Picta.*—A very tender but pretty Hybrid of dwarf and dense habit and very richly coloured, the green leaf being literally covered with markings of a very light yellow and rose tints; must be grown in the shade, and cuttings raised under glass; the old variety, Croton "Pictum," is often sold as Roseo-Picta.

Croton Queen Victoria.  Croton Regina.
" Queensland.  " Reedii.
" Rex.  " Rodeckiana.
" Royal Prince.  " Rotundifolia.

*C. Rubescens*, an introduction from the South Sea Islands, with lanceolate leaves; the midrib and veins are yellow with freckles of the same colour passing through rosy red on the ribs and orange red on the freckling to deep green with rich crimson lines and spots; wants shade, and cuttings require care.

Croton Rubro-lineatus.

*C. Schomburgkiana.*—This is similar in description to the "Princess of Wales," only the colouring is pale yellow, white and brilliant crimson; must be grown in the shade and "stopped" if required to branch; cuttings must be raised under glass.

*C. Sir Ashly Eden* has very handsome twisted leaves of a graceful drooping habit, about eighteen inches long and one and half inches in breadth; the colour is green; the midrib and margins are deep magenta, the underside of the leaf is crimson, but many of the leaves are entirely marked with magenta, which makes it a grand plant; wants plenty of shade, being delicate; cuttings should be put under glass.

  Croton Sovereign.   Croton Sunset.
   „  Spectabilis.   „  Speciosus.
   „  Splendidus.   „  Speckle.
   „  Spencki.    „  Spiralis.

       Croton Stewarti.

*C. Superbiens*, a very richly coloured variety, a native of New Guinea; the leaves are oblong acute, with the base rounded; they begin to colour with yellowish markings on a green ground and finish off on the matured leaves with a ground colour of dark bronze intermixed with coppery portions, while the costa and veins are picked out with crimson, making a very handsome plant for table decoration; wants shade, and cuttings root easily.

  Croton Shuttleworthii.  Croton Tri-colour.

*C. Trilobus, Earl of Derby*, is a very slow-growing three-lobed foliage Croton of dwarf habit; the stem and the leaf-stalk are bright yellow, and this colour extends along the midrib and diffuses itself over two-thirds of the leaf, which subsequently takes on bright red markings as the leaf matures: this plant must be "stopped" to branch; must have plenty of shade, and from its dwarf habit, slow growth, and rich colouring is suitable for table decoration; cuttings succeed easily.

*C. Trilobus, Lord Cairns.*—This is like the "Earl of Derby," only with leaves of much brighter colours, the mature leaves being entirely covered with bright crimson; it is hardy and can be placed out in the open garden except in the very hot months; it can be propagated easily.

  Croton Trilobus Alberti.  Croton Trilobus Disraeli.
   „   „  Traveller.  „  Torquatus.
   „  Tortilis.     „  Truffantianus.

*C. Triumphans (Harwoodianus)* was introduced from the New Hebrides, the long leaves have a longish tapered point somewhat re-curved; the leaves are rolled backwards, are deep green in colour with a yellow line on either side of the midrib; the principal veins are also marked out in the same colour; the costa is bright crimson which increases in intensity in the mature leaf, while the other portions turn bronze green; must be grown in the shade; cuttings succeed easily.

Croton Undulatum.     Croton Variabilis, (falcatus).
„ Variegatum.     „ Veitchii, Nos. 1 & 2.
„ Vedalli.     „ Volutus, Nos. 1 & 2.

*C. Vittatus* has oblong leaves nine inches long by two inches wide, with long leaf-stalks coloured yellow and bright red; the fine green leaves have a band running laterally along the bases of the primary veins, which are of a creamy yellow colour; as the leaves mature, the red in the leaf-stalk extends along the midrib of the leaf, giving it a brighter appearance; wants shade; cuttings succeed well.

*C. Warrenii* has very long narrow spiral leaves, sometimes thirty to thirty-two inches in length, pendant and arching; the dark green leaves are fantastically mottled and marked with rich crimson, carmine, and orange yellow; this plant grows very slowly and will only branch when "stopped;" requires plenty of shade; cuttings succeed easily.

Croton Washingtonii.     Croton Weismannii.

*C. Williamsii.*—This is a very richly coloured variety; the foliage begins to characterise at a very early stage; the leaves are ten to twelve inches in length by three or four inches wide; the young leaves are green with bands of yellow, but these colours quickly disappear as the leaf matures, when the leaf is found to be of a reddish bronze marked with rich violet crimson and magenta; the underside of the leaf is also coloured with a shade of crimson imparting altogether a rich appearance; this plant branches freely, and is very good for table decoration; although a fast grower will not stand much sun; cuttings root easily.

Croton Wilsoni.     Croton Wrightii.
Croton Youngii.

# FOLIAGE PLANTS.

### ALOCASIAS.

There are above fifteen varieties of this plant in the trade, all of them are easily grown in Compost Number 3*; many of these plants require to be grown under the shade of trees, or in the fern house; their leaves are of imposing dimensions, and a few of them have beautifully variegated stems and leaves; some varieties of this plant propagate themselves (like "Gigantea," "Lowii" and "Macrorrhiza-Variegata"), that is, young shoots grow round the parent plant, which spring from the roots; when these have established themselves well, and grown three or four leaves, they should be removed from the parent plant (between October and February being the most suitable time); other varieties like "Metallica" and "Zebrina" grow bulbs which will be found among the roots when making the annual transplantations; these bulbs should be collected and sown in shallow seed pans filled with fine river sand, when they will germinate.

The kinds offered for sale are named as under:—

    Alocasia Amabilis.    Alocasia Chelsoni.

*A. Gigantea.*—This is a grotesque-looking plant, growing to a great height; the leaves have numerous projections like digits, and the edges of the leaf are slightly undulated; the leaves, like the plant, are of huge dimensions.

    Alocasia Illustris.    Alocasia Jenningsii.

*A. Johnstoni (Cyrtosperma Johnstoni).*—This is a beautifully variegated description; is a native of the Solomon Islands (in the Pacific Ocean); has arrow-shaped leaves, olive green,

---

\* COMPOST No. 3.—Fine river sand, three parts; vegetable mould, one; and decayed manure, one part. This compost is well adapted for bulbs in general. Dahlias seem to grow well in it, but require liquid manure occasionally.—*Hints to Amateur Gardeners, by A. T. Jaffrey.*

variegated and veined with bright rosy red; the leaf-stalk is furnished with whorls, and the stem is darkly mottled.

Alocasia Lowii.   Alocasia Macrorrhiza-Variegata.

Alocasia Marshallii.

*A. Metallica*, so called from the metallic hue of the leaves which are peltately attached to the leaf-stalk and slightly cupped; the primary veins are depressed and are marked distinctly in a deeper colour than the ground colour of the leaf; this plant is delicate and requires care; propagated by bulbs found among the roots.

Alocasia Pieta.   Alocasia Singaporensis.
„   Sedenii   „   Sikhimensis.

*A. Thibautiana* has immense leaves of a deep olive greyish green, with a midrib of a peculiar grey white tint with grey veins branching from it; the leaves are of a lasting description, being of a firm stout leather-like texture.

Alocasia Veitchii.   Alocasia Violacea.

*A. Zebrina*, so called from the stem being variegated; known to native gardeners as the Snake Caladium.

### ANTHURIUMS.

These plants belong to a very picturesque family and are remarkably adapted for decorative and show purposes; the huge leaves are in some cases very beautifully marked, and some have a lustrous velvety appearance; new varieties are continually being introduced, especially by Mr. W. Bull of Chelsea, from New Grenada, Brazil, Colombia and South America; the majority of these handsome plants which have been imported to this country grow easily; they propagate very slowly by suckers or shoots, but they can also be propagated very rapidly by removing a portion of the bulb of the old plant, cutting or dividing it in pieces about one inch square, with one or more eyes in each piece and sowing them in shallow seed pans with fine river sand; this process requires skill and experience, and should be tried on the common varieties at first, and when sufficient experience has been gained in rearing these, rarer varieties may be propagated by this method; no plant, less than two years old, should be operated on in this way and no more than two-thirds of the bulb of the parent plant should be cut away, and in doing this, the roots of the old plant must be saved uninjured as far as possible: the portion cut away should be washed *clean* of all earth or manure, then the whole of the roots adhering to it must be removed, and the bulb divided and sown as already directed. The whole of these plants must be grown in the shade.

The varieties commonly met with in Indian collections are—

*A. Andreanum*, a magnificent plant from the United States of Colombia, of tufted habit with cordate dark green leaves.

*A. Crystallinum.*—This is now very common and may be seen in almost every collection; it is, nevertheless, very handsome, having large leaves of a rich but dark olive green with the principal veins marked out on either side by bright silvery white bands. The young leaves are of a shade of bronze.

*A. Crystallinum Williamsii.*—This plant is very much like the above except that the leaves are considerably elongated.

*A. Dechardi*, a robust variety admired for its snow-white flowers, which are fragrant.

| Anthurium Grande. | Anthurium Patini. |
|---|---|
| ,, Insigne (*this is a new tri-lobed variety*). | ,, Hybridum. |
| | ,, Ornatum. |
| | ,, Regale. |
| ,, Magneficum. | |

*A. Scherzerianum.*—This plant is chiefly admired for its large brilliant scarlet flowers.

Anthurium Trilobum.   Anthurium Williamsii.

*A. Veitchii.*—This plant has leaves nearly three feet long and a foot broad, with a glossy metallic but waved appearance.

*Warocqueanum.*—This is a fine variety with leaves from twenty-five to thirty inches in length by eight or nine inches broad, of rich velvety green, on which the midrib and veins are marked in a lighter colour forming a fine contrast.

### ARALIAS.

This family, like the Panax, is very much used for table decoration; will stand the sun only in the cool season and, like Crotons, are propagated by cuttings; the foliage is very varied, being in some instances variegated with creamy white, and in others reddish crimson; the leaves also assume many irregular shapes, some being very minute in size while others are the reverse; as these plants are easily grown, they are worthy the attention of Amateurs.

## DRACÆNAS.

These plants belong to a very elegant showy family, and are now so numerous that leaves of almost any shade of creamy white, green or red, can be obtained, mixed or unmixed, with other tints; most of them propagate themselves by suckers, but by a division of the bulbs, like those of Anthuriums, they can be very easily increased; in six or seven months the bulb of a Dracæna can be divided if the weather is cool enough, the pieces cut from that portion of the bulb removed must be put into seed pans with fine river sand to grow.

*Dracæna Goldieana* is considered the Queen of this group; it comes from Western Tropical Africa; the leaf-stalks are of a greyish colour, with a furrow along the upper side; the leaf-blade is cordate-ovate with a yellowish green rib marbled and branded with alternate silver grey and dark green bands, the reverse of the leaf having a reddish purple colour.

## MARANTAS.

This is a group of very ornamental foliage plants easily propagated by division of the bulbs, or by the suckers thrown out by the parent tree.

The Arrowroot plant belongs to this family, and is known as "Maranta Arundinacea."

## PANAX.

These are ever-green plants with remarkably varied leaflets; some of them are of a dense bushy habit, the leaves being as numerous as they are minute; a few of them are plumelike in character, and these are unsurpassed for table decoration; can be propagated without any trouble from cuttings during any time of the year.

## PALMS AND CYCADS.

It is a matter for surprise that with a climate so suitable for their growth, and with so many natives at hand, these plants, which are undoubtedly the noblest and most majestic of the vegetable kingdom, have suffered so much neglect; their name is Legion and their luxuriance, grandeur, and adaptation for table and other decorative purposes unsurpassed, yet beyond a few common varieties, they are almost unrepresented in most collections, and the absence of the finer kinds in our Annual Shows and in our gardens is an error that must be put right without loss of time; no known plant is capable of imparting the oriental grandeur, that a pile of palms can, to a tropical garden; the numerous dwarf kinds with miniature, but nevertheless perfectly graceful forms, are admirably suited for the decoration of the drawing and dining room, while the larger kinds are suitable for entrances, verandahs and conservatories, the natives being grown out in the open garden.

The most economical method of obtaining a collection is to raise the same from seed which is obtainable at very reasonable rates from the Royal Botanical Gardens at Calcutta, Mauritius and Ceylon; the seed should be received in May or June if possible, and put into nursery pots or pans, each description separately, because young palms look very much alike, and if mixed up cannot be distinguished easily by Amateurs until after the leaves begin to characterise; the soil in which the palm seeds are to be sown should contain very little manure, therefore take three baskets of earth from any part of the garden free from stones and gravel, mix one basket of red earth and one of river sand, to which add half a basket of horse manure, and you have a soil suitable for their growth; after the seed has been sown, water the pots or pans regularly from a can; the seed takes months to germinate, varying very much according to the species, so that watering should not be discontinued because some of the seed has germinated, and the others show no signs of putting in an appearance.

Palms, as a rule, grow very slowly, so to expect to propagate them from the seed to be obtained from plants raised from seed, is quite out of the question; but, fortunately, some kinds, remarkably the cane or Calamus palms, throw out shoots or young plants by the side of the parent tree: these may be separated during the rains from the parent, but care must be taken to first see that the young plants have formed independent roots for themselves through which they can absorb the nutriment necessary for their existence.

The following is a list of palms, nearly all of which can be obtained either by seed or in small seedling plants from Indian Nurseries at a comparatively cheap rate, but any one wishing to possess a first-class collection, must make up his mind to pay from five to fifteen guineas a dozen for them in England, besides the cost and risk of bringing out to this country rare specimens (which are quoted from two to five guineas each) to be handed over to the tender mercies of a native gardener who would be sure to kill them with mistaken kindness if not with starvation.

# LIST OF PALMS AND CYCADS THAT HAVE SUCCEEDED WELL ON THE PLAINS.

*Areca Aurea*, one of the finest and most graceful of the nut palms, with stems of a yellowish colour, easily raised from seed.

*Areca Baueri*, also known as "Seaforthia Robusta."

*Areca Disticha*, known in some collections as "Wallichia Disticha," easily raised, and will grow in any situation.

*Areca Gracilis*, a very fine palm, can be grown for a long time in a small pot or vase, is very like "A. Lutescens."

*Areca Horrida*, a narrow-leafed variety; will grow without much care and in any situation.

*Areca Lutescens*, a very graceful palm; propagates very rapidly by shoots grown in the vicinity of the parent stem; wants shade.

*Areca Madagascarensis*, a hardy variety with narrow long leaves scantily distributed on the stem.

*Areca Oleracea*, hardy palm, can be grown out in the open; requires careful treatment while young.

*Areca Rubra*, so called from the reddish tint of the stems and midribs of the leaves; must have shade.

*Areca Triandra*, a large-leafed variety, very distinct and handsome; wants shade.

*Areca Catechu*, the betel-nut palm of India, native of Ceylon.

*Areca Verschaffeltii*, also known as "Hyophorbe," an elegant variety; the reverse of the leaf-stock has a creamy yellow stripe, and the midrib of the leaves are of the same colour.

*Arenga Obtusifolia*.

*Arenga Saccharifera*, the sugar palm of this country.

*Arenga Wightii*, a fine dwarf palm from the Coimbatore District; will grow easily and in any situation.

*Astrocaryum Argenteum*, (known as the silver palm), a very fine variety, native of Colombia, with the leaf-stalks and reverse side of the leaves covered with a silver white scurf, the upper surface being bright green; seeds not obtainable, must be procured in seedling plants.

*Bowenia Spectabilis Serrulata*, a remarkable Cycad, native of Australia, being the only plant of this family with bipianate fronds; the leaves are large, handsome and serrated at the margins; very rare.

*Calamus Ciliaris*, a fine cane palm, propagates easily.

*Calamus Jenkinsoni.*—This cane is very handsome and throws up shoots very rapidly.

| | |
|---|---|
| Calamus Ceylon, sp., (native cane of Ceylon). | Calamus Roxburghi, (native cane of Ceylon). |
| „ Leptospodix. | „ Java, sp. |
| | „ Malacca, sp. |
| *Caryota Sobolifera*. | Caryota Obtusifolia. |
| „ Urens, the Sago palm, a native of Ceylon. | „ Cunninghami. |

*Ceroxylon Andicola*, the wax palm of South America.

*Chamærops Fortunei*, known also as "Excelsa" in some collections.

*Chamærops Humilis*, a very useful palm for decorative purposes.

| | |
|---|---|
| Chamærops Gracilis. | Chamærops Richardiana. |
| *Cocos Flexuosa*. | Cocos Chilensis. |
| „ Nucifera, is the Cocoanut palm of India. | „ Plumosa. |

*Cocos Weddelliana*, rather tender, but one of the most elegant of the palm family, with leaves of a rich green colour, very suitable for table decoration, being a slow grower, and dwarfish in habit; wants shade.

*Corypha Alata*.

*Corypha Australis*, fine, useful palm, known also as "Livistonia Australis," very hardy.

*Corypha Umbraculifera*, native of Ceylon, raised easily from seed, and will grow in any situation.

*Cycas Circinalis*, hardy Cycad, very common.

*Cycas Media*, a good Cycad from New Holland, producing a grand crown of foliage of large size which vary in different trees of the same species.

Cycas Revoluta.      Cycas Rumphii.

*Cycas Undulata*, a very fine Cycad that will grow without much trouble.

*Dæmonorops Fissus.*

*Dæmonorops Palembanicus*, a very elegant palm, a native of Java; the young leaves are of a bright cinnamon-brown which gradually become deep green by age; requires shade.

*Dæmonorops Plumosus*, one of the most elegant and graceful of palms, very plume-like in appearance and admirably adapted for table decoration; must be grown in the shade.

*Elæis Guineensis.*—This is the oil palm, a native of Africa; will grow in any situation.

*Euterpe Edulis.*—This is the cabbage palm of Brazil, and is also known as "Oreodoxa Sancona."

*Geonoma Gracilis.*

Geonoma Speciosa.      Geonoma Spixiana.

*Jabæa Spectabilis.*—(Cocos Chilensis.)
*Kentia Belmoreana.*—Kentia Fosteriana.

Kentia Canterburyana.

*Kentia Wendlandiana*, a very noble-looking palm, with large handsome leaves serrated (or toothed) at the apex; native of Queensland; will grow in any situation.

Latania Aurea.      Latania Borbonica.

*Licuala Spinosa*, propagate very rapidly by suckers or shoots, and is very hardy.

Licuala Peltata.

*Livistona Australis.*  *Livistona Mauritiana.*
,,  Chilensis.   ,,  Oliviformis.
,,  Hoogendorpii, a   ,,  Rotundifolia,
very broad-leaf-  known in some
ed variety.   collections as
,,  Jenkinsii.   (Subglobosa).

*Macrozamia Cylindrica*, a nicely-marked Cycad from Queensland; must be grown in the shade.

*Macrozamia Denisoni.*

*Macrozamia Perowskiana*, very tender and very slow in growth; requires shade.

*Maximiliana Regia.*

*Oreodoxa "Acuminata"* and *"Regia,"* both are fine narrow drooping-leafed palms, growing very easily and rapidly.

*Phœnix Acaulis.*

*Phœnix Compacta*, dwarf Hybrid obtained by crossing two other Phœnix, sp., very tender.

*Phœnix Dactylifera*, the common date of India.

Phœnix Reclinata.

*Phœnix Rupicola*, the best kind of Phœnix yet discovered, very graceful and ornamental and can be grown without any trouble whatever.

*Phœnix Sylvestris*, a sugar-yielding palm, native of Ceylon.

*Phœnix Andamans*, sp.

*Pritchardia Grandis*, a truly grand palm with very large handsome leaves; a young palm of this species was shown at our Horticultural Exhibition among other rare palms and plants, which obtained a prize; it attracted much attention; it is scarce, but no collection should be without it as it is easily grown and can be obtained from Calcutta in seedling plants.

*Ptychosperma Elegans.*—See Seaforthia Elegans.

Sabal Adamsoni.  Sabal Minor.
,,  Blackburniana  ,,  Palmetto.

*Seaforthia Elegans*, a very good and easily-grown variety, known also as "Ptychosperma Elegans," a native of Ceylon.

*Seaforthia Robusta*.—See Areca Baueri.

*Stevensonia Grandifolia*, also known as "Phœnicophorium Sechellarum"; easily raised from seed.

*Thrinax Elegans*, a very showy palm, well suited for exhibition.

    Thrinax Glauca.    Thrinax Parviflora.
    Zamia Cylindrica.    Zamia Denisoni.

*Zamia Miquelii* ("Spiralis,") a native of Queensland; has very elegant fronds, erect with a slight spiral twist; it is also known as "Zamia Fraseri."